The Insider's Guide to Film Finance

To Theodora and Alexandra

The Insider's Guide to Film Finance

Philip Alberstat BSc BA LLB (London)

AMSTERDAM • BOSTON • HEIDELBERG • LONDON • NEW YORK • OXFORD
PARIS • SAN DIEGO • SAN FRANCISCO • SINGAPORE • SYDNEY • TOKYO

Focal Press is an imprint of Elsevier

Focal Press is an imprint of Elsevier
The Boulevard, Langford Lane, Kidlington, Oxford, OX5 1GB
30 Corporate Drive, Suite 400, Burlington, MA 01803, USA

First edition 2004
Reprinted 2005, 2007, 2008

British Library Cataloguing in Publication Data
A catalogue record for this book is available from the British Library

Library of Congress Cataloging-in-Publication Data
A catalog record for this book is available from the Library of Congress

ISBN: 978-0-240-51661-5

For information on all Focal Press publications
visit our website at www.elsevierdirect.com

Transferred to Digital Printing in 2009

Contents

Foreword

Barely a day goes by without some film related story making the pages of the average newspaper. We are not just talking about the reviews ghetto, but the lifestyle, travel and business sections. With some films and film companies having become brands in their own right, the corporate divorce between Disney and Pixar was treated to front page treatment.

What does this tell us? Film has become big news, big business and dominated by the studio big-boys. Maybe.

But at the same time part of its fascination is that film making is also a cottage industry and a craft industry. There are layers of detail to which the simplistic approach fed to newspaper readers cannot do justice.

The independent film community is made up of highly motivated individuals, struggling to put together financing, logistical and legal puzzles that would defeat many a 3D chess player. Frankly it is a miracle that any independent film ever gets made. Even more of a miracle that any of them are any good at all.

Clearly, it is beyond the scope of this book to tell anyone how to make a good film or a commercially successful one. It would be both patronizing and foolhardy to try. After all, some of the best brains in the business have come horribly unstuck attempting to do that.

But neither is it quite true that 'nobody knows nothing', as ace screenwriter William Goldman once suggested. Studios maximize their chances through a combination of 'portfolio theory' and marketing muscle. Independents can maximize their chances, if not of success, then at least of surviving the production experience by using some of the right techniques. A little knowledge can go a long way.

That means getting a film's budget in line with its recoupment potential; it means knowing what to ask your lawyer and when; and it means understanding the choices you make when opting for equity over debt, pre-sales over independent finance; or shooting on location in Ireland over studios in Luxembourg.

The Insider's Guide to Film Finance is intended to answer many of these questions. Written by a film lawyer whose role it has often been to raise and structure film finance, the book addresses problems with simplicity and clarity; with theory matched by practicalities; with checklists, case studies and sample documents.

It will not prevent anyone from making mistakes but, used wisely, it should enable the averagely intelligent newcomer to avoid making all the basic errors. And for the more experienced player it provides a yardstick against which they can measure their financial, legal and chess-playing creativity.

Take some of Phil Alberstat's advice and, who knows, you could end up making the newspapers sooner than you thought!

Patrick Frater
International Editor, *Screen International*

About the Author

Philip Alberstat is a media finance and production lawyer specializing in film, television and broadcasting. He has worked on films such as *The 51st State*, *Goodbye Mr Steadman*, *Beyond The Sea* and numerous television programmes and series. He is on the editorial board of *Entertainment Law Review* and is the author of the *Independent Producers' Guide to Film and TV Contracts* (2000), and *Law and the Media* (2002).

Philip is involved in raising finance for film and television productions and negotiating and structuring film and television deals. He undertakes corporate and commercial work and handles the intellectual property aspects of broadcasting and finance transactions. He has also executive produced numerous film and television productions. In 2004 he won an Emmy Award as a Producer of the film, *The Incredible Mrs. Ritchie.*

Philip joined Osborne Clarke as a partner in February 2002. Prior to that he was Head of Legal and Business Affairs with one of the largest independent TV production companies in the UK. He was previously Head of Media at Baker & McKenzie and began his career at Olswang. He was winner of the Lawyer/Hifal Award for Solicitor of the year in 1997 and is listed in Legal Experts in the area of Film Finance/Media.

List of Contributors

Alan Harris (BCom, BSc, MBA, ACCA), Managing Director, Atlantic Film Group

Alan is Managing Director of Atlantic Film Productions Limited, a specialist company that is involved in development and production of feature films.

Some of the features with which Atlantic has been involved include *Imagining Argentina* (with Myriad Pictures starring Antonio Bandaras and Emma Thompson), *Citizen Verdict* (starring Jerry Springer) and *Nicholas Nickleby* (with MGM Studios).

Alan was formerly Financial Director at Grosvenor Park Media where he completed several hundred million pounds worth of feature film transactions and advised on the setting-up of many international co-productions.

Alan is an expert on international film structuring and financing and has lectured at such prestigious venues as UCLA, Screen Producers Guild of Australia, The Luxembourg Film Finance Forum, The UK Producers Association for Cinema and Television and the New Zealand Screen Producers and Directors Association.

Rob Sherr

Rob is the Commercial Banking Manager and an Assistant General Manager at Bank Leumi (UK) plc. He has been in banking for 27 years during which time he has largely been involved with commercial lending. He joined Bank Leumi in 1999 as Head of Media, having spent the previous nine years working at Coutts & Co. In 1993 he became one of the founding managers of Coutts' Media Banking Office.

Under Rob's guidance, Bank Leumi participated in the development of completion bonded finance to video games developers and to structuring the advance finance of net producer benefit under sale and leaseback.

Lucy Walker

Lucy Walker joined Osborne Clarke in 1998 and is currently an associate in the banking and finance group. Lucy specializes in film finance together with general finance, leasing and regulatory work (including issues relating to cards and payment systems, and the regulatory issues affecting consumer credit and banking and financial services).

She has acted for Barclays Bank plc on a series of structured film finance transactions and has also advised both funds and producers on a wide spectrum of production and distribution finance arrangements, fundings and sale and leaseback transactions.

Acknowledgements

The author would like to thank the following people who helped make this book possible.

Alan Harris, Rob Sherr and Lucy Walker for contributing their respective chapters.

James Shirras, from Film Finances Inc., for allowing me to use his sample documents in chapter six.

Freeway Entertainment Group for allowing me to use their Collection Agreement in chapter seven.

Tanya Scoot for her hard work and diligence on the manuscript.

Cécile Bouchet for her research assistance.

Dr D.T. McVicar for his research assistance.

My publishers, Beth Howard and Christina Donaldson, who waited so patiently.

Denis Heroux.

Bud and Betty for their hard work, patience and research assistance.

A Note From the Author

This book is designed to help non-lawyers understand legal issues frequently encountered in the film industry.

The book provides readers with an understanding of both basic and complex legal principles, enabling them to better communicate with their lawyer.

Nothing in this book should be construed as legal advice. The information provided is not a substitute for consulting with an experienced lawyer and receiving advice based on the facts and circumstances of a particular transaction.

The sample agreements contained in each chapter need to be tailored and modified to fit the specific circumstances of each transaction. These agreements are based on legal principles that often change and vary by case law, statutes and laws of different jurisdictions.

Introduction

Money frees you from doing things you dislike. Since I dislike doing nearly everything, money is handy.
Groucho Marx
1890–1977

The unpredictable nature of making movies means that negotiating a film finance deal can be a minefield. For producers, the strategies and structures of financing arrangements are as numerous as the films that are made. The aim of this book is to attempt to demystify some of the complexities of the film industry and specifically a film financing transaction. One of the most common complaints from the banking industry sector is the apparent misapprehension of film makers as to the role banks play in the financing of films.

This book will focus on the world of independent film making where producers working outside the Hollywood studio system put together films by an assortment of international, bilateral and multilateral co-production treaties, pre-sales, equity investment, tax funding, gap financing and whatever other means it takes to get their films made. A great deal of creativity is required in putting together the necessary elements to attract finance to any particular production.

Rather than a guide of where to get the money, this book will look at the technical and legal issues involved once a producer has the money to produce his or her film. For many producers, finding money for their films can take years. Sourcing funds for production can be a long, arduous battle. Countless meetings, attendance at film festivals, promises, broken promises, changes in tax legislation, actors dropping in, dropping out and countless other variables. The process can take months, years, even a lifetime. Financing is one of the most crucial areas of the film industry, but one that has often not been given the importance it deserves.

Once a producer has cobbled together all of the finance for a production, the battle has just begun. Imagine the scenario – after five years of hard work and travelling the globe, a British producer has several pre-sales with foreign distributors in place, a co-production deal with a Canadian co-producer who will bring 40 per cent of the budget from an assortment of tax credits, a television sale, various subsidies, a distribution deal, Telefilm Canada subsidy, a sale and leaseback deal in the UK, equity from private investors, UK Film Council money, a UK broadcasting deal and a UK theatrical deal. At last, a fully financed film! The question is, how does the producer then turn all of these contracts from paper into cash?

With all of these deals in place, the fun part of film making begins. Lawyers, bankers, civil servants, more lawyers, more bankers and perhaps even more civil servants for the producer to deal with. Gone are the days when two or three sources of finance will green-light production of a film. Fortunately or perhaps unfortunately, multiparty financing of independent films is the norm. For a creative producer taking the step from development to assembling the finance is a difficult and time-consuming process. What many creative producers are not prepared for is the next step, into the mysterious world of financiers, bankers and lawyers. On the face of it, banking and finance for the film industry appears to be a highly specialized world. However, most banks in the film business are basic commercial banks. They simply lend cash for a certain period of time, would like a fee and some interest and, of course, they would like their money back. The fundamental purpose of a bank is to make money. Many banks see film financing as a basic banking product. Although they can play a vital role in the financing of a given production, banks do not invest in films.

From a lawyer's perspective, film financing involves many different aspects of law. Issues such as intellectual property, contracts, insurance, employment and other areas can sometimes make closing a film financing transaction very difficult.

Each chapter of this book will look at an integral part of a film financing transaction. Chapter one looks at underlying rights, such as a book, a script or other works of intellectual property, which will form the basis of a bank's or financiers' security. When a bank makes a loan to a film producer, all they really have is an interest in a book or script and some film that is 35 mm wide and 1 mm thick. This chapter analyses the importance of rights ownership and specifically looks at the chain of title in a film and a title opinion.

Chapter two, Co-productions, is written by Alan Harris, an experienced financier and producer, and looks at how bilateral and multilateral treaties are an essential tool in financing films. The chapter will analyse some of the major issues that need to be considered prior to closing a financing deal involving two or more co-producers.

Chapter three is written by Rob Sherr, a banker with many years of film financing experience, who will give an insider's view of the banking process. The chapter will look at how a bank interacts with a producer and analyses a film financing transaction from a bank's perspective.

Chapter four, with contributions by Lucy Walker, an experienced banking and finance lawyer, contains various banking documents that are essential in a film financing transaction. Each agreement has commentary and notes at the bottom of the relevant clause or a general summary of what the document does. The commentary and notes will look at issues that should be considered and how these issues are relevant and impact on a film financing transaction.

Chapter five looks at the ever-difficult and somewhat contentious interparty agreement. Some say this agreement acts as the missing pieces and mortar of the film financing puzzle. However, others say that this complex agreement is just a make-work project for lawyers.

Chapter six looks at completion guarantees. The completion guarantee or bond is an essential part of any film financing transaction. The chapter looks at the completion guarantor's relationship with the financier and producer, with an in-depth look at the actual completion bond and completion agreement.

In chapter seven, the expression 'he who has the gold makes the rules' is quite appropriate. Collection agents have become a necessity because of complex financing structures and multiple financiers who all have expectations of repayment and an accounting of their investment in a film. This chapter looks at important aspects of collection management and has a collection agreement, courtesy of Freeway Entertainment, attached.

Chapter eight is a natural follow-on to chapter seven as it looks at the complexities of recoupment. Tiers, corridors and other aspects of collecting revenues from the sale and distribution of films are analysed.

Chapter nine is an in-depth look at gap financing, with examples of various financing structures. Gap financing is a popular way for producers to finance their films when it may be difficult to pre-sell distribution rights.

Chapter ten looks briefly at alternative financing structures, such as sale and leaseback, that have been popular in the UK. Gawain Hughes, an experienced corporate lawyer, contributes an interesting section on limited liability partnerships. The final sections of the book contain a helpful glossary of film financing terms, recommended reading and helpful websites.

The legal bit! This book is not a substitute for expert legal advice. It is only a guide, and law and practice evolve and change very quickly. Before acting on any of the sample agreements or documents in this book, you should consult a lawyer with appropriate qualifications and expertise in this area of law for advice.

1 Underlying Rights

Never judge a book by its movie.
J. W. Egan

Financing Intellectual Property Rights

One of the fundamental elements of the film business is the buying and selling of rights: rights in books, scripts, treatments, magazine articles, short stories and various other forms of intellectual property. It is customary for a producer or production company to initially option the underlying rights in a project that is based on an existing form of intellectual property. For economic reasons, the cost of an option is much less than buying the rights. As a rule of thumb, producers generally pay 10 per cent per year of the purchase price. If the purchase price is £50,000 then a producer will pay £5,000 for a year-long option. This gives the producer a year to decide whether they want to exercise the option and purchase the rights. Producers usually negotiate the right to extend the option for another year by paying an additional fee, i.e., another 10 per cent. In most cases, the initial option fee is on account of the purchase price so, in the example above, if the producer decides to exercise the option during the first option period, he will have to pay only £45,000 for the rights, as he has already paid the £5,000 option fee.

An Option Agreement must be in writing and must be signed by the person who owns the underlying work (the person who owns the copyright).

From a financier's or a banker's perspective, the ownership of rights is paramount for any film financing transaction. From personal experience as an entertainment lawyer, many film-financing transactions are delayed because producers have not acquired all of the rights necessary to satisfy the requirements of the financier or bank.

Assuming that a producer has raised all the funds needed to finance their film, a bank or financier will send the producer a term sheet or deal memorandum offering to lend money and help finance their production. This is usually done so that a producer will agree the material deal points with the bank or financier. The term sheet/deal memo will contain all the relevant commercial issues and will generally set out a list of condition precedents required by the bank before lending any money. (See chapter four for a sample term sheet/offer letter.)

In relation to rights, most term sheets have a condition precedent provision as follows:

The borrower must provide original or certified copies of the rights documents and/or evidence that the borrower has title to the rights.

Another variation can read:

The borrower must provide the rights documents confirming that the borrower has full and unfettered title to produce the film based on the screenplay.

Banks will require a full chain of title in relation to any film they decide to finance. The chain of title documents that the producer must provide, may, depending on the type of underlying rights, include any or all of the following:

a. An Option Agreement
b. An Option Extension Agreement
c. Assignment or Purchase Agreement
d. Short Form Option Agreement
e. Short Form Assignment Agreement
f. Assignment of Copyright
g. Quit Claim
h. Writer's Agreement
i. Publisher's Release
j. Life Story Rights Agreement.

All film deals are different, so the particular underlying rights documents required by the bank vary depending on the facts. A film based on a book with a screenplay written by multiple writers over a long period of development with various drafts will have more documents in the chain of title than a film based on an original screenplay by one writer.

It is common practice and sometimes a requirement by financiers to record documents at the United States Copyright Office. Most long form option agreements for copyright works include a short form option agreement and short form assignment. These documents are for registration purposes and do not contain all of the commercial terms agreed between the parties. By recording these documents, this enables others to see that the producer has an interest in an underlying work.

In many film financing deals, the bank and other financiers will require the producer's lawyer to provide a chain of title opinion. The producer's lawyer will be required to review all of the underlying rights documents and give an opinion that the producer owns or has acquired all the rights that are necessary to exploit the film. In addition, the opinion will also have to confirm that the producer has the right to assign all rights (or certain rights) under the chain of title documents. Lawyers generally qualify and limit the scope of/and who can rely on their opinion.

The following is a checklist of important clauses in an option/assignment agreement that are necessary for the due diligence process to be completed by a bank or bank's lawyer. If a producer has entered into an agreement with a writer or owner of an underlying work and has not included most of the following clauses then a bank or financier will require the producer to re-draft their documentation. This can result in lengthy negotiations with agents or lawyers. In many cases, the closing of the financing is delayed as a result. The following is a checklist which the bank or financier's lawyers will focus on while reviewing an option and assignment agreement.

1. **Parties to the Agreement**
   It is common for a producer at the outset of the development process to enter into an agreement with a writer or rights owner with a company that may be different from the entity, usually a single purpose company (SPV) set up to make the film. A producer will be required to assign the option or any rights that have been assigned from the original company to the new SPV.
2. **Consideration for the Option**
   All sums due under the agreement should be paid and the producer may be required to provide proof of that payment in the form of a receipt or acknowledgement in writing from the rights owner.

3. **Option Period**
   The agreement will set out how long the option period runs for and whether it has expired. Believe it or not, in many deals an option may have expired, even though all parties to the deal are in agreement with one another. A simple solution in this circumstance is to draft an extension agreement that is attached to the original option agreement. This option extension agreement will then form another document in the chain of title.
4. **Exercise of Option**
   If the option has been exercised in writing and all payments are made under the assignment then there should be a written document that records this.
5. **Assignment**
   Since copyright is a form of property, it can (subject to certain exceptions) be bought and sold, charged, licensed and dealt with, in any way the original owner may choose. It is essential that the rights that the producer is trying to acquire are freely assignable. Not only should the rights be assignable, but the agreement entered into by the producer, intending to assign or give the producer the right to do so, should also be assignable to a potential financier as security.
6. **Entire Agreement Clauses**
   Just what it says. That the agreement is the complete understanding between the parties, it supersedes all other agreements and cannot be modified except in writing and signed by both parties.
7. **Governing Law**
   This clause sets out which country's laws govern the agreement and in most cases if there is a dispute, where the dispute will be adjudicated.

The assignment/purchase agreement

1. **Parties to the Agreement**
   See option agreement notes.
2. **Rights Granted**
   This is the clause that is of most concern to a bank or potential financier. At one time, producers would acquire all rights in the underlying work for the full period of copyright. This would enable the producer to exploit the rights by all means and in all media without any restrictions whatsoever

and without the obligation to make any further payments except to certain performers in relation to residuals, repeat fees, or other collection organizations.

Now that deals have become much more complex, both in the acquisition of rights and in the financing process, producers often may obtain limited rights to make only one film. If this is the case, it is prudent to negotiate in advance, upon payment of a further fee, the right to make prequels, sequels or other derivative works based on the underlying rights.

The financier's or banker's lawyer reviewing this clause in an agreement will set out, in detail, all the rights that the producer is entitled to exploit. The report will set out if there are any reserved rights, such as publication, stage or radio rights or any rights that the producer is not entitled to.

3. **Duration and Extent of Rights Granted**
The agreement must contain a clause that sets out how long the producer can exploit the underlying rights. For feature films it is advisable to acquire as many rights as possible for the full period of copyright. A short duration will ultimately affect the sales agent's or distributor's ability to exploit the finished film. Most financiers or end users such as distributors will not acquire rights in a film unless the producer has all rights in the underlying work and subsequent film for the full period of copyright or at least a substantial amount of time that will enable the sales agent or distributor to recoup their investment by making appropriate long-term licences/sales of the film.
4. **Right to Make Changes**
In order for the producer to fully exploit the rights, they will have to ensure that there is a waiver of the author's or writer's moral rights and with an express right to alter and adapt the underlying work.
5. **Consideration**
The due diligence process will ensure that all payments have been made or will be paid on the first day of principal photography. This clause will also set out what is being paid for, i.e. film rights, TV rights or separate payments for different types of exploitation.
6. **Representation and Warranties and No Infringement**
Standard representations and warranties that the writer is the owner of the copyright, the work is original, has not breached

any third party rights and that the rights have not be assigned to anyone else, will be required in the agreement.

7. **Indemnity**
   The agreement should contain a clause that requires each party to agree an indemnity against all losses that may arise as a result of the other parties' breach. Since the producer will be assigning the benefit of the agreement to a bank or financier then that assignee will want the right to rely on any indemnities that have been given.
8. **Credit Provisions**
   The credit provisions will be checked to ensure that prior to delivery of the film, the writer or author will receive their agreed credit. This provision should state that any inadvertent failure to give a credit will not enable the individual entitled to that credit to seek an injunction against the producers or subsequent theatrical distributor. If this was the case, then a writer who was entitled to a credit that was not given for whatever reason could actually stop the film from being released. Usually this type of clause sets out that the only remedy for missing credits are monetary damages.
9. **Assignment**
   A bank or financier will require that the producer is able to transfer or assign the agreement to the bank or financier in order to take a charge or mortgage over the rights. This ultimately enables the bank or financier to enforce repayment in certain circumstances. A charge or mortgage will be meaningless if it cannot be assigned to a lender. See chapter four for further explanation of charges.

The Chain of Title Opinion

A chain of title opinion letter is usually required by a bank or financier as a condition precedent for closing the financing on a film production. Not only do banks require the chain of title opinion, but any other financier or participant who is at risk in a film transaction may ask to be named as a beneficiary to the opinion. The opinion acts as an additional form of comfort that all of the underlying rights are in order and that there is no likelihood of potential litigation or a claim being made. The following is an example of a form of opinion letter that is given by a producer's lawyer to a bank involved in the financing of a feature film. Please note that an opinion given by a lawyer in relation to the underlying rights in a feature film will always be based on the particular circumstances and rights involved in the development of that specific film.

Sample Chain of Title Opinion Letter

Dated:

Dear Sirs

[Name of Bank] (**the 'Bank'**)
[Name of Producer] (**the 'Producer'**)
[Name of Film] (**the 'Production'**)

We act in the capacity of UK production counsel to the Producer in connection with the production and financing by the Producer of the Production.

As such counsel, we have examined or reviewed the following agreements relating to the acquisition by the Producer of all rights and copyright in and to the screenplay in respect of the film currently entitled '[ ]'

1. Option Agreement dated [ ]
2. Option Extension Agreement dated [ ]
3. Option and Purchase Agreement dated [ ]
4. Short Form Option dated [ ]
5. Short Form Assignment of Copyright dated [ ]
6. Certificate of Authorship dated [ ]
7. Assignment Agreement dated [ ]
8. Exercise Letter dated [ ]
9. Quit Claim dated [ ]
10. Second Option Extension dated [ ]

(Collectively the '**Chain of Title Documents**')

In connection with this opinion, we have not reviewed documents other than the Chain of Title Documents referred to above.

We have assumed that in respect of all documents referred to herein, all signatures are genuine, all documents submitted as originals are authentic, all documents submitted as certified copies conform to the original document and such documents are authentic. We have further assumed the legal competency of any individual executing such documents.

We have also assumed that the Chain of Title Documents have been executed and delivered by the parties therein in accordance with the laws of the jurisdiction or jurisdictions applicable thereto.

Based upon and relying on the foregoing, and subject to the assumptions, qualifications and limitations expressed herein, we are of the opinion that:

1. By virtue of the Chain of Title Documents, the Producer owns or has acquired all rights which are necessary to exploit the Production in all media throughout the world, and the Producer has the right to assign all rights under the Chain of Title Documents to the [NAME OF BANK IN MOST CASES BUT SOME EXCEPTIONS]
2. No person, firm or corporation has any agreement or option or rights capable of becoming an agreement for the purchase of the rights contemplated in the Chain of Title Documents.

The foregoing opinions are subject to the following qualifications:

1. Copyright in [may wish to state jurisdiction] arises upon the creation of the work by the author or composer and subsists even in the absence of the legal formality of copyright registration. We have conducted no copyright searches in respect of this matter. Under the laws of [Name of country] an assignment may be affected even in the absence of the legal formality of copyright registration. Therefore, even a search of the copyright registers may not reveal all copyrighted works such as are contained in the Production.
2. This opinion is based upon the laws of [England and Wales] and therefore do not express an opinion under the laws of any other jurisdiction other than the laws of the jurisdictions referred to above.
3. We are of the opinion that all moral rights of parties contributing copyright works to the Production have been waived.
4. The validity, enforceability and binding nature of the Chain of Title Documents is subject to (i) any applicable bankruptcy, insolvency, moratorium, organization, personal property or similar laws at the time in effect affecting the rights, powers, privileges, remedies and/or interests of creditors generally.
5. Equitable remedies, such as specific performance and injunctions, are in the discretion of the applicable court of competent jurisdiction before which such remedies are sought. Without limiting the generality of the foregoing, a court may consider the conduct or course of conduct of the parties and require that the parties act with reasonableness.
6. We express no opinion with respect to the availability of any particular remedy and the ability to recover certain costs, damages and expenses, whether by reason of indemnity,

contribution or otherwise, is subject to the discretion of the court regardless of whether enforcement is considered in equity or at law. In particular, nothing in this opinion is to be taken as indicating that the remedy of, or any order for, specific performance or the issue of any injunction will be available.

7. There may be material added to the script based on underlying works and contemplating the use of music, other works, translations, locations and personal appearances. Consequently, our opinion is in respect of the [Chain of Title Documents] only. The Producer's ownership of certain rights in the completed Production will be subject to the Producer's full and proper clearance of all underlying works, music, translations, personal appearances and other matters subject to clearance during production and in accordance with a valid errors and omissions policy of insurance and such an insurer's recognized clearance procedures.
8. A number of the agreements entered into by the Producer may contain obligations to extend participation, credit and profit participation to other parties as well as obligations of the Producer which are customary in the film industry. This opinion is given assuming that all such obligations have been fulfilled to date or will be fulfilled by the Producer and are not encumbrances to ownership of the Production.

This opinion is rendered solely for the benefit of [Name of bank, financier or the parties that require an opinion] in connection with [Name of film] and not for the benefit of any other person and may not be used, circulated, quoted from, published or otherwise referred to for any other purpose and may not be relied upon by any other person without our prior written consent in each instance. This opinion is rendered as of the date set forth above and we are under no obligation to revise, supplement or update the opinions contained herein to take into account any changes in facts or changes in law which are brought to our attention after the date hereof.

Yours faithfully

[Name of Lawyer, Law Firm]

Sample Chain of Title Documents

1. Certificate of Authorship
2. Short Form Option Agreement
3. Short Form Assignment Agreement
4. Quit Claim and Notice of Ownership of Copyright and Other Rights

Certificate of Authorship

Reference is made to the film currently entitled [ ] (the 'Film') I, [Name of Writer] hereby certify that I wrote the original screenplay entitled [ ] ('the Work') and that pursuant to various assignment agreements, [ ] ('the Producer') owns all right, title and interest throughout the world in and to said Film based on the Work and the results and proceeds of my writing services in accordance with the said agreement and the Producer shall be deemed the author and sole owner of the Work and all other literary works, drafts and revisions thereto written by me and the right to use, adapt and change said Work and derivative works thereof.

The above rights have been signed in perpetuity.

____

[Name]

Writer

On [ ], before me, a notary public or solicitor, personally appeared [Name of Writer], known to me personally or proved to me on the basis of satisfactory evidence, to be the person who executed the within instrument, as the individual who executed the within instrument.

Witness my hand and official seal [ ]
NOTARY PUBLIC

Short Form Option Agreement

KNOW ALL MEN BY THESE PRESENTS: That in consideration of the payment of [£1] and other good and valuable consideration, receipt of which is hereby acknowledged, the undersigned, [ ] (**Author**), does hereby grant to [ ] ('Producer') and its assigns, successors, licensees and transferees forever, the exclusive and irrevocable right and option to purchase from the undersigned all audiovisual rights of every kind, now known or hereafter devised, including, without limitation, the sole and exclusive film, television musical, merchandising and commercial tie-up rights, and all allied and ancillary rights, throughout the universe, in perpetuity, in and to that certain original, [published] [unpublished] [novel] [screenplay] described as follows:

TITLE: [ ]

AUTHOR: [ ]

COPYRIGHT REGISTRATION : [ ]

The undersigned and Producer have entered into that certain literary option/purchase agreement (the 'Agreement'), dated [ ], relating to the transfer and assignment of the foregoing rights in and to said literary work. Without limiting the generality of the foregoing, this Short Form Option Agreement shall be deemed to include, and shall be limited to, those rights of whatever nature which are included within the Agreement, which is not limited, added to, modified or amended hereby, and this Short Form Option Agreement is expressly made subject to all of the terms, conditions and provisions contained in the Agreement.

IN WITNESS WHEREOF, the undersigned has executed this instrument as of
[ ], 200[ ].

[ ]
(**Name of Author/Writer**)

Short Form Assignment Agreement

KNOW ALL MEN BY THESE PRESENTS: That in consideration of the payment of [£1] and other good valuable consideration, receipt of which is hereby acknowledged, the undersigned, [ ] (**Author**), does hereby sell, assign, grant and set over unto [ ] ('Producer') and its assigns, successors, licensees and transferees, all audiovisual rights of every kind, now known or hereafter devised, including, without limitation, the sole and exclusive film, television, musical, merchandising and commercial tie-up rights, and all allied and ancillary rights, throughout the universe, in perpetuity, in and to that certain original, [published] [unpublished] [novel] [screenplay] described as follows:

TITLE: [ ]
AUTHOR: [ ]
COPYRIGHT REGISTRATION : [ ]

Including all contents thereof all present and future adaptations and versions, and the theme, title and characters thereof, everywhere throughout the universe.

The undersigned and Producer have entered into that certain literary option/purchase agreement (the 'Agreement'), dated as of [ ], relating to the transfer and assignment of the foregoing rights in and to said literary work. Without limiting the generality of the foregoing, this Short Form Assignment shall be deemed to include, and shall be limited to, those rights of whatever nature which are included within the Agreement, which is not limited, added to, modified or amended hereby, and this Short Form Assignment is expressly made subject to all of the terms, conditions and provisions contained in the Agreement.

IN WITNESS WHEREOF, the undersigned has executed this Assignment on
[ ].

[ ]
(**Name of Author/Writer**)

Acknowledgement

On [ ], 200[ ], before me, [ ], personally appeared [ ], personally known to me (or approved to me on the basis of satisfactory evidence) to be the person(s) whose name(s) is/are subscribed to the within instrument and acknowledged to me that he/she/they executed the same in his/her/their authorized capacity(ies), and that by his/her/their signature(s) on the instrument the person(s), or the entity(ies) upon behalf of which the person(s) acted, executed the instrument.

WITNESS my hand and official seal.

[ ]
Signature of Notary

Quit Claim and Notice of Ownership of Copyright and Other Rights

This agreement (the 'Agreement') is entered into and is effective as of [ ] by and between **ABC Films Limited**, (the 'Producer') and **Y** ('Y'):

WHEREAS:

A. By Agreement dated as of [ ], Y entered into an Option Agreement (the '**Short Form Option**') with **Producer**, whereby Producer acquired an option to purchase the screenplay (the 'Screenplay') currently entitled [ ] written by Y;
B. By Agreement dated as of [ ], the Short Form Option was extended until [ ] (the '**Option Extension**');
C. By Agreement dated as of [ ], Y entered into a Literary Option and Purchase Agreement pursuant to which Y agreed to sell and Producer agreed to purchase the Screenplay on the terms and subject to the conditions set out therein (the '**Purchase Agreement**') so that Producer could produce a feature length motion picture based on the Screenplay (the '**Film**');
D. By Agreement dated as of [ ], the Producer assigned all right, title and interest in and to the Short Form Option and the Option Extension to Y (the '**Assignment**');
E. The Short Form Option, the Option Extension, and the Assignment are collectively referred to as the '**Agreements**';
F. The Producer wishes to remise, release and quit claim any and all of its rights acquired from Y under the Agreements.

NOW THEREFORE THIS AGREEMENT WITNESSES that in consideration of the obligations and undertakings of the parties hereunder and for other good and valuable consideration, the receipt and sufficiency of which is hereby acknowledged, the parties agree as follows:

Quit claim

a. The Producer remises, releases and quit claims all right, title and interest in and to the Screenplay and the Film granted pursuant to the Agreements, and for greater certainty, confirms that it is not currently and hereafter shall not subsequently be entitled to any revenues from the exploitation of the Film.

b. The Producer further quit claims any and all copyright interest in connection with the Film.
c. The Producer hereby agrees to execute any and all further documents and assurances that Y may reasonably request to effect, protect, evidence or continue the quit claim of the Film set forth above.
d. The parties acknowledge and agree that upon the execution of this Agreement, the Agreements shall be deemed terminated. Thereupon each of the parties shall have released and do hereby release, the other from and against any and all obligations and claims of any kind and nature under the Agreements.
e. The Assignment is hereby nullified.

Representations and warranties

The Producer hereby represents and warrants to Y with respect to the Screenplay as follows:

f. Except as set out above, it has not sold, transferred, assigned or otherwise disposed of any of its right, title and interest in and to the Screenplay.
g. It has the right and capacity to enter into and perform this Agreement.
h. There are no liens or encumbrances on the Screenplay, and no claims have been made or litigation instituted or, to the best of its knowledge, threatened with respect thereto.
i. It has not produced or authorized the production of any motion picture, television or dramatic presentation in any media whatsoever based on the Screenplay.
j. Prior to the effective date hereof, it did not breach any, and performed all of the obligations which it was required to perform under the Agreements, and all sums which had accrued and were payable pursuant to the provisions of the Agreements were paid.
k. To the best of its knowledge, it has not done or omitted to do any act or thing that will impair, alter, diminish the rights herein assigned, granted, quit claimed and otherwise transferred to Y.

Indemnification

l. The Producer shall defend, indemnify and otherwise hold Y, his successors, heirs, assigns and licensees free and harmless from and against any and all liabilities, claims, demands, damage, fees, expenses and costs (including reason outside attorneys; fees and disbursements) arising out of or resulting from any breach by The Producer of any of its representations, warranties or agreements contained in this Agreement.

Other documentation

m. The parties hereto shall each execute and deliver to the other such further documents, if any, as are reasonably required to carry out and effectuate the purposes and intent of this Agreement.

Notices

n. Notices required by this Agreement shall be in writing. Any notices hereunder shall be given by personal delivery, or by mailing by registered or certified mail or by telecopying the same to the appropriate party at the addresses set forth below:

To [ ]

To Producer: [ ]

c.c. [ ]

Any notice mailed, personally delivered or telecopied as aforesaid shall be deemed to have been given on the date of mailing or telecopying or the date of personal delivery.

Binding on successor and assigns

o. This Agreement shall be binding on and inure to the benefit of the parties hereto and their respective successor, heirs, licensees and assigns.

Governing law

p. This Agreement shall be construed and enforced in accordance with the laws of [ ] applicable to contracts entered into and performed therein.

Counterparts

q. This Agreement may be executed in one or more counterparts, each of which shall be deemed an original, but all of which shall be taken together shall constitute one and the same instruments. Delivery of an executed counterpart of the Agreement via telephone facsimile shall be effective as delivery of a manually executed counterpart.

Entire agreement

r. This Agreement contains the entire understanding of the parties hereto and replaces any and all former agreements, understandings and representations and contains all of the terms, conditions, understandings and promises of the parties hereto, relating in any way to the subject matter hereof. This Agreement may not be modified except in writing signed by the parties.

IN WITNESS WHEREOF the parties have executed this Agreement effective as of the date and year first set forth above.

By: [ ]

Its: [ ]

[ ]

PRODUCER HEREBY ACKNOWLEDGES THIS AGREEMENT

Per:
[ ]

Per: [ ]

2 Co-productions

Alan Harris

Things were fine between us, until the litigation started.
UK Producer discussing his relationship
with a Canadian Co-producer

Introduction

Increasingly over the past few years one of the most important items in the producer's toolbox has been an understanding of co-production treaties and conventions.

The British Government has entered into co-production treaties with other countries in Europe and around the world with the purpose of encouraging a pooling of creative, artistic, technical and financial resources among producers of those countries.

Films produced under the terms of a co-production treaty qualify as national content in the country of each participating co-producer and thus make the production eligible for applicable tax benefits from each co-production territory.

Co-production treaties fall into two categories:

1. Bilateral treaties where the UK has official co-production treaties;
2. Bilateral or multilateral structures under the European Convention.

Official Co-production Treaties

These include treaties agreed between Great Britain and Canada, Australia, New Zealand, France, Germany, Italy and Norway.

The treaties vary in their individual requirements and guidelines. Some require that the production qualifies under a points system (i.e., Australia), where points are awarded to key participants who are nationals of one or other of the co-producing countries, while other treaties have less onerous qualification requirements.

See the table for highlights of the individual treaties.

UK's bilateral treaty partners	*Minimum contribution*	*TV and video*	*Provision for co-producers from other country(ies)*	*Provision for financial participation only*	*Studio and labs*
Australia	30%	Yes	Yes	No	Normally majority country
Canada	40%	Yes	Yes	No	Most in majority country
France	20% for bilateral projects; 10% for some multilateral	No	No	No	Most in majority country
Germany	30%	No	No	No	Most in majority country
Italy	20% for bilateral projects; 10% for multilateral	No	Yes	Yes – typically 20% for bilateral; 10–25% for multilateral	Most in majority country
New Zealand	20%	Yes	Yes	No	Most in majority country
European Convention on Cinematographic Co-production	20% for bilateral projects;10% for multilateral	No	Yes (third party contribution not >30%)	Yes – 20–25% for bilateral; 10–25% for multilateral	In the states which are partners in the co-production, proportional to their investment

European Convention

The Council of Europe's Convention on Cinematographic Co-production came into force in 1994. The Convention has been ratified by more than twenty European countries, including the UK. As with the official co-production treaties, a production that is produced in accordance with the terms of the Convention will be entitled to receive national status and national benefits from each of the co-producing countries.

If one of the co-producers is a British company, the film will be entitled to receive certification as a British film and, accordingly, the producer will be entitled to benefit deriving from a sale and leaseback transaction.

Treaty requirements

The Convention applies to theatrical feature films only. It provides that a film co-produced by a company that is established in the UK and one that is established in one of the other signatory countries of the Convention will be entitled to national treatment in each co-producing country if the film is produced under the terms of a co-production agreement between the two producers and in accordance with the requirements of the treaty. Generally, each co-producer must contribute at least 20 per cent of the financing to the production of the film. This applies to a two-way co-production. If it is a three-way co-production it may be 70 per cent:20 per cent:10 per cent. The co-production agreement must stipulate that the co-producers are joint owners of the original picture and sound negative.

Points system

In addition, the Convention establishes a points system to measure the European nature of the co-production. The Convention requires a minimum of 15 points out of a total possible 19 points awarded on the basis of European nationality in creative and technical categories. The points available to a production are:

- Director: 3 points
- Scriptwriter: 3 points
- Composer: 1 point
- First role: 3 points
- Second role: 2 points
- Third role: 1 point
- Director of Photography: 1 point
- Sound Recordist: 1 point
- Editor: 1 point
- Art Director: 1 point
- Shooting location: 1 point
- Post-production: 1 point

Exceptions

Two issues are relevant in the determination of points required under the Convention. First, the performer points awarded for the first, second and third roles are determined by the number of days worked, not by prominence of credit or financial compensation to the performers. Accordingly, a film with a non-European star need not lose three points for the appearance of that star if he or she is on set fewer days than one of the European performers.

Second, a film that achieves fewer than 15 of the total possible 19 points and is otherwise produced in accordance with the Convention may be granted status under the Convention on a discretionary basis if, having regard to the demands of the screenplay, the film nonetheless reflects a European identity.

Co-production Agreement

When either seeking, or being approached by, potential co-production partners it is important, before opening negotiations, to check out the potential co-producer and the project.

Unless the producer is known to you it is advisable to explore the following points:

- check company background and do a company search;
- ask other producers or production companies in that country;
- check out their production credits;
- determine who they have already approached re: financing/co-production;
- ensure that the underlying rights to the script are clear;
- check out the viability of the financing plan. Ask to see any contracts for 'committed' funding;
- check the production budget closely;
- ensure that the timescale for pre-production, production and post-production are realistic.

One of the first tasks, even before the co-production agreement is drawn up, is the agreement between the co-production partners as to the roles they are each to perform on the production. The treatment of most other areas to be addressed in the agreement will relate to these roles and responsibilities.

Second, as a prerequisite to the agreement, one must establish the proportions in which the co-producers will share ownership of, and benefits, from the production. Whereas this should ideally reflect the effort and financial risks that the originating co-producer may have taken in developing the project prior to entering into the co-production, it must also give more than a passing nod to the limits and thresholds of the co-production treaty or convention under which the project is structured.

Co-production agreements are fairly complex but they all have a similar working skeleton upon which hangs the basic premise of the agreement between the parties. Here I outline a fairly basic but standard co-production agreement and explain the elements therein.

The agreement

The agreement is made on a certain [DATE] between [PARTY 1] and [PARTY 2].

Recitals

[PARTY 1] and [PARTY 2] agree to produce a film entitled [FILM] written by [WRITER]. It is intended to be produced as a [CO-PRODUCTION STRUCTURE] between [COUNTRY 1] and [COUNTRY 2].

A. Definitions and interpretation

Included in here are meanings of words and expressions included in the agreement. This section outlines such definitions as:

[BUDGET]
[THE BANK]
[DELIVERY DATE]
[THE TREATY]
etc.

B. Agreement to co-produce

(Roles and responsibilities of each co-producer)
This outlines what each co-producer must do to fulfil their side of the co-production, i.e., submit an application to the relevant authority for co-production status; agree to provide their contributions to the budget, etc.

This can also be where the implications of refusal for co-production status from any one of the co-production country authorities can be addressed.

C. Rights ownership

i. Underlying Rights. Here the co-producers acknowledge the ownership of the underlying rights and the division of those rights to each co-producer.
ii. Copyright Ownership/Distribution Rights. The completed production is made up of many separate copyrights, copyright in the underlying rights; in the script; in the key artistic elements, etc. Here the agreement addresses these matters.

D. Production of the film

Here the agreement outlines specific elements of the film's production such as [COMMENCEMENT DATE], [DELIVERY DATE], [SHOOTING LOCATION], [POST LOCATION], etc.

Sometimes this section also includes the name and nationality of some of the principal cast and crew as these may need to be agreed so that the production can qualify under the treaty or convention being used.

E. The financing of the film

This section outlines where and how the film is to be financed. It outlines the financial contributions to be advanced from each co-producer and when they fall due. This is extremely important and must be calculated in conjunction with the co-production structure being used, as some treaties require a minimum amount to be contributed by a co-producer.

It is also where the cash flow of the film is outlined, the bank and the account are named and any compliance issues of handling the transactions are dealt with.

F. Management of the production

This section deals with the management of the production. It looks at the issue of joint responsibility and usually outlines which co-producer has the ultimate say should there be a disagreement.

It will discuss the engagement of individuals, cast and crew and the structure for this engagement. Also the issue of insurances, E&O (errors and omissions) and completion guarantees, etc., access to the locations, studios and facilities, delivery and registration of the film.

It will also confirm that the two co-producers are not linked by common management or control, which is a requirement in all co-production treaties and conventions.

G. Receipts

This area usually references the Finance and Distribution Agreement and deals with the application of receipts from the exploitation of the film.

H. Credits

Here the co-producers agree to the wording and form of the credits, usually also encompassing the nationality credit, i.e., 'A [COUNTRY 1] – [COUNTRY 2] Co-production'.

I. Termination and force majeure

Should either co-producer commit a material breach of the agreement or go into liquidation the consequences of this are discussed in this section.

This section also deals with the impact of a delay in the production or delivery date and exactly when the Agreement is terminated, the responsibilities and liabilities of each co-producer.

J. No partnership

The Agreement does not constitute a partnership between the two co-producers.

K. Assignment

Subject to rights of each co-producer, this area states that neither co-producer is entitled to assign, charge or licence the Agreement to any other party without prior approval of the other co-producer.

L. Entire agreement

Basically this states that the agreement should be read in its entirety and that each party waives any right to seek remedy for mistakes or misrepresentations.

M. Notices

This is a standard legal inclusion about when something is deemed to have been delivered. When dealing with transactions and time-sensitive documents it is obviously vital to understand exactly when something can be legally termed delivered.

N. Governing law

This states the legal jurisdiction in which the Agreement has been drawn up and will be governed by should there be any dispute.

Schedule 1. Production Specifications

Schedule 2. Budget

Schedule 3. Cashflow Schedule

The Co-production Agreement

THIS AGREEMENT is made the [ ] day of [ ] 200 [ ]
BETWEEN:

(1) **[CO-PRODUCER 1]**, [ADDRESS] ('[ ]' or the '[ ] Co-producer');

AND

(2) **[CO-PRODUCER 2]**, [ADDRESS] ('[ ]' or the 'UK Co-producer');

Recitals

A. UK CO-PRODUCER and [ ] (together referred to as 'the Co-producers') intend to co-produce a full length feature film provisionally entitled '[ ]' ('the Film') based upon the original screenplay written by [ ].
B. The Co-producers intend to produce, complete and deliver the Film in accordance with the terms and provisions of the Agreement between the Government of the United Kingdom of Great Britain and Northern Ireland and the Government of [ ] concerning the Co-production of Films dated [ ] (the 'Treaty') and to apply to the relevant authorities for recognition of the Film as an official co-production under the Treaty.
C. The Co-producers are entering into this Agreement for the purpose of setting out the terms and conditions pursuant to which they will finance, co-produce, and seek to obtain official co-production status for the Film.

THE PARTIES NOW AGREE as follows:

A. Definitions and interpretation

a. In this Agreement the following words and expressions shall, unless the context otherwise requires, have the following meanings respectively:

'the Bank' [ ]or such other bank as may be approved by the parties hereto as the bank at which the Production Account will be held;

'the British Contribution'	sums amounting in the aggregate to [%] per cent of the Budget or [%] of the Cost of Production;
'the Budget'	[ ] which is the estimated cost of producing and delivering the Film as the same shall be approved by the Co-producers annexed hereto as Schedule 2;
'the Cashflow Schedule'	the cashflow schedule for the Film as approved by the parties hereto and annexed hereto as Schedule 3;
'the Contribution(s)'	the British Contribution and/or the [ ] Contribution as the context permits;
'the Cost of Production'	the final total aggregate cost of all items included in the original Budget actually incurred in the making, completion and delivery of the Film in accordance with this Agreement, certified correct pursuant hereto;
'the Delivery Date'	shall mean [ ];
'the Film'	the sound and colour theatrical feature film and sound-track associated therewith, tentatively entitled '[ ]' based on the Screenplay, which the Co-producers intend to produce in compliance with the specifications set out in this Agreement;
'the [ ] Contribution'	sums amounting in the aggregate to [%] of the Budget or [%] of the Cost of Production;
'the [ ] Territory'	[ ], all of the countries composing [ ], for all rights,

	and [ ] for television and videogram rights only and air companies, trains, and oil rigs flying the flag of any country in the [ ] Territory.
'the Production Schedule'	the production and post-production schedule for the Film as approved by the parties hereto;
'the Relevant Authority'	the authority responsible for the approval and administration of official co-productions under the Treaty in each of the Co-producers' countries;
'the Remaining Territory'	all parts of the world other than the [ ] Territory and the United Kingdom Territory;
'the Screenplay'	the original screenplay for the Film written by [ ];
'the Treaty'	the Agreement between the Government of the United Kingdom of Great Britain and Northern Ireland and the Government of the [ ] concerning the Co-production of Films dated [ ]
'the United Kingdom Territory'	the United Kingdom of Great Britain and Northern Ireland, and Eire and air companies, trains, and oil rigs flying the flag of any country in the United Kingdom Territory.

b. Any reference in this Agreement to the Film or a film shall, unless the context otherwise requires, be deemed to include a reference to any soundtrack associated with such film.

c. Words denoting the singular shall include the plural and vice versa, words denoting any gender shall include every gender, and words denoting persons shall include corporations and vice versa.

d. Any reference in this Agreement to any statute, statutory provision, delegated legislation, code or guideline shall be a reference thereto as the same may from time to time be amended, modified, extended, varied, superseded, replaced, substituted or consolidated.

e. The Clause headings and sub-clause headings in this Agreement are for the convenience of the parties only and shall not limit, govern or otherwise affect its interpretation in any way.

B. Agreement to co-produce

The Co-producers hereby agree that they will each in consultation with the others, apply to the Relevant Authority in their country for recognition of the Film as an official co-production under the Treaty within the time limits set out in the Treaty, and subject to the terms hereof, the Co-producers agree to advance their respective Contributions to the Budget in accordance with the Cashflow Schedule and to do or cause to be done all things of every kind necessary to co-produce, complete and deliver the Film and otherwise deal with the Film in accordance with this Agreement and in compliance with the provisions of the Treaty and with any special conditions imposed by the Relevant Authority.

Notwithstanding the foregoing, as a strict condition precedent to each Co-producer's participation in the co-production of the Film hereunder, each Co-producer shall provide evidence that it has secured sufficient financing to cover its full contribution to the Budget by no later than [DATE].

C. Rights ownership

f. The Underlying Rights

The Co-producers acknowledge that the underlying rights in the Work and the Screenplay have been acquired by [ ] and the amounts paid by [ ] in relation thereto shall be deducted from the [ ] Contribution and each party hereto shall thus have an undivided interest in such underlying rights in the same proportion as its interest in the Film hereunder (i.e., [%] for [ ] and [%] for UK CO-PRODUCER).

g. Copyright Ownership

As co-producers under the Treaty the Co-producers will be co-owners of the copyright in the Film when made and accordingly (and where appropriate by present assignment of future copyright) for the full period of copyright and all renewals and extensions thereto wherever possible, and, to the extent permitted by law, in perpetuity:

i. In the [ ] Territory, [ ] shall be the exclusive and sole owner of the entire copyright, title and interest in and to the Film including, without limitation, all rights of commercial exploitation, and all proceeds derived therefrom for the full period of copyright and all extensions and renewals thereof; and
ii. In the United Kingdom Territory, UK CO-PRODUCER shall be the exclusive and sole owner of the entire copyright, title and interest in and to the Film including, without limitation, all rights of commercial exploitation, and all proceeds derived therefrom for the full period of copyright and all extensions and renewals thereof;
iii. with regard to the Remaining Territory the Co-producers shall be entitled to and shall retain a percentage of the copyright and all other rights in the Film and all proceeds derived therefrom pro rata to their respective Contribution and the Co-producers each hereby make the assignments necessary to achieve such joint ownership for the full period of copyright and all extensions and renewals thereof.

h. Distribution Rights

It is hereby acknowledged that all distribution rights in the Film in the Remaining Territory shall be granted to a mutually agreed sales agent. For the avoidance of doubt any and all receipts and revenues derived by the Co-producers arising from the exploitation of the Film and all allied and ancillary rights in the Remaining Territory shall be allocated to the Co-producers in the same proportions as their contributions respectively.

D. Production of the film

i. Principal photography of the Film is scheduled to commence on [ ] and it is agreed between the Co-producers that the scheduled delivery date for the Film shall be on [ ] ('the Delivery Date').

j. The Co-producers have agreed to engage the following individuals for the Film, or where no individual is yet agreed, have agreed to engage an individual of the nationality referred to:

Role	*Nationality*	*Name*
Director		
Scriptwriter		
Composer		
Principal Actors:		
First Role		
Second Role		
Third Role		
Fourth Role		
Fifth Role		
Sixth Role		
Seventh Role		
Cameraman		
Sound Recordist		
Editor		
Art Director		

k. Principal photography of the Film shall take place in [ ] and post-production of the Film shall take place in the UK.

l. All Co-producers shall contribute technical and artistic elements of their own nationality, and all reasonable endeavours shall be made to ensure that each Co-producer's contribution in terms of creative personnel, technicians, actors and technical equipment shall be proportionate to the investment by that Co-producer in the Film.

m. At least ninety per cent (90 per cent) of the footage included in the Film shall be shot specially for the Film.

n. The sound-track for the Film shall originally be recorded in [LANGUAGE] and an additional version of the sound-track shall be produced prior to the Delivery Date dubbing the Film in English and UK CO-PRODUCER shall have access to all materials necessary to manufacture the English version of the Film.

o. The Co-producers undertake to ensure that, upon completion of the Film, all persons connected with the development and production of the Film and its sound-track shall have been duly paid.

p. To the best of the knowledge and belief of each of the Co-producers, no part of the Film (including its title) infringes or violates the trademark, copyright, patent or other rights of any person or entity.

q. To the best of the knowledge and belief of each of the Co-producers, no part of the Film by sight or sound contains any defamatory matter.

r. The Co-producers will keep each other fully informed with regard to the progress of the Film's production.

s. The Co-producers shall keep full and accurate records and books of account relating to the Film and each Co-producer shall be entitled to audit, inspect and copy all and any documents and agreements relating thereto.

t. The Co-producers agree to permit the completion guarantor to be accorded customary rights with respect to the Film including, without limitation, takeover, recoupment and first position security assignment rights.

u. The Co-producers shall mutually agree on the participation of the Film at any international film festivals and/or markets and shall agree on the maximum expenditure to be incurred in relation to the same and shall share such expense in the same proportion as their contribution to the Budget.

E. The financing of the film

v. The Co-producers' Contributions

The Co-producers shall each be responsible for advancing or causing to be advanced a proportion of the monies required for the financing of the cost of the production of the Film; [ ] shall advance or cause to be advanced not less than the [ ] Contribution, being [ ] ([ ]) net of all taxes, levies and duties, if applicable, in accordance with the Cashflow Schedule; UK CO-PRODUCER shall advance or cause to be advanced not less than the British Contribution, being [ ] ([ ]) net of all taxes, levies and duties, if applicable, in accordance with the Cashflow Schedule. Each Co-producer will participate in any excess of the Budget on a pro-rata basis of its contribution.

w. Cashflow

The sums to be advanced or caused to be advanced by each of the Co-producers shall be advanced at the times and by the instalments and in the currencies set out in the agreed Cashflow Schedule for the Film, provided that if the exigencies of production require amendments to such Cashflow Schedule each party will vary its advances of its Contribution accordingly, and shall be deposited in a bank account at the Bank, which account shall operate in accordance with a bank mandate approved by the parties hereto, and shall be known as the '[ ]' Production Account ('the Production Account'). The Production Account shall be operated only for the purposes of production of the Film in accordance with the Budget and the Cashflow Schedule and in accordance with the provisions of this Agreement.

x. Completion of Contributions

The financial contributions of the Co-producers to the Cost of Production shall be completed no later than sixty days following the Delivery Date.

y. Refusal of Co-production Status

If the Film is refused conditional approval as a co-production film by the Relevant Authorities, then the Co-producers shall negotiate in good faith to try to agree terms upon which to proceed to production of the Film without co-production status, Provided That if no agreement has been reached between the Co-producers fourteen (14) days after the date of such refusal (or such longer period as shall be agreed by them) then production of the Film shall be deemed abandoned, and each Co-producer shall be liable for a proportion of the costs incurred, with the approval of all parties, in connection with the development and pre-production of the Film, such proportions being equal to each Co-producer's proposed Contribution to the Budget.

z. Failure to Meet Conditions/No Public Exhibition

If:

i. the Film is granted conditional approval of co-production status and fails to comply with the conditions of such approval; or

ii. the Film is given final approval of co-production status, but is refused permission for public exhibition in the United Kingdom Territory or the [ ] Territory

then the financial liabilities of the Co-producers in relation to the Costs of Production shall be proportionate to each Co-producer's Contribution to the Budget pursuant to this Agreement.

aa. If the circumstances set out in Clauses z(i) or z(ii) arise as a result of a failure by one of the Co-producers to comply with its obligations hereunder or under the Treaty or any special conditions imposed by the Relevant Authority, then the defaulting Co-producer shall be solely responsible for the additional financial liabilities arising directly from such default.

F. Management of the production

bb. Joint Responsibility

Except as otherwise provided in this Agreement, the Co-producers shall have joint responsibility for managing all aspects of the production of the Film, including all financial and creative decisions. In the event that the Co-producers shall fail to agree on any matter after reasonable consultation then, subject always to the provisions of this Agreement and the requirements of the Treaty and any special conditions imposed by the Relevant Authority, and to the constraints of the Budget and the Production Schedule, the decision of [ ] shall prevail. The Co-producers shall each keep others fully informed on all matters relating to the Film.

cc. Application to Relevant Authorities

The Co-producers shall forthwith apply to the Relevant Authority in their country with a view to obtaining a provisional approval for the Film as a co-production project under the Treaty. Each Co-producer shall be responsible to its respective national Relevant Authority for the submission of all relevant information in connection with the co-production and for endeavouring to comply with any terms or conditions upon which any approvals by such authorities have been or may be given.

dd. Engagement of Individuals

Each of the Co-producers shall be primarily responsible for the engagement (on terms to be agreed between them) of the respective nationals whose services are required and utilized for the production, completion and delivery of the Film. All such engagements as aforesaid must be within the financial and other terms as required and stipulated by the Budget and the Production Schedule. If the terms of such engagements cannot be agreed between the Co-producers the decision of [ ] shall be final. All contracts shall be in a form usual in the film industry and shall be consistent with this Agreement and with the requirements of any financiers. Such contracts shall contain a grant of rights to permit the widest legally permissible exploitation of the Film. Such grant of rights shall specifically include an assignment of and an unrestricted authorization of exploitation of all performers' property rights, including (but not limited to) exploitation of the Film by means of rental and lending, and the contracts shall include an acknowledgement that the payment provided in the contracts includes an element representing equitable remuneration for the authorization of rental and lending. Further, all contracts for production of the Film shall include a waiver of moral rights, to the extent (if any) that such waiver is legally permissible. Each Co-producer shall be solely responsible for payment of any music performing rights or local charges and levies pursuant to laws in its exclusive territory in connection with the exploitation of the Film rights.

ee. Insurance

The Co-producers agree to obtain and maintain all such insurances as are customarily maintained by producers of first class films including the following:

i. Errors and omissions insurance (for a period of not less than three (3) years);
ii. Public and employer's liability indemnity;
iii. Indemnity against loss of or damage to negative stock;
iv. Indemnity against accident, illness or death of the director and principal cast members and such other individuals as the Co-producers shall consider advisable;
v. A completion guarantee;
vi. Such other insurances as may be prudent in the circumstances of the production of the Film or as may be required by law.

All insurances shall name all of the Co-producers as insured and shall have limits of liability, be subject to such deductions and exclusions and shall be maintained for such period as shall be agreed between the Co-producers (or if the Co-producers shall fail to agree, as shall be determined reasonable by [ ]). The Co-producers shall notify each other of any occurrence which may give rise to an insurance claim and shall consult concerning its settlement. No Co-producer shall do or permit to be done anything whereby any of the policies entered into may lapse, or become, in whole or in part, void or voidable.

ff. Access

Representatives of each of the Co-producers shall be given unrestricted access to all locations, studios and facilities at which the Film is produced and shall have the right to inspect daily rushes of the Film and during post-production to view all cuts of the Film.

gg. Delivery of the Film

i. During Production of the Film, all materials will be held at a mutually agreed laboratory in the joint names of the Co-producers and each Party shall be furnished with an irrevocable laboratory access letter granting access to such materials on terms to be agreed in good faith and set out in the laboratory access letter. The original negative of the Film shall belong to the Co-producers jointly as tenants in common in proportion to their respective Contributions.

hh. No Common Management

The Co-producers confirm that they are not linked by common management or control.

ii. Registration of the Film

Each Co-producer shall register the Film and all relevant contracts with the relevant national authorities in its own country and shall bear itself the costs of such registration unless such costs are included in the Budget.

G. Receipts

jj. The Co-producers acknowledge that any and all benefits received from the Relevant Authorities in respect of the Film shall be the sole property of the Co-producer to which such benefit is paid.

kk. All receipts from the exploitation of the Film shall be applied on the basis set out in the Financial Arrangements.

H. Credits

The Co-producers agree that there will be accorded in the Film and all paid advertising or publicity issued or paid for by all or any of them in connection with the Film credits. In particular the credits shall mention the nationality of each party hereto and the [ ] version must include the credit:

An [ ]-Anglo Co-production

and the English version of the Film must include the credit:

An Anglo-[ ] Co-production

and the international version must include the credit:

An [ ]-Anglo Co-production

The Co-producers expressly acknowledge the right of any distributor, sub-distributor or assignee of the Film rights hereunder to appear in the credits of the Film.

I. Termination and force majeure

11. If any Co-producer shall:

i. commit a material breach of this Agreement and (if capable of remedy) shall fail to remedy the same within 7 days of written notice notifying the breach and requiring its remedy; or

ii. go into liquidation (other than for the purposes of solvent amalgamation or reconstruction) or become insolvent or bankrupt or have a liquidator, receiver, administrator or other similar official appointed over any of its assets or fail to satisfy any final judgement within 7 days thereof or shall cease to carry on all or a substantial part of its business or anything analogous and having substantially similar effect to any of the foregoing events shall happen under the laws of the jurisdiction of incorporation of any party hereto,

the other Parties (the 'Non-Defaulting Parties') shall provide the Defaulting Party with notice of such default (the 'Default') by registered mail and the Defaulting Party shall have eight (8) calendar days from the date of receipt of such notice to cure the Default. If the Defaulting Party fails to cure the Default within such eight (8) day notice period, the Non-Defaulting Parties shall have the right to terminate this agreement, and without prejudice to any other damages available in equity or at law, shall further have the right to substitute the Defaulting Party with another producer of the same nationality as the Defaulting Party (the 'Replacement Party') for the purposes of the co-production of the Film. In such event, all amounts contributed to the co-production of the Film by the Defaulting Party up until and including the date of Default, shall be treated as a last priority credit of the Defaulting Party against all proceeds deriving from the exploitation of the Film by the

Replacement Party, such credit to be payable to the Defaulting Party only after the Replacement Party has recouped its entire investment in the Film, including, without limitation, financial charges, etc.

mm. If the Co-producers shall be delayed in or prevented from completing and delivering the Film or if either party shall be delayed by or prevented from performing its obligations in accordance with this Agreement by reason of any act delay or omission caused by circumstances beyond its control including (without limitation to the foregoing) strikes, lockouts, labour disputes, labour shortages, accident, fire, explosion or inability to obtain materials, facilities, transportation or power then and in any such event the party so delayed or prevented shall not be liable to the other for such delay or failure nor shall it give rise to a breach of this Agreement. It is further agreed that if any single occurrence as aforesaid shall continue for a consecutive unbroken period of sixty (60) days or more the parties unaffected may terminate the interest of the other party in this Agreement.

nn. The Co-producers agree that in the event of termination of this Agreement, the right, title and interest of the defaulting Co-producer in and to the Film, all physical materials relating to the Film and the production thereof, and all monies in the Production Account shall be transferred to the other Co-producers jointly, without the necessity of further legal formality, but the Co-producers agree that whichever of them is the defaulting Co-producer will forthwith execute any confirmatory documents reasonably required by the other Co-producers.

J. No partnership

Nothing in this Agreement is intended to or shall be deemed to constitute a partnership between the Co-producers and save as contained herein no Co-producer shall have any authority to bind the others or pledge the others' credit in any way.

K. Assignment

Subject to the terms of this Agreement and to each Co-producer's right to associate a third party co-producer to the co-production (provided that any such association does not jeopardize the Film's eligibility for qualification under the Treaty), no Co-producer shall be entitled to assign, charge or license this Agreement or any of its rights hereunder to any third party without the prior approval of the other Co-producers other than each Co-producer's right to enter distribution, sub-distribution, license and rights assignment agreements in its exclusive territory and any right to receive revenues which may be assigned to a subsidiary or associate or parent company or a company succeeding to 100 per cent of the assets of such assigning Co-producer Provided That any such approved assignment, charge or licence shall not relieve the assigning party of its obligations hereunder.

L. Entire agreement

oo. This Agreement (including the Schedules hereto, which are deemed a part of this Agreement) constitutes the entire agreement between the parties hereto in respect of the subject matter hereof and no terms, obligations, representations, promises or conditions, oral or written, express or implied, have been made or relied upon other than those contained herein.

For the avoidance of doubt each party irrevocably waives any right it may have to seek a remedy for:

i. any misrepresentation which has not become a term of this Agreement; or

ii. any breach of warranty or undertaking (other than those contained in this Agreement) whether express or implied, statutory or otherwise;

unless such misrepresentation, warranty or undertaking was made fraudulently.

pp. The parties to this Agreement acknowledge that in the event of a breach of this Agreement any application to enjoin or restrain the production, distribution, exhibition, advertising or exploitation of the Film or any rights therein or derived therefrom would be excessively disruptive and unreasonably damaging to the Film and the other parties' and third party's interests therein and consequently the parties agree not to apply for any such relief and accept that the recovery of damages in an action at law will provide a full and appropriate remedy for any loss or damage incurred by them as a result of any such breach.

qq. No variation of any of the terms or conditions hereof may be made unless such variation is agreed in writing and signed by all of the parties.

M. Notices

Any notice required to be given under the provisions of this Agreement shall be in writing and in English, shall be copied by the sender to all of the other Co-producers and shall be deemed to have been duly served if hand delivered or sent by facsimile or other print-out communication mechanisms or, within the United Kingdom, by pre-paid special or first class recorded delivery post, or, outside the United Kingdom, by pre-paid international recorded airmail, correctly addressed to the relevant party's address as specified in this Agreement and any notice so given shall be deemed to have been served (unless actually received at an earlier time in which case the time of service shall be the time of such actual receipt):

rr. if hand delivered at the time of delivery;

ss. if sent by facsimile or other print-out communication mechanisms, at completion of transmission if during business hours at its destination, or at the opening of business on the next business day if not during business hours (and for this purpose 'business hours' means between 09.00 and 17.30 and 'business day' means Monday to Friday, excluding bank or other public holidays in the country of the addressee) but subject in the case of facsimile and other print-out communication mechanisms, to proof by the sender that it holds a transmission report indicating uninterrupted transmission to the addressee and in each such case to dispatch of a copy of the notice by pre-paid post as provided above on the same day as such transmission (or the next business day in the country of the sender if such notice is transmitted outside post office hours); or

tt. if sent by pre-paid post as aforesaid, forty-eight (48) hours after posting (exclusive of the hours of Sunday), if posted to an address within the country of posting and seven (7) days after posting if posted to an address outside the country of posting.

N. Governing law

This Agreement shall be construed and performed in all respects in accordance with, and shall be governed by, the laws of [ ] and the parties irrevocably submit to the exclusive jurisdiction of the Court of [ ].

IN WITNESS whereof the parties hereto have executed this instrument the day, month and year first above written.

SIGNED and

DELIVERED by

[ ]

in the presence of:

[ ]

Name: [ ]

Address: [ ]

Occupation: [ ]

SIGNED and

DELIVERED by

[UK CO-PRODUCER]

in the presence of:

[ ]

Schedule 1. Production specifications

The Film shall be a 35 mm sound and colour film provisionally entitled '[ ]' originally recorded in the English language and complying with the following specifications:

i. The Film as produced by the Co-producers will accord with the Screenplay save only for such changes as may be agreed between the Co-producers and permitted by the provisions of any agreement relating to the financing and production of the Film.
ii. Film stock: filmed in Kodak with Dolby sound.
iii. Aspect ratio: Panavision.

iv. Running time including main and end titles: 100 min.

v. Rating:

[ ]: not more restrictive than [ ]

United Kingdom: not more restrictive than [ ]

vi. Laboratory:

Schedule 2. Budget

Schedule 3. Cashflow schedule

3 Banking the Deal

Rob Sherr

I'm not doing this for love!
Unnamed banker during negotiations
with producer for a loan

Introduction

It is very important to recognize the bank's role in the deal. In many respects the role is simple, although accommodating a bank into the financing structure can be complex. The reason lies with the bank's chosen position as provider of senior debt finance. In simple terms, this means that the bank is prepared to lend strictly on the basis that it expects to be fully repaid, without facing any unreasonable risk and, in doing so, to receive a small return on its cost of capital.

This approach influences the bank's attitude towards distribution agreements, its reliance upon the completion guarantee, its attitude towards co-financiers and its cautious approach to calculating its interest reserve. Practically, this also often results in the bank being the last to put in its funding and the first to be repaid.

Getting the bank to the stage where it is prepared to lend can be somewhat tortuous, but I hope that this chapter will provide some clues to help the process along.

Getting to the Term Sheet

Putting together the finance of a film can be likened to completing a jigsaw puzzle. However, most often there is no picture on the front of the box to illustrate how the final puzzle should look. For all the parties, it is therefore important to obtain the terms of the deal on offer. This, at least, will give an outline of the picture and will help identify areas of conflict that will need to be resolved.

As far as the bank is concerned, at the term sheet stage you are not seeking a commitment but an understanding of what will be required. Accordingly, the amount of information required by the bank is not vast but will include the following:

- background of the producer;
- budget;
- finance plan;
- synopsis;
- details of director, key cast, production crew;
- details of completion guarantor;
- details of co-producers;
- deal memos on pre-sales;
- details of sales agent;
- sales estimates.

This information should allow the bank to issue a term sheet. The term sheet will not offer a commitment to provide the finance, but it will indicate a willingness to consider providing a facility and will set out the terms upon which the bank is prepared to take the deal forward. The detail provided within the term sheet will vary from bank to bank but should include the details below as a minimum.

- *Amount* – this will also confirm the currency in which the facility is to be made available. The amount will incorporate the allowance made by the bank for its financing costs (see below).
- *Purpose* – financing the production costs of the film.
- *Arrangement fee* – this may vary depending on the security offered to the bank.
- *Interest rate* – this will be a margin above cost of funds. The cost of funds is typically expressed as LIBOR (the London Interbank Offer Rate) and is the rate at which banks lend to each other.
- *Security* – this will include an assignment and charge over the film, an assignment of current and future distribution agreements, a completion guarantee and an assignment of the usual comprehensive insurance policies (including errors and omissions insurance). Other security may be required depending on the structure of the finance.
- *Other conditions* – this will include the likely conditions precedent, the basis upon which the bank will calculate its interest reserve and the basis upon which distribution

agreements will be discounted for security purposes. These are expanded upon below.

From Term Sheet to Cash Flow Forecast

The term sheet should provide sufficient information to enable the financing structure to proceed. Within the financing plan, an assumption will have been made as to the amount of bank debt required and the term sheet will indicate whether sufficient funds can be raised from the bank, given the security (collateral) that is to be made available. The key determinates of this will be as follows.

The acceptability of the distribution agreements

Banks will tend to split distribution agreements into three categories:

1. *Primary collateral* – these will be with counterparties of undoubted standing and will include all the US Major Studios. It may be that a lesser counterparty is prepared to support its payment obligation with a letter of credit. A letter of credit transfers the obligation to pay to a bank and in most cases this will be considered primary collateral. Other conditions will apply, such as the completion guarantor adopting the contract, the contract being properly assigned and payment being due without any set off. Banks will lend up to 100 per cent of the face value of this collateral.
2. *Secondary collateral* – these will be with acceptable counterparties of lesser standing. In addition to the conditions mentioned within primary collateral, contracts will only be deemed to be acceptable provided a signature payment of 20 per cent has been paid. Banks will lend up to 50 per cent of the remaining value of this collateral.
3. *Tertiary collateral* – these will be contracts that are not considered acceptable. Banks tend not to apply any value to these contracts although they will form part of the bank's security.

Other acceptable security

At the time of writing (March 2004) there is an active market in providing advance funding on the net producer benefit arising out of a UK sale and leaseback agreement. Some banks are prepared to look at these agreements in the same way as they look at distribution agreements and it may be possible to obtain up to 100 per cent of the estimated net producer benefit. The principal conditions applying will be: the issuance of preliminary approval of co-production status by the Department for Culture, Media and Sport (if applicable) and appropriate wording within the completion bond to mitigate the British Qualifying risk. The legislation relating to films with a budget under £15,000,000 is due to expire in July 2005.

The calculation of the interest reserve

An interest reserve is the reserve set aside by the bank to meet the financing costs of the facility it is making available. The size of this reserve is critical as this money will not be available for any other production cost. It is an expense not covered by the completion guarantee (save where the completion guarantor has requested an accelerated draw down of the facility) and the bank will therefore adopt a cautious approach when calculating the figure. The following factors will be taken into account.

A. Timing of the draw down

The Bank may be required to draw all the money down on day one and place these funds into a production escrow account. In this instance, interest will accrue on the borrowing throughout the term of the production and until it is repaid. Most often, however, the loan is drawn down during the production period. The dates upon which the loan is to be drawn down will be pre-agreed and approved by the completion guarantor.

In view of the fact that the completion guarantee does not become effective until all the money has been advanced to the production (that is, the strike price has been met), the bank will usually insist that its money goes in last. This is advantageous to the producer as the interest will be lower as a result.

B. Cost of funds

This is the cost to the bank of making the finance available and is typically expressed as LIBOR, the London Interbank Offered Rate. LIBOR is available in all major currencies and the rate is fixed everyday in London at 11.00 h. Each draw down under the loan will be fixed for a period (usually 1 or 3 months) at the LIBOR rate that applies on the day. The LIBOR rate can be fixed in advance through financial hedging instruments but this has a cost, as a non-returnable premium is payable. Most often, therefore, the rate is not hedged but, to protect itself from increases in the LIBOR rate, the bank will build an anticipated increase into the interest reserve calculation, typically of 2 per cent.

C. Interest margin

The interest margin is the rate that is applied above LIBOR and represents the bank's return on its loan. The rate will vary depending upon the perceived risk of the transaction to the bank. In the event that the contract being discounted is a major studio agreement, the studio may insist that the interest margin does not exceed a maximum figure.

D. Repayment date

The bank will look at the very worst-case scenario in estimating the final repayment date. Accordingly, an assumption will be made that the full force majeure and arbitration periods allowed for in the completion guarantee will be required. A further period will then be added to recognize any likely delays in the distributor meeting its payment obligation. Roughly speaking, 180 days may be added to the delivery date as part of the interest reserve calculation.

E. Foreign exchange

It may be that whilst you have a distribution agreement in one currency, you may need to spend the funds in a different currency. In such circumstance, there will be an exchange risk. The example below illustrates this.

Pre-sales totalling US$5,000,000 have been made.

The exchange rate between US dollars and sterling is 1.65.

The production is being shot in the UK with the budgeted cost, including interest, of £3,000,000, which the bank is prepared to lend.

18 months later the film is delivered.

Bank borrowing stands at £2,950,000, representing an underspend of £50,000.

The bank receives US$5,000,000 from the pre-sales.

The rate between US dollars and sterling that day is 1.8.

The bank converts the dollars to sterling and receives £2,777,777, suffering a shortfall of £172,223.

To prevent this situation from arising, the bank will insist that the foreign exchange risk is covered. The example above is a simple one with three possible ways of hedging the exchange risk available.

1. The loan could be converted into dollars on day one. This has two potential disadvantages:
   - interest will be paid on the full advance from day one;
   - the LIBOR rate for US dollars may be higher than the LIBOR rate for sterling.
2. A forward foreign exchange agreement can be entered into to convert the sterling loan to dollars at an agreed date in the future. The disadvantages of this are:
   - the rate may be such that the amount available to spend in sterling is lower than the budget;
   - there is no certainty as to the date of repayment. This is not necessarily a major problem as a foreign exchange contract can be arranged so that it is exercisable between dates.
3. A series of forward foreign exchange agreements can be taken out to coincide with the dates upon which the loan is to be drawn down. This method is more complex than the other two but certainly represents the best solution when more than two currencies are involved.

The bank will be able to assist you with your decision.

F. Legal cost contingency

The bank will hold an additional amount back in case it needs to make use of legal advice. The amount will tend to be influenced by the size and complexity of the transaction. This sum is in addition to any legal costs that will have been incurred in putting the facility in place.

From Cash Flow Forecast to Commitment

The cash flow will be recalculated many times and will not be finalized until the day of draw down.

In the meantime, the bank will have undertaken its due diligence upon all the parties to the transaction and, provided it is satisfied, an approach will be made to its credit committee to obtain commitment. Solicitors will be instructed and a loan agreement will be produced setting out in greater detail the terms that had previously been set out in the term sheet.

Conditions precedent

The loan agreement will incorporate a list of all the conditions that will need to be fulfilled before the loan can be drawn down. The length of the list will vary from transaction to transaction but typically will contain between 15 and 40 conditions. Below are some general headings into which these conditions fall and a brief explanation of some individual matters that will need attention.

1. *Account opening documents.* The bank's account opening requirements must be fulfilled. These will include the completion of the application to open the account together with the mandate to operate the account, certain incorporation documents (e.g., Certificate of Incorporation and Memorandum and Articles of Association or partnership deed) and documents to identify the principals (shareholders or partners), executive officers (directors) and the authorized signatories.

   A word of warning: this sounds straightforward but banks are very particular about this documentation. Leave plenty of time to fulfil this condition, especially as this includes satisfaction of the individual bank's anti-money laundering procedures.
2. *Corporate governance documents.* These will include incorporation documents (see above) and various resolutions.
3. *Security documents.* These will include charges and assignments over the film and any distribution agreements, an interparty agreement, a collection agreement, a laboratory pledge holders agreement and a completion guarantee.
4. *Insurances.* The bank will need to see evidence that it is a named loss payee under all the film insurances, including the production insurance, errors and omissions insurance and any third party liability insurance.
5. *Opinions.* This will include an opinion letter on chain of title. It may also be necessary to obtain opinion on documents entered into by parties in other legal jurisdictions.

6. *Other.* This will include such matters as receiving a final certified copy of the budget and cash flow, satisfaction of repayment of any pre-production facilities and may also include matters relating to specific types of lending such as advance financing of sale and leaseback.

All these conditions precedent have been met. There are some things that you can do that will help move matters along. Here are some simple tips.

- Give yourself as much time as possible. A period less than eight weeks is definitely too short.
- Ensure that the film rights are properly vested in the rights holding company.
- Identify any potential conflicts early on and get them resolved.
- Give early warning on any potential difficulties in meeting any of the conditions.
- Ensure that you fully understand the requirements of the bank – don't be afraid to ask.
- Encourage the solicitors acting to identify early on who is responsible for producing which document.
- Encourage the creation of a conditions precedent schedule showing the status of each document and then its regular circulation.
- Make sure your solicitor is driving the transaction forward and that all parties are communicating.

Closing Time

Once the bank's solicitor is satisfied that all conditions have been met, the loan can be drawn down. The bank will insist that certain payments are made out of the first draw down. These may include:

- the completion guarantor's fees;
- any payments to discharge finance provided for pre-production;
- the bank's arrangement fee;
- the bank's legal fees;
- insurance fees.

After draw down, contact with the bank will lessen, although the bank will have certain monitoring requirements to ensure that the production of the film is on track. Not least of these is the provision of regular cost reports, with the bank's requirements usually matching those of the completion guarantor. The bank may raise certain questions but, generally speaking, as long as the cost reports are received in a timely manner they will let you get on with things, sit back, wait for repayment and look forward to the next deal.

4 Banking Documents

Lucy Walker and Philip Alberstat

I don't care, I do not want to be an investor in this movie.
Unnamed banker to producer during lengthy conference call

Banks and Security Documents – An Introduction

This chapter looks at the form and content of the agreements that a bank typically will require a borrower to enter into in connection with a secured loan facility for the purposes of financing a film transaction.

This chapter is written on the basis that a film production partnership, or company, is the borrower and that the bank, as security for its loan facility, requires a charge and assignment over the borrower's rights in the film and key contracts in connection with the film. The content and principal terms of a standard facility letter will be explored together with an explanation of the nature of security and the terms of the bank's security documents and the form and content of other documents that may be required by a bank, such as a letter of credit by a third party bank.

Generally, a borrower will approach a bank and request its terms, or best offer, in respect of the amount and type of loan facility that the borrower wishes to borrow from the bank. Depending on the bank's own internal protocol for approving borrower facilities, it may be able to give an agreement in principle to the borrower fairly swiftly, particularly if there is a pre-existing relationship between bank and borrower. In nearly every case however, any offer made by a bank will be expressed to be subject to credit committee approval (which is the bank's internal control mechanism for vetting the credit worthiness of borrowers) and negotiation of satisfactory loan and security documentation.

The primary document is usually the facility letter, which is the document that contains the main contractual terms and governs the relationship between bank and borrower regarding the loan facility. The terms and conditions relating to any security given by the borrower in favour of the bank, together with any other necessary contractual arrangements normally will be documented in separate agreements as this chapter explains.

Registration of Security

Where a company (that is a company formed under the Companies' Acts) or a limited liability partnership ('LLP') creates a registerable security interest over its property and assets then, under section 395 of the Companies' Act, that mortgage, charge or security document must be registered at Companies' House within 21 days of the date of its creation. Section 396 of the Companies' Act 1985 lists what constitutes a registerable security interest. A charge and assignment by way of security as set out in this chapter would be registerable if the borrower was a company or LLP.

If a company or LLP fails to register a registerable security interest within the 21 day time limit then the security interest is void against a liquidator, administrator or other creditor of the company or LLP. This is a matter of great importance for any bank or lender. As we have seen earlier in the chapter, the primary purpose of taking security from a borrower for its loan obligations is to ensure that the bank has recourse to specified secured assets for realization, in the event that the borrower fails to repay. Effectively, a security interest ringfences the secured assets from any other property and assets of the borrower and (subject to certain contractual arrangements and conditions) gives the bank exclusive recourse to those secured assets, in priority to other creditors of the borrower. Equally, registration gives the bank priority over the interest of any other lender registering a later charge in relation to the same secured assets. Crucially, in the event that the borrower was in liquidation or administration, a properly registered and enforceable security interest would also prevent a liquidator or administrator of the borrower from using or realizing the secured assets for the benefit of any other creditors of the borrower.

Failure to register a security interest means that the bank loses its priority interest in the secured assets and undermines to a very large extent the purpose of taking the security in the first place. Registration is effected by completion of a simple form (Companies Form M395 – see Companies' House website for further details: http://www.companieshouse.gov.uk) which must then be filed at Companies' House accompanied by the original security document and the requisite registration fee.

The register of security interests, known as the register of mortgages and charges, created by each company or LLP is available for public inspection. On the basis of the importance of registration, it is common for a bank to take responsibility for registration of any registerable security created in its favour.

Health warning!

The documents used in this chapter are only a guide. Many of the clauses contained within have been shortened or have specific sections deleted. These documents are for teaching purposes only. Always consult an experienced lawyer before entering a film financing transaction with a bank.

Bank Facility Letter

From: [Name of Bank]
To: [Producer]
Date: [ ] 200[ ]

Dear Sirs,

The bank has agreed to provide you with production finance of up to [amount of Facility] [£] (the '**Production Finance Facility**') in respect of the Film (as defined below) inclusive of all applicable interest, costs and fees subject to the following terms and conditions and repayable in accordance with the Repayment Schedule:

This is the introductory paragraph to the Facility Letter which is addressed to the Borrowers. The paragraph should contain an indication of the Bank's willingness to lend, either on a committed or an uncommitted basis and the amount of the facility should also be stated.

A. Definitions

In this Facility letter, the following expressions shall have the following meanings, unless the context otherwise requires.

'Account'
'Bank'
'Borrower'
'Borrowing'
'Budget'
'Cashflow'
'Charges'
'Completion Guarantee'
'Completion Guarantor'
'Co-producers'
'Co-production Agreement'
'Delivery of the Film'
'Distribution Agreement(s)'
'Distributor'
'Distributor Notices'
'Facility'
'Facility Letter'
'Film'
['Gap Amount'] (if applicable)

'Insurance Policies'
'Interparty Agreement'
'Laboratory'
'Laboratory Pledgeholder's Agreement'
'Letter(s) of Credit'
'Producer'
'Production Agreements'
'Production Finance Facility'
'Repayment Date'
'Repayment Schedule'
'Rights'
'Rights Documents'
'Sales Agent'
'Sales Agency Agreement'
'Sales Estimates' (Gap deals only)

The definitions section is self-evident, but operates to set out the full meaning of any defined terms that are used throughout the Facility Letter, and also to clarify the interpretation of certain terms and phrases as they are used.

B. Purpose

The Facility is to be used to assist the Borrower by the provision of the production finance to be utilized exclusively for the proper costs of production of the Film in all respects in accordance with the provisions of this Facility Letter.

Unless a bank has agreed to lend monies for general purposes, it will usually lend monies to a Borrower for a specific purpose; for example, to pay certain production costs in respect of a film. Nevertheless, a bank will not accept any responsibility for ensuring that the monies are actually applied for that purpose. The 'purpose' clause gives the bank the best of both worlds in that the Borrower is placed under a contractual obligation to apply the facility for the specified purpose but the clause also makes it clear that the bank is not under any obligation to check or ensure that the monies are actually used in this way.

C. Conditions precedent

No Drawing may be made under the Facility until the Bank has received the following (which shall be originals or certified copies as the Bank shall require) in relation to the Films:

i. The Rights Documents and/or evidence that the Borrower and/or either of the Co-producers, as the case may be, have title to the Rights, together with such legal opinions in relation thereto as the Bank may require;
ii. The Production Agreements fully executed or in agreed format, in which case any subsequent variations to their standard form provisions are subject to the Bank's prior approval;
iii. Evidence satisfactory to the Bank of the subsistence of the Insurance Policies, including the Completion Guarantee, and evidence that any fee due there under to the Completion Guarantor and/or the insurers shall be paid prior to or out of the first Drawing under this Facility Letter;
iv. [The Letter(s) of Credit, fully issued, in form and substance satisfactory to the Bank];
v. Evidence of the following duly executed agreements:
   1. The Co-production Agreement;
   2. The Sales Agency Agreement;
   3. The [any other(s)] Agreement(s);
   4. The Distribution Agreement(s).
vi. Together with evidence of satisfaction of all the conditions precedent of all the aforementioned agreements, satisfactory in all respects in form and substance to the Bank;
vii. Evidence of the subsistence of duly executed Distributor Notices duly executed by the parties thereto;
viii. The Laboratory Pledgeholder's Agreement duly executed by the Laboratory and the other parties thereto;
ix. The duly executed security documentation referred to in paragraph (e) below satisfactory in all respects in form and substance to the Bank;
x. Evidence that all relevant pre-production approvals required of the Sales Agent and the Borrower, pursuant, respectively, to the Sales Agency Agreement, have been satisfied or waived prior to the date hereof;
xi. Written confirmation from the Completion Guarantor that all funds required to be paid towards the production of the Film before drawing is to be made under the Facility in accordance with the Cashflow (such funds being equal to the 'Strike Price' under the Completion Guarantee less the Production Finance Amount) have been so paid;

xii. [Evidence that the Sales Estimates have either been reviewed and approved by an independent expert to be appointed by the Bank prior to the date hereof; (this applies only to gap deals)];
xiii. Certified true copy of a resolution of the Borrower accepting the terms and conditions of the Bank's security documentation;
xiv. The Borrower's original Certificate of Incorporation and Memorandum and Articles of Association, or certified copies thereof;
xv. The Borrower's acceptance of this offer signed on the Borrower's behalf as evidence of its acceptance of the terms and conditions stated herein; and
xvi. A mandate in the Bank's approved form duly signed on the Borrower's behalf.

When agreeing to make available a facility to a borrower, a bank needs assurance that its understanding of the factual and commercial circumstances relating to the borrower and any connected transaction is correct. Conditions precedent act as the bank's proof that agreements, financial circumstances and other relevant matters are correct and exist in accordance with the bank's expectations. Essentially, this clause is a list of evidence that the bank needs to see before it is willing to make available the facility. Collectively, these items are known as conditions precedent because delivery of these items is a condition of the availability of the facility. If the borrower failed to deliver any item and/or the bank was not happy, then it would be entitled to withhold availability of the facility. Sometimes a bank may be happy to receive certain agreements or items after the availability date, in which case they are known as conditions subsequent. The status of these items is exactly the same as a condition precedent except that the bank is acknowledging that they may be delivered within a certain time frame subsequent to the facility being made available.

The nature of the conditions precedent and/or conditions subsequent required by the bank will reflect the purpose for which the facility is required and, usually, the nature of the borrower's business. In film finance transactions, it is usual to require items such as the relevant distribution and production agreements, recoupment schedules, chain of title documentation, cast agreements, together with evidence of the borrower's due incorporation and/or organization and other items such as the bank's security requirements.

D. Offer period

This offer will be available to the Borrower for acceptance until [ ] from the date of this Facility Letter, after which date the offer will lapse [unless extended in writing by the Bank].

A bank may attach certain conditions to the time-frame within which a borrower may actually draw down the facility. This caters for circumstances in which both the bank and the borrower might sign the agreement but where the borrower does not require the Facility monies on day one of the facility letter. Therefore, for the sake of certainty for both bank and borrower this clause specifies the period during which the facility will be available.

E. Security

i. The obligations of the Borrower to the Bank under this Facility Letter shall be secured by security in the Bank's preferred form as follows:
   (a) The Completion Guarantee;
   (b) The Charges;
   (c) The Interparty Agreement;
   (d) The Laboratory Pledgeholder's Agreement;
   (e) Such Distributor Notices as may be relevant; and

Any future security which the Bank may from time to time hold for the Borrower's liabilities relating to the Film.

ii. For the avoidance of doubt, the Borrower acknowledges that all security held and to be held by the Bank for the Borrower's liabilities shall, unless the relevant security document expressly states otherwise, secure all the Borrower's liabilities to the Bank for whatsoever purpose.

iii. The Borrower hereby undertakes at the request of the Bank to execute such deeds, documents, mortgages, charges, assignments, notices, communications and other securities or agreements whatsoever as the Bank may require for the purpose of securing the obligations of the Borrower under this Facility Letter or for protecting, perfecting or enforcing the rights and remedies of the Bank under this Agreement or under any security document.

In most cases, a bank will require security for repayment of the facility that it is making available to a borrower. The purpose of security is to give the bank recourse to certain assets of the borrower (or to assets of a third party in the case of a guarantee or third party security) in the event that the borrower fails to repay the facility. The security clause (E) of the facility letter specifies the nature of the security required by the bank, namely a charge covering the Borrower's rights in the Film and an assignment of the benefit of the Borrower's rights and remedies under the Distribution Agreement and any connected guarantee or letter of credit. The nature of security agreements is explored later in this chapter.

Clause (E)(iii) contains what is commonly referred to as a 'further assurance' undertaking. When a bank makes a decision to lend, it will assess the value of the assets offered to it by way of security against the amount of the required facility. This assessment is normally expressed as a percentage and it is common for banks to monitor that the security cover for the amount of the Facility always exceeds a certain percentage. The purpose of this clause is to give the bank a right at any time to require the borrower to execute further security for its obligations under the facility letter in the event that the bank felt uncomfortable about the level of available security cover. Equally, it gives the bank a general power to require the borrower to enter into further security agreements in the event that any defect or problem was found in relation to any existing security or if further documentation was required to supplement, amend or perfect any existing security held by the bank.

F. Right to draw funds

This clause is very straightforward as its sets out the way in which a borrower may actually request the facility monies to be drawn down from the bank. The clause does contain protections for the bank however, as it makes clear that if an event of default has occurred or if the borrower is otherwise in breach of the facility letter, the bank shall not be obliged to make any monies available to it.

G. Interest

The Borrower shall pay interest on the Facility from time to time outstanding of [%] per annum.

This clause sets out the rate of interest applicable to the facility. Obviously, the borrower is required to pay back both the principal amount of any facility plus the accrued interest. This clause should detail the applicable rate of interest, explains the way in which interest is calculated and the dates on which the borrower must repay the amount of accrued interest to the bank. In some cases, a borrower may repay accrued interest on payment dates that are different to the scheduled repayment dates for the principal amount of the Facility.

H. Maximum amount of facility/increased costs

A bank is similar to any other corporate entity in that it is subject to tax on its profits against which it may set off its losses and it is also subject to special statutory requirements imposed on banks in order to ensure that, for the protection of bank customers, a bank has adequate capital reserves at any given time. When making available a Facility a bank will always calculate the rate of return or, put simply, amount of profit, that it will earn as a result of lending to the borrower. The purpose of this clause is to protect the bank in the event that any change in law or taxation as applicable to the bank results in any reduction in the bank's rate of return. In these circumstances, the bank is entitled to recover from the borrower additional amounts so as to preserve its anticipated rate of return.

I. Fees and costs

A bank will always charge a fee for making available a facility and may well seek to recover its legal and other costs from the borrower. These items are specified and described in this clause. It is important for the borrower always to check the terms and dates on which any fees or expenses will be payable. It is common practice for the bank to deduct its fees and expenses from the principal amount of the Facility made available to the borrower. Potentially, this could result in the borrower actually receiving a net amount less than the headline amount of the facility.

J. Repayment/pre-payment

This clause describes how and when the borrower must repay the facility. There are many repayment possibilities and, usually, repayment is structured to match the borrower's projected ability to repay. Some facility letters may require a borrower to make scheduled repayments of principal and interest throughout the term of any facility. Other facility letters may require a borrower to make regular scheduled repayments of interest but with the principal amount of the facility only falling due for repayment in a single bullet repayment at the end of term. Alternatively, other facilities may require a combination of these options.

Many facility letters will also include an option for the borrower to 'pre-pay' the facility. Pre-payment differs from repayment in that repayment relates to scheduled repayments of the facility. Pre-payment refers to early repayment of a facility. Some facilities may permit the borrower to pre-pay the facility either in whole or in part, prior to the anticipated repayment dates. A bank will always specify terms and conditions that may apply to pre-payment.

K. Representations, warranties and indemnity

In many respects, the purpose of this clause correlates with the purpose of the conditions precedent clause. A bank will lend on the basis of a certain set of facts as presented to it by the borrower. Whilst the conditions precedent constitute documentary evidence of those facts, the representations and warranties are statements made by the borrower confirming the set of facts is true. Again, as with conditions precedent, the nature of the representations to be made by the borrower will closely reflect the nature of the borrower's business and the purposes for which the facility is to be made available. Representations and warranties may cover basic issues such as the due incorporation of the borrower (assuming the borrower is a company); and the borrower's financial condition, together with more specialized representations and warranties relating to the ownership of the film, due performance of items such as the production agreement and the distribution agreement and that, for example, the screenplay does not contain any defamatory or libellous material.

L. Covenants

This clause contains covenants that are essentially promises by the borrower in favour of the bank to do or undertake certain actions. Covenants will vary in subject matter in accordance with the nature of the borrower's business and the purposes for which the facility is required. Some covenants may aid the flow of information between the bank and the borrower, for example a covenant by the borrower to provide the bank with specified information regarding the progress of the film; covenants by the borrower agreeing to maintain insurance over the film and its other assets; covenants by the borrower agreeing not to amend certain key agreements in relation to the film such as the distribution agreement and/or the production agreement; covenants by the borrower informing the bank upon the occurrence of any event of default; and covenants by the borrower for the purpose of protecting the bank's security (known as the negative pledge clause under which the borrower agrees not to mortgage, charge or assign any of its assets in favour of a third party save with the prior written consent of the bank).

M. Information

N. Payments

O. Events of default

Events of default are the levers by which the bank is entitled to demand repayment of the facility. This clause contains a list of those events that constitute a default. Mostly, events of default will be obvious, for example, if the borrower failed to make any repayments under the facility on the due date, if any kind of insolvency event affected the borrower, if the borrower otherwise breached any of its obligations under the agreement and the more general event of default, being any event that would be likely to have a material adverse effect on the ability of the borrower to comply with its obligations under the facility letter. A borrower should always look very closely at the events of default as a borrower may be able to negotiate with the bank for 'grace periods', which essentially allow a borrower additional time to make payment and/or perform its obligations. Grace periods prolong the period before which any failure by the borrower to perform actually becomes a default.

P. Illegality

Q. Borrower's liability

R. Notices

S. Waiver

T. Law and jurisdiction

Yours faithfully,

[ ]
For and on behalf of
Bank

Accepted on the terms and conditions stated herein, pursuant to a resolution of the Board of Directors, a certified true copy of which is attached hereto.

[ ]
For and on behalf of the Borrower

Schedule 1. The Budget

Schedule 2. The Cashflow

Schedule 3. The Insurance Policies

Schedule 4. The Rights Documents

Schedule 5. Production Agreements

Schedule 6. Laboratory Pledgeholder's Agreement

Charge and Assignment

Charge dated

Parties

1. **[Bank]** acting through its branch at [ ] (the **'Bank'**);
2. **[Borrower]**, (registered no: [Borrower registered number]), of [Borrower address] (the **'Borrower'**).

Recitals

A. The Bank has agreed to make available to the Borrower a loan facility of up to [amount] (the **'Facility'**) in accordance with a facility letter dated on or about the date of this Charge (the **'Facility Letter'**) for the production and completion of the Film (as defined in Clause 1.1);

B. The Borrower has agreed to execute this Charge as security for the repayment of the Facility together with interest thereon and all other sums from time to time owing to the Bank from the Borrower.

This clause sets the background and explains the purpose of the Charge. As mentioned earlier in connection with the loan facility, the Borrower is giving the assets covered by the Charge as security for repayment of the monies owed to the Bank under the Facility Letter. The Charge apportions certain of the Borrower's assets so that the Bank has recourse to those assets in the event that the Borrower fails to repay the Facility.

Operative provisions

1. Interpretation

1.1 In this Charge, the following expressions shall have the following meanings unless the context otherwise requires:

'Bank' includes persons deriving title under the Bank;

'Borrower' includes persons deriving title under the Borrower or entitled to redeem this security;

'Charge' means this charge and any and all schedules, annexures and exhibits attached to it or incorporated by reference;

'Charged Assets' means, to the extent of the Borrower's right in and title to such assets, the Film, the Rights, the Co-production Agreement, the Sales Agency Agreement, the Distribution Agreement, the Letter of Credit and all property and assets charged or to be charged under this Charge in favour of the Bank and all other property and assets which at any time are or are required to be charged in favour of the Bank under this Charge;

'Distributor' means [ ];

'Event of Default' shall mean those events defined as events of default under the Facility Letter;

'Facility Letter' means the facility letter referred to in Recital (A) above;

'Film' means the feature film provisionally entitled '[Film]', short particulars of which are set out in **Schedule 1**;

'Letter of Credit' means the letter of credit dated on or about the date of this Charge and issued by [ ] in favour of the Borrower in respect of the obligations of the Distributor to the Borrower under the Distribution Agreement;

'Physical Materials' means the materials required to be delivered to the Sales Agent pursuant to the Sales Agency Agreement, and the Distributor pursuant to the Distribution Agreement, together with all physical properties of every kind or nature of or relating to the Film whether now in existence or hereafter made and all versions thereof, including, without limitation, exposed film, developed film, positives, negatives, prints, answer prints, special effects, pre-print materials, soundtracks, recordings, audio and video tapes and discs of all types and gauges, cutouts, trims and any and all other physical properties of every kind and nature relating to the Film in whatever state of completion, and all duplicates, drafts, versions, variations and copies of each thereof;

'Receiver' means any receiver or manager or administrative receiver appointed by the Bank either solely or jointly (and if more than one on the basis that they may act jointly and severally) under or by virtue of this Charge or any other security interest of the Bank or the Bank's statutory powers;

'Rights' means the rights in respect of the Film short particulars of which are set out in **Schedule 1**;

'Sales Agent' means [Sales Agent legal name] of [Sales Agent address];

'Sales Agency Agreement' means the sales agency agreement entered into by the Borrower with the Sales Agent on [date] in connection with the distribution of the Film in the Territory;

'Secured Amounts' means all monies or liabilities which shall for the time being (and whether on or at any time after demand) be due, owing or incurred to the Bank by the Borrower whether actually or contingently and whether solely or jointly with any other person and whether as principal or surety, including interest, discount commission or other lawful charges and expenses which the Bank may in the course of its business charge in respect of any of the matters aforesaid or for keeping the Borrower's account and so that interest shall be computed and compounded according to the usual mode of the Bank as well after as before any demand made or judgement obtained hereunder; and

'Source Material' means, to the extent of the Borrower's right in and title to the following, all underlying literary, dramatic, lyrical, musical, artistic and other material including, without limitation, the format, all titles, trade marks, designs, and logos used in or in connection with the Film.
For the purposes of this Charge, all capitalized expressions not otherwise defined herein shall have the meanings ascribed to them in the Facility Letter.

1.2 Any reference in this Charge to any statute or statutory provision shall be construed as including a reference to that statute or statutory provision as from time to time amended, modified, extended or re-enacted, whether before or after the date of this Charge, and to all statutory instruments, orders and regulations for the time being made pursuant to it or deriving validity from it.

1.3 Expressions used herein that are defined in The Copyright, Designs and Patents Act 1988, shall, unless the context otherwise requires, have the meaning attributed thereto in that Act.

The definitions should be the same as those found in the Facility Letter.

2. Charge and security assignment

2.1 The Borrower hereby covenants to pay or discharge to the Bank the Secured Amounts in accordance with the provisions of the Facility Letter.

2.1.1 As continuing security for the payment and discharge of the Secured Amounts and for the performance of the obligations of the Borrower under the Facility Letter and this Charge, the Borrower with full title guarantee hereby unconditionally and irrevocably assigns absolutely to the Bank by way of security throughout the world (and insofar as necessary by way of present assignment of future copyright pursuant to s.91 of the Copyright Designs and Patents Act 1988) the Borrower's right, title and interest in and to:

a. the Rights (subject to and with the benefit of the Sales Agency Agreement, and the Distribution Agreement);
b. the Sales Agency Agreement and all of the Borrower's right, title, benefit and interest to and in the same including, without limitation, any and all sums of money whatever payable to or on account of the Borrower by the Sales Agent pursuant to the Sales Agency Agreement;
c. the Distribution Agreement and all of the Borrower's right, title, benefit and interest to and in the same including, without limitation, any and all sums of money whatever payable to or on account of the Borrower by the Distributor pursuant to the Distribution Agreement;
d. the benefit of all policies of insurance now or in the future taken out by the Borrower in respect of the Film and/or the Rights, including the Insurance Policies; and
e. the Letter of Credit;
f. charges by way of a first fixed charge to the Bank the Borrower's right, title and interest in and to:

i. the Film (as both presently existing and to be created or acquired);
ii. the Physical Materials;
iii. the proceeds of all policies of insurance now or in the future taken out by the Borrower in respect of the Film and/or the Rights, including the Insurance Policies;
iv. all sums from time to time standing to the credit of the Collection Account; and

g. charges by way of a floating charge any and all of the Borrower's rights and interest detailed in sub-clauses 2.1.1 above if and to the extent that the first fixed charge may fail for any reason to operate as a fixed charge.

2.1.2 The Borrower hereby undertakes to hold in trust for the Bank any monies paid to the Borrower by the Sales Agent pursuant to the Sales Agency Agreement, and by the Distributor pursuant to the Distribution Agreement or by any insurers pursuant to the Insurance Policies and will notify the Bank forthwith upon the receipt of any such monies and immediately credit the same to the Collection Account to be paid subject to the Recoupment Schedule and the Collection Agreement.

Clause 2 is where the Borrower actively creates charges and assigns its assets in favour of the Bank. The assets being charged and assigned are described and listed in this clause. In a film transaction, the items such as the rights and physical materials and soundtrack in relation to the film, the benefit of agreements such as the co-production agreement and the right to receive the income streams from agreements such as the sale agency agreement and the distribution agreement, and in this particular case, the benefit of the Letter of Credit (which is, itself, security for the payments to be made by the Distributor under the Distribution Agreement).

Where, under the Charge and Assignment the Borrower assigns in favour of the Bank the right to receive the income payable under agreements such as the Sales Agency Agreement and the Distribution Agreement, the Bank may well require that any such income is paid directly to the Bank into a blocked account. This means that the Borrower will be unable to withdraw or utilize any of those monies thus protecting the Bank's collateral. Alternatively, as set out in this clause, the Borrower will, upon receiving those monies, hold the monies on trust for the Bank and pay them directly into the collection account (which may or may not be charged in favour of the Bank).

3. Enforcement

3.1 The security and charge created pursuant to this Charge shall become enforceable at any time after the occurrence of an Event of Default.

3.2 In addition to the foregoing provisions of this Clause, the Bank may at any time after an Event of Default is declared appoint in writing a Receiver or Receivers of the Charged Assets on such terms as to remuneration and otherwise as it shall think fit, and may from time to time remove any Receiver and appoint an alternative receiver.

3.3 If a Receiver is appointed, such Receiver shall be the agent of the Borrower and have all the powers set out in **Schedule 1** to the Insolvency Act 1986 and, in addition, shall have the power:

a. to take possession of, get in and enforce the Charged Assets;

b. to take any steps that may be necessary or desirable to effect compliance with any or all of the agreements charged or assigned pursuant to this Charge and to carry on, manage or concur in carrying on and managing the business of the Borrower or any part of the same in relation to the Film, and for any of those purposes to raise or borrow from the Bank or otherwise any money that may be required upon the security of the whole or any part of the property or assets charged or assigned by this Charge;

c. to institute proceedings and sue in the name of the Borrower and to appoint managers, agents and employees at such salaries as the Receiver may determine;

d. to sell or license or concur in selling or licensing the interest of the Borrower in the Charged Assets or otherwise deal therewith and on such terms in the interest of the Bank as the Receiver thinks fit;

e. to appoint and discharge managers, advisers, officers, agents, contractors, workmen and employees for any of the aforesaid purposes for such remuneration and on such other terms as the Bank or the Receiver shall think fit;

f. to do all such other acts and things as may be considered to be incidental or conducive to any of the matters or powers aforesaid and which he lawfully may or can do; and

g. to make any arrangement or compromise and enter into any contract or do any other act or make any omission which he shall think expedient in the interest of the Bank and to do any other act or thing which a Receiver appointed under the Law of Property Act 1925 or the Insolvency Act 1986 would have power to do subject to the provisions of this Charge, provided always that nothing contained in this Charge shall make the Bank liable to such Receiver as aforesaid in respect of the Receiver's remuneration, costs, charges or expenses or otherwise.

3.4 At any time after the security created hereunder becomes enforceable, the Bank or a Receiver may (but shall not be obliged to) do all such things and incur all such expenditure as the Bank or such Receiver shall in its sole discretion consider necessary or desirable to remedy such default or protect or realize the Charged Assets or its interests under this Charge, and in particular (but without limitation) may enter upon the Borrower's property and may pay any monies which may be payable in respect of any of the Charged Assets, and any monies expended in so doing by the Bank or the Receiver shall be deemed an expense properly incurred and paid by the Bank, and the Borrower shall reimburse the same on demand to the Bank.

This clause describes the circumstances in which the Charge will become enforceable. Upon the occurrence of an event of default under the Facility letter, the Bank will be entitled to enforce the Charge and assert its rights to receive, sell or otherwise deal with the assets charged and assigned in favour of the Bank under the Charge. The Bank has the power to deal with the Charged Assets in any way that it thinks fit and to apply them in repayment of the loan facility and/or in repayment of the Bank's costs and expenses as the Bank may decide. The Bank also has the power to appoint a Receiver over the Borrower and this clause also sets out wide powers to enable the Receiver to get in and realize (essentially, into cash) the Charged Assets.

4. Covenants and warranties

4.1 The Borrower hereby warrants, undertakes and agrees for the benefit of the Bank as follows:

a. that it is the sole, absolute legal owner of the Charged Assets and that none of the Charged Assets are the subject of any mortgage, charge, lien, pledge, incumbrance or security interest other than any such arising in favour of the Bank;

b. that the execution of this Charge by the Borrower will not conflict with or cause a breach of any agreement, instrument or mortgage to which the Borrower is a party or which is binding on the Borrower or its assets;
c. that it has acquired the Rights, which are unencumbered subject to the Sales Agency Agreement, the Distribution Agreement [and the Completion Guarantor's Security];
d. not, without the prior written consent of the Bank, to sell, transfer, dispose of or part with possession or control of or attempt to sell, transfer or dispose of the Charged Assets or any part of them or any interest in them, nor directly or indirectly create or permit to exist or be created any mortgage, charge, lien, pledge, incumbrance or security interest upon or in the Charged Assets or any part of them;
e. to maintain the Physical Materials in good and serviceable condition (fair wear and tear excepted) and not to permit the same to be used, handled or maintained other than by persons properly qualified and trained;
f. not, without the prior written consent of the Bank, to make any modification or permit any modification to be made to the Film or the Rights if such modification may have an adverse effect on the security of the Bank whether under this Charge or otherwise;
g. promptly to pay all taxes, fees, licence duties, registration charges, insurance premiums and other outgoings in respect of the Film and the Rights or any part of any of them, and on demand to procure evidence of payment to the Bank;
h. to obtain or cause to be obtained all necessary certificates, licences, permits and authorizations from time to time required for the production of the Film and the protection of the Rights in accordance with the provisions of the Sales Agency Agreement and the Distribution Agreement and not to do or permit to be done any act or omission whereby the Film or its production, distribution, broadcast or exhibition would contravene any relevant rules and regulations for the time being in force;
i. immediately to notify the Bank of any material loss, theft, damage or destruction to the Physical Materials and/or breach of the Rights or any part of them;

j. to give the Bank such information concerning the location, condition, use and operation of the Physical Materials as the Bank may reasonably require, and to permit any persons designated by the Bank at all reasonable times to inspect and examine the Physical Materials and the records maintained in connection with them;
k. immediately to notify the Bank in writing if it becomes aware of any claims made by a third party with respect to the Film and/or the Rights and to use its best endeavours to protect and preserve the Rights;
l. not to enter into any agreements relating to the distribution or exploitation of the Film or any of the Rights without the prior written approval of the Bank, such approval not to be unreasonably withheld or delayed;
m. not to modify or vary or waive any of its rights pursuant to the Sales Agency Agreement, or the Distribution Agreement or the Laboratory Pledgeholder's Agreement or breach or terminate any such agreements;
n. that it has no knowledge of any notification or assertion of any prior claims by any third party in priority to the Bank's to any of the advances or other payments required to be made pursuant to the Sales Agency Agreement or to the Borrower's or any other party's right to compensation or other payment under the Distribution Agreement;
o. to keep all necessary and proper accounts of its dealings with the Sales Agent under the Sales Agency Agreement, and the Distributor under the Distribution Agreement and such accounts shall at all reasonable times be open to the inspection of the Bank or of any Receiver appointed under this Charge or of any person authorized by the Bank or any such Receiver;
p. that it will in a timely manner perform its obligations under the Sales Agency Agreement and the Distribution Agreement and will comply with all laws and regulations from time to time relating to the Sales Agency Agreement and the Distribution Agreement or affecting their enforceability; and
q. that it shall procure that all sums charged or assigned to the Bank hereunder shall be paid to the Bank or as the Bank may direct from time to time.

4.2 The Borrower further covenants:
   a. not to do anything nor to allow anything to be done whereby any policy or policies of insurance on the Film and/or the Rights may be or become void or voidable or whereby any such insurances might be prejudiced, cancelled, avoided or made subject to average;
   b. to renew (or procure the renewal of) all insurances (where applicable) at least 14 days before the relevant policies or contracts expire, and to procure that the approved broker shall promptly confirm in writing to the Bank when each such renewal has been effected;
   c. promptly to pay or procure for the payment of all premiums, calls, contributions, or other sums payable in respect of all such insurances and to produce all relevant receipts when so required by the Bank, failing which the Bank may pay such premiums itself and the amount of the premiums and all costs, charges and expenses relating to that payment shall be repaid by the Borrower to the Bank, and until so repaid shall be added to this security;
   d. upon the happening of any event giving rise to a claim under any insurances, forthwith to give notice to the appropriate insurers and to the Bank; and
   e. to reimburse the Bank the cost to the Bank of effecting any policy of insurance to protect the interest of the Bank in the Film and/or the Rights as mortgagee.

4.3 Prior to the date hereof and on the occasion of each renewal of the insurances required pursuant to Clause 4.2, the Borrower shall procure that its insurance brokers issue to the Bank a letter confirming the subsistence of the insurances in accordance with the terms hereof.

4.4 The Bank shall apply monies received pursuant to a claim for an actual, agreed or constructive total loss of the Physical Materials in the following order:
   a. in or towards repayment of any part of the Secured Amounts as the Bank decides; and
   b. the surplus (if any) to be paid to the Borrower or other person entitled thereto.

4.5 The Bank shall apply all monies received pursuant to a claim for any other loss in paying directly for repairs or other charges in respect of which such proceeds were paid, or in reimbursing the Borrower for any such repairs or other charges.

4.6 The Bank shall not be obliged to make any enquiry as to the nature or sufficiency of any payment made under any of the Sales Agency Agreement, or the Distribution Agreement or to make any claim or take any other action to collect any money or to enforce any rights and benefits assigned to the Bank or to which the Bank may at any time be entitled under this Charge.

The covenants and warranties contained in this clause operate in a very similar manner to the covenants and undertakings found in the Facility Letter. Again, they represent an assertion by the Borrower that certain factual circumstances that have induced the Bank to enter into its arrangements with the Borrower are true and contain promises by the Borrower to protect the Charged Assets and to supply certain information to the Bank.

5. Set-off

This clause gives the Bank a right of set-off which enables the Bank at any time, to set-off any credit balance held by the Borrower with the Bank against any debit balance, namely the amount of the Facility.

6. Grant of time or indulgence

This clause provides protection for the Bank by making it clear that any delay or failure on the part of the Bank to exercise any of its rights and remedies under the Charge, shall not constitute a waiver of those rights and remedies.

7. Assignment

The Bank shall be entitled to assign, transfer, charge, sub-charge or otherwise grant security over or deal in all or any of its rights, title and interest in this Charge.

8. Protection of third parties

8.1 No purchaser, mortgagee or other third party dealing with the Bank and/or any Receiver shall be concerned to enquire whether any of the powers which they have exercised or purported to exercise has arisen or become exercisable or whether the Secured Amounts remain outstanding or as to the propriety or validity of the exercise or purported exercise of any such power, and the title of a purchaser or other person and the position of such a person shall not be prejudiced by reference to any of those matters.

8.2 The receipt of the Bank or any Receiver shall be an absolute and conclusive discharge to any such purchaser, mortgagee or third party, and shall relieve such person of any obligation to see to the application of any sums paid to or by the direction of the Bank or any Receiver.

9. Protection of the bank and receiver

9.1 Neither the Bank nor the Receiver shall be liable to the Borrower in respect of any loss or damage which arises out of the exercise or the attempted or purported exercise of or the failure to exercise any of their respective powers.

9.2 Without prejudice to the generality of Clause 9.1, entry into possession of the Film or the Rights or any part of them shall not render the Bank or any Receiver liable to account as mortgagee in possession, and if and whenever the Bank or any Receiver enters into possession of the Film or the Rights or any part of them they may at any time go out of such possession.

10. Power of Attorney

It is standard for a charge or security document of this type to contain a power of attorney. Under this clause, the Borrower appoints the Bank as its attorney to sign any documents and take any action on behalf of the Borrower as required under the Charge. This provides the Bank with protection in circumstances where the Borrower is, for example, being uncooperative or where relevant signatories are unavailable. In such cases the Bank could sign for and on behalf of the Borrower as the Borrower's Attorney under the power given by this clause.

11. Indemnity

The indemnity clause contains a promise by the Borrower to compensate the Bank for all expenses incurred by the Bank in connection with the preparation and completion of the Charge, together with any other expenses incurred by the Bank in connection with the Charge. Typically these costs and expenses might include items such as receiver's fees and the Bank's legal fees and other costs connected with enforcement of the Charge.

12. Further assurance

The Borrower shall on demand execute any document and do any other act or thing which the Bank may reasonably specify for perfecting any security created or intended to be created by this Charge or which the Bank or the Receiver may specify with a view to facilitating the exercise, or the proposed exercise, of any of their powers.

13. Other security

This security is in addition to, and shall not be merged in or in any way prejudice or be prejudiced by, any other security, interest, document or right which the Bank may now or at any time hereafter hold or have as regards the Borrower or any other person in respect of the Secured Amounts.

14. Waivers, remedies cumulative

The powers which this Charge confers on the Bank are cumulative and without prejudice to its powers under general law, and may be exercised as often as the Bank deems appropriate. The rights of the Bank and the Receiver (whether arising under this Charge or under the general law) shall not be capable of being waived or varied otherwise than by an express waiver or variation in writing; and, in particular, any failure to exercise or any delay in exercising on the part of the Bank or the Receiver any of these rights shall not operate as a waiver or variation of that or any other such right; any defective or partial exercise of any such right shall not preclude any other or further exercise of that or any other such right; and no act or course of conduct or negotiation on the part of either the Bank or the Receiver or on its or their behalf shall in any way preclude either the Bank or the Receiver from exercising any such right or constitute a suspension or variation of any such right.

This clause protects the rights and remedies of the Bank, by making it clear that the Bank may exercise its rights as many times as it thinks fit. The Bank's rights are always cumulative.

15. Bank's costs and expenses

The Bank has a power under this clause to recover all of its costs, charges and expenses from the Borrower.

16. Discharge and re-assignment

Upon repayment in full to the Bank of the Secured Amounts, the Bank will, at the request of the Borrower, release the charges created under this Charge and re-assign to the Borrower all rights in and to the assets assigned pursuant to Clause 2 hereof, including, without limitation, the Sales Agency Agreement and the Distribution Agreement.

17. Power of sale

18. Invalidity of any provision

If at any time any one or more of the provisions of this Charge becomes invalid, illegal or unenforceable in any respect under any law, the validity, legality and enforceability of the remaining provisions shall not in any way be affected or impaired thereby.

19. Notices

20. Governing law

This Charge shall be governed by and construed in accordance with the laws of England, the courts of which shall be the courts of competent jurisdiction.

Duly Executed as a Deed the day and year first above written.

Schedule 1

The film

The full length feature film having a provisional running time of between [ ] and [ ] minutes and entitled '[FILM]', to be produced by the Borrower [jointly with [Co-Producer 1] and [Co-Producer 2] pursuant to the terms of the Co-production Agreement,] together with all tangible property now in existence and owned by the Borrower or hereafter created or acquired by the Borrower for use in the production of the Film.

The rights

All proprietary, statutory, contractual and common law rights throughout the world acquired by the Borrower whether as owner, maker, author or otherwise, in and to the Film and any other videotape, computer film, computer disk, film and any sound recordings made in the course of the production of the Film, including the Source Material, and without prejudice to the generality of the foregoing but subject to the Sales Agency Agreement, the Distribution Agreement, [and the Completion Guarantee Security]:

1. The sole, exclusive and irrevocable right to distribute, reproduce, exhibit, license and otherwise exploit and deal in and with the Film and any and all parts of the Film by all methods and means in any and all media systems and processes now known or in the future devised.
2. All rights of copyright in the original screenplay of the Film and in all other literary, artistic, dramatic and musical works created or to be created for and whether or not used and/or contained in the Film and, in respect of the music, all rights including the right to synchronize the same with and incorporate the same in the Film and to exploit the music and the Source Material independently of the Film (except for musical performing rights if the composer is a member of the Performing Right Society).
3. All ancillary publishing, spin-off and merchandising rights of every kind and nature in or to the Film, including but not limited to novelization and publishing rights and commercial tie-ups and sponsorship.

4. All rights of the Borrower pursuant to any agreement, arrangement or contract made with any person, firm or company in connection with or relating to the production or distribution of the Film.

Schedule 2

Part I: Form of Notice of Assignment/Irrevocable Payments Instructions

See example later in this chapter.

Part II: Form of Acknowledgement of Notice of Assignment

See example later in this chapter.

DULY EXECUTED AND DELIVERED as a **DEED** by	[ ] [ ] Director
and for and on behalf of **[BORROWER]**	[ ] Director/Secretary

Signed and acknowledged
by [ ]
duly authorized signatory
for and on behalf of
[Bank]

Letter of Credit

To: [Beneficiary]
From: [Issuer]

Dear Sirs

Irrevocable Letter of Credit – [*insert name of film production partnership or company*]

On the terms and subject to the conditions set out below, [Issuer] hereby issues this irrevocable Letter of Credit in favour of the Beneficiary at the request of the Distributor.

The introductory paragraph relates to issuance of the letter of credit in favour of the Beneficiary. In this example, the letter of credit has been issued at the request of the Distributor. In film transactions, letters of credit and/or guarantees are frequently used as security for the payment obligations of, for example, the Distributor under the Distribution Agreement. In this example, the Distributor will have certain payment obligations to the Production Partnership under the Distribution Agreement between the Production Partnership and the Distributor. The letter of credit, or guarantee, is effectively a promise by the Issuer to pay the Beneficiary (the Production Partnership) in the event that the Distributor fails to make payment under the relevant Distribution Agreement.

1. Definitions

In this Letter of Credit and in the Schedules hereto, except where the context otherwise requires, the following expressions have the following meanings:

'Abandonment Amount'
'Account'
'Beneficiary'
'Business Day'
'Certificate of Delivery'
'Distribution Agreement'
'Distributor'
'Expiry Date'
'Film'
'Holding Company'
'Issuer'

'L/C Demand'
'LC Table'
'Minimum Guarantee Payment'
'Non-delivery Pre-payment Date' [ ]
'Payment Amount'
'Payment Date'
'Subsidiary' has the meaning given to it in section 736 of the Companies Act 1985 (as amended).

The definitions set out the full meaning of defined terms and phrases used throughout the letter of credit. The use of defined terms is essential to ensure that there is no ambiguity or inconsistency in the letter of credit.

2. Undertaking to pay

The Beneficiary may make L/C Demands under this Letter of Credit in accordance with this Clause.

The undertaking to pay (clause 2) contains the actual promise by the Issuer to pay the Beneficiary in the event of a failure by the Distributor to pay certain amounts owed. This clause contains a lot of detail as to the terms and conditions upon which the Issuer will be obliged to meet its promise under the letter of credit. In many cases, the payments owed by the Distributor under the Distribution Agreement will be structured over a certain period of time, perhaps as much as a 20-year period. On this basis, the payment obligations of the Issuer under the letter of credit need to match the payment obligations of the Distributor. The undertaking to pay also contains provisions for payment of interest that will have accrued on the payment amounts owed by the Distributor. The letter of credit also contains specific provisions dealing with the amount that would be payable by the Issuer to the Beneficiary in the event that a demand was made because the film had not been completed and delivered. This amount is known as the 'Abandonment Amount'.

In most cases the Issuer will require to see certain documentation in support of any demand for payment made by the Beneficiary. Under the example letter of credit, the demand must be in an agreed format together with a certificate of delivery in circumstances where a demand is made after the film has been completed and delivered.

3. Termination of obligations

The Issuer shall be released from its obligations under Clause 2 (without prejudice to any then outstanding liability of the Issuer to the Beneficiary as a result of a L/C Demand complying with the terms of this Letter of Credit having already been made) on the earlier to occur of:

A. the date (if any) notified by the Beneficiary to the Issuer in writing as the date upon which the obligations of the Issuer hereunder are to be released and this Letter of Credit is returned; or
B. if no L/C Demand shall have been presented under Clause 2 by that date which is forty-five (45) Business Days after the first Payment Date under the LC Table and the Beneficiary shall not by such date have delivered to the Issuer a Certificate of Delivery (which delivery shall be deemed made if the Certificate is delivered by hand to the Issuer's address set forth above and/or one business day after the Certificate is sent by first class post to the Issuer's address set forth above); or
C. upon payment in full by the Issuer pursuant to a L/C Demand.

This clause contains provisions for the benefit of the Issuer, setting out the circumstances in which the Issuer may be released from its obligations to make payment under the letter of credit. For example, the Beneficiary may choose to release the Issuer by giving written notice and the obligations of the Issuer may terminate once the Beneficiary has been paid out in full.

4. Payments

Save as required by law or any competent authority, all payments under this Letter of Credit shall be made:

A. without set-off or counterclaim whatsoever; and
B. free and clear of any deduction or withholding for or on account of any taxes.

In addition, all payments, under this Letter of Credit shall be made in pounds sterling and in immediately available funds and for value on the due date.

Clause 4 contains specific provisions relating to payments made under the letter of credit and the possible application of any taxes or increased costs in relation to those payments. Briefly, the Issuer is obliged to make any payments owed to the Beneficiary under the letter of credit, gross. This means that in the event that the Issuer was required by any law to make any deduction or withholding on account of tax from any amounts payable under the letter of credit then the amount of deduction or withholding would be for the account of the Issuer alone. In other words, the Issuer would still be liable to pay all amounts under the Letter of Credit gross, as if such deduction or withholding had not been made. Therefore, this represents an additional cost for the Issuer as its actual liability in these circumstances would be the amounts payable under the letter of credit plus the amount of any required deduction or withholding.

5. Assignment

Clause 5 contains provisions allowing the Beneficiary to assign the benefit of the letter of credit to any person. In practice, this means that the Beneficiary gives away its rights to receive any payments under the letter of credit to a specified third party. In a film transaction, this clause is usually necessary because a bank lending to the film partnership will require security. The film partnership is Beneficiary of both the right to receive payments under the Distribution Agreement and the right to receive payment under the letter of credit. Therefore, this gives the film partnership two income streams to offer to its lending bank as security. It can, therefore, assign in favour of its lending bank the benefit of the letter of credit together with the benefit of the right to receive payments under the Distribution Agreement. The nature of the charge and assignment is discussed elsewhere in the chapter.

6. Disclosure of information

This clause is very straightforward and provides for the disclosure and sharing of any relevant information in connection with the letter of credit or about the acquisition and distribution of the relevant film.

7. Security review

The security review clause, clause 7, contains provisions for the benefit of the Beneficiary that enable the Beneficiary to review the adequacy and value of the security represented by the letter of credit. The general right of review is applicable on or after the fifth anniversary of the date of the letter of credit and there is also a specific provision which applies at any time following the second anniversary of the date of the letter of credit in circumstances where the Issuer's credit rating has fallen below AA[min]. To the extent that the Issuer's credit rating fell below this threshold, it would be of concern to the Beneficiary as it might operate as an early warning that the Issuer may encounter problems meeting any demand made under the letter of credit. In the event that the Beneficiary was concerned for any reason as to the Issuer's ability to pay under the letter of credit, under the security review provisions it could require the Issuer to arrange a substitute letter of credit or require a cash deposit to be placed in a nominated account for the benefit of the Beneficiary as substitute security for the letter of credit.

8. Notices

8.1 Every notice or other communication (other than a L/C Demand) under this Letter of Credit:

A. shall be in writing delivered personally or by pre-paid registered or recorded letter or, in the case of any communication other than a notice from the Beneficiary to the Issuer releasing the Issuer from its obligations hereunder in accordance with the terms of Clause 3(A) (which shall be delivered by hand in writing), by fax confirmed by letter;

B. shall be deemed to have been received, in the case of a letter, when delivered personally or on actual receipt and, in the case of a fax, at the time of receipt of the confirming letter; and

C. shall be sent to the addressee at its address or fax number as set out below or to such other address or fax number as is notified by the addressee in accordance with this Clause 8:

The Issuer
Address: [ ]
Fax No: [ ]
Attention: [ ]

The Beneficiary
Address: [ ]
Fax No: [ ]
Attention: [ ]

8.2 A notice or other communication (including a L/C Demand) received on a day that is not a Business Day or after 5.00 p.m. shall be deemed to be received on the next following Business Day.

8.3 Each L/C Demand shall:
A. be delivered personally or by pre-paid registered or recorded letter to the Issuer at the address specified in Clause 8.1(C) marked 'FOR THE URGENT ATTENTION OF [ ]'; and
B. be deemed to have been received when delivered in accordance with this sub-clause.

9. Waivers and amendments

9.1 Writing required
A waiver or amendment of a term of this Letter of Credit will only be effective if it is in writing signed by both parties.

9.2 Expenses
Each party agrees to reimburse the other party for the expenses that second party incurs as a result of any proposal made by the first party to waive or amend a term of this Letter of Credit.

10. Miscellaneous

10.1 Exercise of rights
If either party does not exercise a right or power when it is able to do so this will not prevent it exercising that right or power. When it does exercise a right or power it may do so again in the same or a different manner. Each party's rights and remedies under this Letter of Credit are in addition to any other rights and remedies it may have. Those other rights and remedies are not affected by this Letter of Credit.

10.2 Counterparts
This Letter of Credit may be signed in any number of separate counterparts. Each counterpart shall constitute an original and all counterparts, when taken together shall constitute a single document.

10.3 Contracts (Rights of Third Parties) Act 1999
The parties to this Letter of Credit do not intend that any term of this Letter of Credit should be enforceable, by

virtue of the Contracts (Right of Third Parties) Act 1999, by any person who is not a party to this Letter of Credit.

11. Reliance

Each of the Beneficiary and the Issuer may rely upon any communication or document reasonably believed by it to be genuine and to have been made or delivered by the proper person or persons.

12. Governing law

This Letter of Credit shall be governed by and construed in accordance with English law.

Yours faithfully

[ ]
For and on behalf of
[ ]

Schedules 1A and B set out the form of demand that must be completed by the Beneficiary in order to make proper demand upon the Issuer.

Schedule 1A: Form of L/C Demand Certificate

To: [ ]
FOR THE URGENT ATTENTION OF: [ ]
[Date]

Dear Sirs

a. L/C Demand
Irrevocable Letter of Credit No [ ]
Dated [ ] 200 [ ] issued by [ ]
In favour of [ ]

We refer to the above Letter of Credit (the **'Letter of Credit'**). Terms defined in the Letter of Credit have the same meanings when used in this L/C Demand certificate.

The Distributor has failed to pay £[ ] ([ ] pounds sterling) in respect of the Payment due on the Payment Date which fell on [*insert date*]. Accordingly, we hereby demand payment of this amount of £[ ] ([ ] pounds sterling) and, in addition, of interest on this the amount as described in paragraph 2.2(B) of the Letter of Credit. In each case, this payment is demanded in accordance with, and is due under, Clause 2 of the Letter of Credit.

Yours faithfully
(Authorized Signatory)

For and on behalf of
[ ]

Schedule 1B: Form of L/C Demand Certificate

To: [ ]
FOR THE URGENT ATTENTION OF: [ ]

[Date]

Dear Sirs

b. L/C Demand
Irrevocable Letter of Credit No [ ]
Dated [ ] 200 [ ] issued by [ ]
In favour of [ ]

We refer to the above Letter of Credit (the **'Letter of Credit'**). Terms defined in the Letter of Credit have the same meanings when used in this L/C Demand certificate.

We are not in receipt of the Certificate of Delivery. Accordingly we hereby demand the amount of £[ ] ([ ] pounds sterling). This payment is demanded in accordance with, and is due under, Clause 2 of the Letter of Credit.

Yours faithfully
(Authorized Signatory)

For and on behalf of
[ ]

Schedule 2 contains the details of the payment obligations under the letter of credit. As mentioned earlier, the payment obligations must match the underlying payment obligations of the Distributor under the Distribution Agreement and the contents of the schedule provide certainty for both the Issuer and the Beneficiary as to the maximum amounts that will be payable under the letter of credit at any given date.

Schedule 2: LC Schedule

Payment Date	*Payment Amount*
[ ]	[£]
[ ]	[£]
[ ]	[£]
[ ]	[£]
[ ]	[£]
[ ]	[£]
[ ]	[£]
[ ]	[£]
[ ]	[£]
[ ]	[£]
[ ]	[£]
[ ]	[£]
[ ]	[£]
[ ]	[£]
[ ]	[£]
[ ]	[£]
[ ]	[£]
[ ]	[£]
[ ]	[£]

Schedule 3 is the form of certificate of delivery in respect of the film. The certificate is important, as the amounts payable under the letter of credit will vary depending on whether or not the film has been completed and delivered.

Schedule 3: Form of Certificate of Delivery

Dated [ ]

The undersigned, [ ] ('Guarantor') hereby certifies and confirms to [ ] (' ') the following in respect of the feature length theatrical film tentatively entitled '[ ]' ('the Film').

1. The Film stars [ ] as '[ ]', [ ] as '[ ]', [ ] as '[ ]' or substitute actresses and/or actors engaged in accordance with the terms of the Interparty Agreement relating to the Film between, inter alia, [ ] and Guarantor. The Film is directed by [ ] or a substitute director engaged in accordance with the terms of the Interparty Agreement relating to the Film between, inter alia, [ ] and Guarantor.
2. The Film, is based on the script dated [ ] written by [ ] ('the Script') subject to minor changes or variations as may be necessitated by exigencies of production (which in no event shall alter the plot, storyline, or the nature of any characters or characters or characterizations) and no changes, modifications, or revisions have been made to the Script (except as provided above) without the express prior approval of [ ], or which changes have not been disapproved in writing by [ ] within Five (5) business days following receipt of request for approval thereof.
3. The Film has a duration of between [ ] and [ ] minutes.
4. The Film is capable of obtaining a MPAA censorship rating which is not more restrictive than 'R' in the United States and of obtaining a BBFC censorship rating which is not more restrictive than '15' in the United Kingdom.
5. The Film [*insert agreed undertakings regarding qualification as British*].
6. Delivery (as defined in the Distribution Agreement dated [ ] between [ ] and the Distributor relating to the Film (the 'Distribution Agreement')) of the Film has been completed fully in accordance with the terms of the

Distribution Agreement (or as otherwise agreed by Distributor).

Guarantor acknowledges that this Certificate is a material document and is a condition precedent to the first payment due to be made under a letter of credit issued by [ ] for the account of [ ] and that [ ] is relying on the truth and accuracy of the statements contained herein.

[ ]
For and on behalf of [ ]
By: [ ]
Its: [ ]

Notice of Assignment and Irrevocable Payment Instruction

From: [Film Partnership as Borrower and Chargor]
(the '**[Film Partnership]**', '**we**' or '**us**')

To: [Party to contract]
(the '**Licensee**' or '**you**')

Date: [ ]

Dear Sirs

'[Film Title]' ('Film')

This Notice is given pursuant to the agreement (the '**Agreement**') made between us and you dated [ ] relating to the Film.

We hereby give you notice that under a deed of charge and assignment dated [ ] we have assigned our right to receive advances or other sums payable by you to us pursuant to the Agreement (the '**Payments**') to the bank ('**Bank**') by way of security, and we hereby give you irrevocable authority and instructions to make the Payments to the Bank in accordance with the instruction set out below. This notice hereby replaces and takes priority over any previous payment instructions given to you whether pursuant to the Agreement or otherwise.

The Payments are to be sent by telegraphic transfer to:

Bank: [ ]
Sort Code: [ ]
Account Name: [ ]
Account Number: [ ]
Address: [ ]

We also hereby notify you that we have no authority, without the prior written consent of the Bank, to waive any provisions of or rights under the Agreement or to modify or amend the Agreement or to enter into any other agreement with you which may in any way affect the Bank's security.

This authority and instruction is coupled with an interest and may not be revoked or altered without the prior written consent of the Bank.

Please sign and return to the Bank (with a copy to us) the attached Acknowledgement of Assignment to indicate your receipt of these instructions and your agreement to the terms set out herein.
By its counter-signature below, you give your consent to the foregoing.

Signed by [ ]
For and on behalf of
[ ]

Signed by [ ]
For and on behalf of
[ ]

Notes to the Agreement

In order for an assignment of the benefit of any agreement or other assets to be legally effective, the party assigning its rights must give written notice to the other party or parties to the agreement. In this particular example, the Notice includes a payment instruction that the other party to the agreement should pay all amounts payable under that agreement direct to the Bank. For example, if giving notice to a distributor following assignment of the benefit of a Distribution Agreement, the distributor upon receipt of this Notice would be obliged to pay all monies payable under the Distribution Agreement direct to the Bank. Owing to the fact that Notice of Assignment is a legal requirement, banks normally insist that the Notice and attendant Acknowledgement of Notice of Assignment are prepared and served on the relevant parties at the same time as the underlying Charge and Assignment itself, is executed.

Acknowledgement of Notice of Assignment

From: [Party to Contract]

To: [Bank name and address]
(the '**Bank**')

Date: [ ]

Dear Sirs

'[Film Title]' ('Film')

We hereby acknowledge receipt of the Notice of Assignment and Irrevocable Payment Instructions (the '**Notice**') dated [ ] relating to the Film and hereby undertake for the benefit of the Bank to comply with the Notice. Capitalized terms used in this Acknowledgement shall bear the meanings ascribed to them in the Notice.

In consideration of £1 and of other valuable consideration (the receipt and adequacy of which we hereby acknowledge), we hereby undertake and agree that:

i. we will not invoke or assert any rights of termination, set-off, cross-collateralization, counter-claim or defence or make any withholding so as to extinguish or reduce the Payments;
ii. we have irrevocably exercised all approval rights which would otherwise be a pre-condition to our making the Payments, and any and all other pre-conditions thereto have either been fulfilled or waived by us, save the condition that 'Delivery', as defined in the Agreement, may be effected on or before the 'Delivery Date', as defined in the Agreement;
iii. the failure by [Film Partnership/Company] (or by any other person or entity) to observe or perform any representation, warranty, term, condition, obligation, covenant or requirement, whether provided for in the Agreement or otherwise (including, without limitation, any failure to comply with any censorship or rating requirements in the Agreement), shall not excuse, constitute a defence to or otherwise adversely affect the timely payment by us to the Bank of the Payments, provided always that Delivery has been made;

iv. we will not modify or amend the Agreement in any way whatsoever;
v. we will send to the Bank duplicates of all notices relating to the Film under the Agreement;
vi. without limiting the generality of the foregoing and notwithstanding anything to the contrary contained in the Agreement or elsewhere, we hereby acknowledge (insofar as our rights and interests are concerned) that we have approved the chain of title relating to the Film and the underlying rights thereto and that (without prejudice to [Film Partnership/Company]'s obligations under the Agreement) we may not refuse to pay all or any portion of the Payments or refuse to accept Delivery by reason of any deficiency with respect to such underlying rights;
vii. without prejudice to [Film Partnership/Company]'s obligations to us under the Agreement, we will not refuse to pay any sum due to the Bank under the Agreement or refuse to accept Delivery by reason of any deficiency with respect to any literary material, music, musical compositions or other intellectual property included in the Film, or any claim arising out of such actual or claimed deficiency, or [Film Partnership/Company] not having obtained title to or licence to use a story, script, music or other rights in connection with the Film (including copyright and title), or the Film or its title infringing or claims being made that the Film or the title infringe the rights of others;
viii. we will not assign the benefit or burden of the Agreement without the prior written consent of the Bank;
ix. we will, at the request of the Bank and at the expense of [Film Partnership/Company], execute and deliver any agreement, document or other instrument as the Bank may reasonably require to evidence, establish, enforce or secure the arrangements and transactions envisaged herein;
x. we will make the Payments directly to the Bank as directed in the Notice and such payments will constitute good and valid discharge of our obligations to make the Payments under the Agreement; and
xi. once paid to the Bank in full, Payments shall not be subject to refund or return to us for any reason.

We further acknowledge that the Bank has taken as an assignment only the Payments and the Bank has not assumed any obligations or liabilities of [Film Partnership/Company] under the Agreement, and we shall look solely to [Film Partnership/Company] for the performance and discharge of such obligations and liabilities.

We hereby consent to the assignment of the right to receive the Payments to the Bank and we agree that the Bank is now entitled to receive the Payments in place of [Film Partnership/Company] until such time as the Bank shall notify us in writing to the contrary.

This Acknowledgement shall be capable of signature in separate counterparts which together shall constitute a single instrument.

This Acknowledgement of Assignment shall be governed by and construed in accordance with the laws of England.

Signed by [ ]
For and on behalf of
[ ]

Signed by [ ]
For and on behalf of
[ ]

Date : [ ], 200[ ]

Notes to the Agreement

This letter is by way of Acknowledgement of the Notice of Assignment and payment instructions and serves as evidence to the Bank that the legal requirement to serve Notice of Assignment has been complied with. The Acknowledgement creates a direct contractual link between the Bank and the relevant party to the Agreement that has been assigned. The Bank will usually require that the Acknowledgement of Notice of Assignment contains certain acknowledgements and undertakings on the part of the relevant party to the agreement. This will include an agreement to pay any sums payable under the agreement direct to the Bank and any other matters that the Bank may consider necessary.

Laboratory Pledgeholder's Agreement

When a bank is involved in a film financing transaction, they will require an agreement from the laboratory that processes the film materials stating that the negatives and all of the materials in possession at the laboratory will be held to the order of the bank and will not be released to the producer without the bank's prior written approval. The bank will give the laboratory permission for any distributors or the sales agents to duplicate negatives to meet their specific print requirements or delivery requirements.

This Laboratory Pledgeholder's Agreement is made on [ ], 200[ ]
Between:

1. **[Film Laboratory] of [ ]**
2. **[Name of Producer] of [ ] ('Producer')**
3. **[Name of Bank] of [ ] ('Bank')**
4. **Completion Guarantor of [ ] ('Guarantor')**
5. **Sales Agent of [ ] ('Sales Agent')**

Addressed to Bank
Dated: as of [ ]

Dear Sirs
[ ] (the 'Film')

We refer to the proposed arrangement with the Producer and the Sales Agent, pursuant to which we have been engaged as the laboratory with respect to the Film (the **'Agreement'**). Capitalized words and expressions used herein shall have the following meanings unless otherwise specified:

a. Definitions and interpretations

'Producers' Materials' shall mean all materials, information, documentation and any other thing whatsoever deposited with us by the Producer in relation to the Film in order for us duly to perform our obligations under the Agreement.

'Delivery Materials' shall mean all materials, information, documentation and any other thing whatsoever which we shall create or produce in relation to the Film in preparation for the delivery of the Film to the Sales Agent or the Producer.

'Materials' shall mean the Producer's Materials and the Delivery Materials.

In accordance with the instructions that we have today received from the Producers and in consideration of the Bank, Guarantor (hereinafter **'you'**) agreeing that the general production services and laboratory work on the Film will be carried out by us and of other valuable consideration (the receipt of which we hereby acknowledge), subject to:

i. The rights of the Guarantor to obtain access to the Materials in accordance with its rights to take over production of the Film (in which event we will accept instructions solely from the Guarantor to the exclusion of all other parties) under the terms of its Completion Guaranty to you dated on or about the date hereof and its Security Agreement (the **'Security Agreement'**) with the Producer dated on or about the date hereof; and
ii. The rights of the Sales Agent to obtain access to the Delivery Materials strictly in accordance with the terms of the sale agency agreement with [ ] dated [ ] (the 'Sales Agent Agreement') and solely for the purpose of properly marketing and selling the Film throughout the world (but provided that the Sales Agent is not at any time in material breach of the Sales Agent Agreement or of the Interparty Agreement between, inter alia, you, the Sales Agent and the Producer of even date herewith (the **'Interparty Agreement'**)); and

In this Agreement, unless the context otherwise requires we agree with you that:

1. We will retain and hold in the name of the Producer but to your order from the time they reach our possession the Producer's Materials and all other materials, documents, information and any other thing whatsoever on deposit with us or placed with us by the Producer after the date hereof relating to the Film.
2. We will also retain and hold in the name of the Producer but to your order from the time each of them is created or produced by us the Delivery Materials to be delivered to the Producer pursuant to the Agreement and by them on to the Sales Agent.
3. We shall keep the Materials on our premises and shall not part with possession of any of the Materials except (a) for the

purpose of cutting, scoring or performing special optical or sound work or similar purposes or (b) otherwise in accordance with your written directions or with your prior written consent. Upon receipt of such written directions or consent, we will deliver the Materials to you or to your nominee named therein.

4. We shall not allow any other person, firm or company other than you or the Guarantor and persons duly authorized by you or the Guarantor to have any access to any of the Materials or to any copy masters or positive prints made from any of the Materials or to any other materials made from them, save that the Producer or the Guarantor may be permitted access to the Materials solely for the purposes of the proper production of the Film and may be supplied with any Delivery Materials (subject to our standard terms of trade) solely for the purpose of proper production of the Film, but shall not be permitted to remove any of the Materials from our premises without your and the Guarantor's prior written consent save as provided in para 3 above.
5. We shall not, without prior written instructions, accept orders from any of the Producers for any of the Materials in connection with the Film other than those orders relating to production requirements and delivery to distributors previously approved by you in writing.
6. We shall not assert any claims against the Materials or any of them other than against the Producer for our charges for work done in relation to the Film pursuant to the Agreement.
7. In the event that we shall receive written notice from you requiring us so to do, we shall not allow the Producer or the Sales Agent or any persons authorized by the Producer or the Sales Agent to have access to any other Materials or to any materials made from them, but we shall at all times continue to permit you, the Guarantor and your and their authorized nominees to have rights of access to the Materials and to any materials made from them.

We acknowledge, undertake and agree that this agreement is irrevocable and may not be altered or modified except with your prior written consent.

Upon written request from the Producer, you shall promptly give us written notice when your security interest with respect to the Film has been terminated. Upon receipt of such written notice, our obligations herein shall continue on the terms set out herein but as if references to you were references to the Producer.

[Any party (if any) (other than the Producer and the Guarantor) entitled to access to the Materials agrees not to exercise that right in such a way as would interfere with the obligations of the Producer and the Guarantor to complete the production of the Film and will comply with the reasonable instructions of the Producers or the Guarantor in that connection.]

The signatories hereto hereby agree and confirm that this agreement shall be governed by the laws of England, and that any disputes arising under any of the provisions of this agreement shall be subject to the exclusive jurisdiction of the Courts of England.

The Producer and the Sales Agent, by its counter-signature, agrees and consents to our entering into this Agreement, and the Guarantor by its counter-signature, confirms its acceptance of the provisions of this Agreement. The Producer further agrees and undertakes that, save as set out in this Agreement, none of the Materials will deliver to any person other than ourselves.

Please confirm your acceptance of the aforementioned by signing and returning the attached copy of this letter.

Yours faithfully

Signed by [ ]
For and on behalf of

[Film Laboratory])
) [ ]
)

Signed by [ ]
For and on behalf of

[Producer])
) [ ]
)

Signed by [ ]
For and on behalf of

[Sales Agent])
) [ ]
)

Signed by [ ]
For and on behalf of

[Bank])
) [ ]
)

Signed by [ ]
For and on behalf of

[Completion Guarantor])
) [ ]
)

5 The Interparty Agreement

An interparty is not an agreement, it's an excuse for lawyers to make money.
Producer's comment after being presented with legal bill from a bank's law firm

Introduction

The discounting of production receivables is the essence of all production financing. Whether for television or film, production receivables can include, among other things, licences to broadcasters, pre-sales or licences to distributors, negative pick-ups, equity investments, tax funds and grants or rebates made available by various institutions. The production receivables for a particular project are typically assigned to the bank by notice of assignment and the proceeds received are used to retire the loan. For significant licences or distribution agreements, where payments are contingent upon delivery, it is common for banks to require the implementation of multiparty agreements involving the producer, the completion guarantor, the bank and the licensee or distributor. This type of agreement is commonly referred to as the Interparty Agreement.

Although sometimes difficult to settle, the Interparty Agreement brings the pertinent parties together and provides the bank with significant comfort that it will receive the amounts owing under their loan, when due. The Interparty Agreement has the effect of modifying the terms of any pre-existing licence or distribution agreement and of accomplishing various matters that are of fundamental concern to a bank. The Interparty Agreement enables all parties to approve and consent to the bank's security interest and will usually have a list of parties in order of priority of their respective security.

The bank analyses the production receivables and determines the circumstances under which these payments must be made or potentially avoided. These circumstances need to be mitigated through the settlement of the Interparty Agreement. The agreement also serves the purpose of bringing the completion guarantor and licensee or distributor together on the issue of what constitutes delivery. The form of Interparty Agreement set out below is one that would primarily be used for a distributor or licensee where the licence fee or advance payable is due on delivery and represents a significant portion of the bank's source of repayment. This type of agreement would not be appropriate for minor licences or for transactions where the bank's advances are to be repaid by multiple sources. In these circumstances, notices of assignment and direction and the distributor's or licensee's acknowledgements may be more appropriate. The form of Interparty Agreement required by a bank will depend on various factors, including the terms of the financing; the amount of the receivables relative to the loan; the identity of the producer, the licensee, the distributor and their track records; the type and terms of the production receivables; and the timing of payments. The following agreement is in relation to a multiparty agreement.

Please note that this is only a sample of an Interparty Agreement. Interparty agreements should be negotiated according to the particular facts and circumstances of each transaction.

Film finance transactions with multiple sources of funds will always have a much more complex recoupment schedule and will generally take much longer to negotiate because of the number of parties to the agreement.

Sample Agreement

Preamble

The preamble introduces the parties and their relationship to each other and briefly describes the purpose for the Interparty Agreement.

THIS INTERPARTY AGREEMENT made the [ ] day of [ ] 200[ ] BETWEEN:
[ ] (hereinafter called the 'PRODUCER') and
[ ] (hereinafter called the 'LICENSEE') and
[ ] (hereinafter called the 'BANK')
[ ] (hereinafter called the 'COMPLETION GUARANTOR')

WHEREAS pursuant to the terms of a loan agreement between the Bank and the Producer dated [ ] (the 'Loan Agreement'), the Bank has agreed to advance funds (the 'Loan') to the Producer for use in connection with the production of a film presently entitled [' '] (the 'Film') in accordance with terms and conditions contained therein;

AND WHEREAS the Producer and the Licensee have entered into an agreement dated as of [ ] (the 'Licence Agreement'), pursuant to which the Licensee will be granted the exclusive right to [DISTRIBUTE] the Film throughout [ ] (the 'Territory');

AND WHEREAS pursuant to the terms of the Loan Agreement, the Producer has provided the Bank with various security agreements including a copyright mortgage (collectively, the 'Security') over all of its right, title and interest and to all tangible and intangible elements comprising the Film (the 'Collateral');

AND WHEREAS pursuant to a completion guarantee agreement ('Completion Guarantee') between the Completion Guarantor and the Bank dated as of [ ] the Completion Guarantor has guaranteed to the Bank that the Film will be duly and timely completed and delivered to the Licensee in accordance with terms and conditions of the Licence Agreements;

AND WHEREAS pursuant to that certain agreement (the 'Producer's Agreement') between the Producer and the Completion Guarantor dated [ ] the Completion Guarantor has agreed to issue the Completion Guarantee;

AND WHEREAS the Producer has agreed to assign to the Bank all amounts payable to it by the Licensee pursuant to the Licence Agreement as security for and as a source of repayment of the Loan;

In consideration of these premises and for other good and valuable consideration, the receipt and sufficiency of which is hereby acknowledged, the parties hereto hereby agree as follows:

The first few provisions below are important for the Bank as they confirm that the Licence Agreement is in full force and effect and that the Licensee has approved all elements of the Film over which it has rights of approval.

The Bank is also assured that any conditions precedent to the Licensee's obligations under the Licence Agreement, other than delivery, have been met. Banks do not usually provide financing until all the conditions precedent have been satisfied. (See chapter four, term sheet/loan letter, for a full list of condition precedents.)

To the extent that any condition precedents have not been satisfied, the Bank may be asked to waive or take a commercial view on some of them.

Depending on the size of the transaction and the importance of the licence or distribution agreement to the financing, it is usually necessary to list the condition precedents in detail for certainty.

1. Matters pertaining to the licence agreement

1.1 The Producer and the Licensee each represent and warrant that, as of the date hereof, no default exists under the Licence Agreement, that the Licence Agreement is in full force and effect and that the Licence Fee (as hereinafter defined) shall be payable to the Bank in the manner set forth therein, as herein modified.

1.2 The Licensee hereby acknowledges, for the benefit of the Bank and the Completion Guarantor only, that it has approved all elements of the Film over which the Licensee has rights of approval (the 'Elements').

1.3 The Licensee acknowledges that any conditions precedent to its obligations under the Licence Agreement (including, without limitation, each of the conditions precedent set forth in Paragraph [ ] of the Licence Agreement) have, as of the date hereof, either been satisfied, or are hereby waived by the Licensee as against the Bank (but not as against the Producer).

1.4 The Completion Guarantor and the Producer each acknowledge and agree that the budget for the Film dated [ ] (The 'Budget') presently provides for the production of any and all delivery requirements for the Film set out in the Licence Agreement.

If not otherwise clear in the Licence Agreement, it is important for the Bank to establish a mechanism by which the Licensee approves any 'open elements' – or elements which must be replaced – and to clarify that the Licensee's obligations cannot be diminished or avoided as a result of its refusal to approve or select a replacement for a certain element in the Film such as cast or crew.

The Bank and the Completion Guarantor will also attempt to have the Licensee's rights extinguished if it does not exercise the same within a specific time period. Additional terms are required where essential elements are involved in the licence.

1.5 With respect to any Element of the Film (if any) which the Licensee has not approved as of the date hereof but has the right to approve under the Licence Agreement ('Open Element'), the Licensee agrees to exercise such approval rights reasonably and in good faith so as not to frustrate the due and timely production, completion and delivery of the Film by the Delivery Date, or Outside Delivery Date, as applicable (as such terms are defined below), in a manner taking into account the allocation of funds in the Budget for such element and the Licensee hereby waives, as to the Bank only, the right to refuse to accept delivery of the Film by reason of the Licensee's failure to have approved any Open Element.

1.6 If any of the Elements (including any individual which has been specified in the Licence Agreement) must hereafter be replaced prior to the completion of principal photography by reason of death, incapacity or default or if the Completion Guarantor takes over the production of the Film and elects to replace any such element, because, in the Completion Guarantor's good faith reasonable opinion, such element is the cause of cost overruns or production delays which would result in the Completion Guarantor's increased liability under the Completion Guarantee, then the Licensee agrees to exercise its approval right with respect to any such replacement in good faith, and as expeditiously as possible so as not to frustrate the production and delivery of the Film (but consistent with the original allocation of funds in the Budget for such position, item or element and provided that such replacement is available and does not have a history of causing substantial costs overruns).

It is essential that the underlying Licence Agreement is not terminated or modified without the prior written consent of the Bank or the Completion Guarantor.

This type of clause is often negotiated so that amendments which are not material to the Bank or the Completion Guarantor may be completed without their involvement:

1.7 Until the Bank has been irrevocably and indefeasibly repaid all sums owing to it pursuant to the Loan Agreement (the 'Obligations'), the Producer and the Licensee hereby agree that the Licence Agreement shall not be terminated, amended or modified or altered in any way without the prior written consent of the Bank and the Completion Guarantor.

The Completion Guarantor has to ensure that it does not have any responsibility for the performance of the obligations of any party under the Licence Agreement unless it has taken over the production of the Film:

1.8 It is expressly agreed by the parties hereto that notwithstanding anything herein to the contrary, the Producer shall remain responsible for the performance of all obligations under the Licence Agreement, and provided that the Bank has not foreclosed upon the Collateral or has not exercised its takeover rights under the Loan Agreement or the Security, neither the Bank nor the Completion Guarantor (provided it has not taken over production of the Film) shall have any obligation under the Licence Agreement by reason of or arising out of this Agreement, nor shall the Bank or the Completion Guarantor be required or obligated in any manner to perform any obligations of the Producer under or pursuant to the Licence Agreement, other than in the case of the Completion Guarantor, only to perform its obligations under the Completion Guarantee. The Bank shall not be required to present or file any claim or to take any other action as a condition to collecting or enforcing the payment of the Licence Fee.

The provisions below constitute notification and direction to the Licensee of the specific assignment by the Producer to the Bank of the Licence Fees payable.

2. Notice of assignment and acknowledgement

2.1

a. The Producer hereby notifies the Licensee that it has irrevocably assigned to the Bank and has granted the Bank a security interest in and to all right, title, and interest in and to the Film, the Producer's rights in and to and under the Licence Agreement, the licence fee payable to the producer in respect of the Film under Paragraph [ ] of the Licence Agreement in the amount of [£] (the 'Licence Fee') and any and all other sums (if any payable thereunder or hereunder (collectively, the 'Bank's Assigned Receipts').

b. The Producer hereby authorizes and instructs the Licensee, and the Licensee hereby accepts and acknowledges the foregoing assignments and agrees:

   i. to make payment of the Licence Fee and any additional Bank's Assigned Receipts directly to the Bank, without deduction, set-off or withholding of any type, at the following address: [ ] Attention: [ ] (or such other address as the Bank may designate in writing);

   ii. to send to the Bank and the Completion Guarantor duplicates of all notices furnished by the Licensee or the Producer under the Licence Agreement;

   iii. to notify the Bank promptly of any conflicting notice received by the Licensee or of any claim by any third party that such third party is entitled to receive all or any portion of the Bank's Assigned Receipts; and

   iv. that the authority, instructions, and directions contained in this Paragraph 2 are coupled with an interest and are in all respects irrevocable and without right of rescission or modification without the written consent of the Producer and the Bank.

The following provisions are added for the benefit of the Producer and the Licensee and require the Bank to release or subordinate its interest once the Licence Fees have been paid to the Bank. Whether a release or a subordination is appropriate depends on whether the receipt of the Licence Fees was sufficient to discharge the loan. In such case, the Bank would release its interest in the Film. If the funds received only represent partial repayment and the proceeds of other production receivables are necessary to fully repay the loan, the Bank can only subordinate or discharge its interest in the Licence Agreement and its rights in respect of the Film in the relevant territory.

3. Application on the assigned receipts

3.1 Upon receipt of the Bank's Assigned Receipts, the Bank shall be entitled to retain and shall immediately apply the same on account of the Obligations. Upon the indefeasible repayment of the Obligations in full, the Bank shall:

i. notify the Licensee, the Completion Guarantor, and the Producer thereof in writing (such notice being herein referred to as the 'Termination Notice') and thereupon the authority, instructions, and directions from the Producer to the Licensee under Paragraph 2 hereof shall terminate, and the Licensee shall thereafter be relieved of its obligations to the Bank under Paragraph 2 hereof; and

ii. deliver to the Licensee, concurrently with the Termination Notice (with a copy to the Producer) any and all reasonable documents necessary to evidence the subordination of the Bank's interest in the Film in the Territory and the Licence Agreement.

The Bank must be certain as to the amount of the receivable it is entitled to. This provision ensures that the Bank receives the full amount of the Licence Fee without any set-off or reduction and reserves all of such rights of the Licensee as against the Producer only.

4. Payments to the bank and rights of offset

4.1 Subject to Mandatory Delivery (as hereinafter defined) being effected, the Licensee hereby agrees to make payment of the Licence Fee to the Bank as provided in Paragraph 2 hereof, in full, without offsets, withholdings, counterclaims or defences which the Licensee may have or claim against the Producer pursuant to the Licence Agreement (including without limitation, any right of cross-collateralization with respect to any other films or programmes), all of which are expressly reserved by the Licensee as against the Producer but only to the extent that the exercise of such rights does not alter, impair or derogate from the Bank's rights to receive timely payment of the Licence Fee in full hereunder. The Licensee shall have no claim against the Bank for return or refund of any funds paid to the Bank hereunder, such rights being reserved by the Licensee as against the Producer as provided elsewhere herein.

It is essential to the Bank that the Licensee's rights in the Film (including copyright) do not vest and that the Licensee does not become entitled to enjoy its rights in the Film until the License has been paid. It is imperative that the Bank (or the Producer on behalf of the Bank) is able to exercise its rights with respect to the Film and re-exploit the rights granted to the Licensee in the event that the Licensee does not pay for the Film. Depending on the jurisdiction, this type of clause is also important to overcome the claims of an administrator, receivers or trustees of a Licensee in circumstances of bankruptcy and insolvency. A provision is added for the benefit of and to comfort the Licensee which permits the Licensee to promote and market the programme prior to vesting. Terms have also been added to confirm the Bank's first priority security and to provide the Licensee with quiet enjoyment of its rights unless and until it defaults.

5. Vesting of rights – acknowledgements of priority

5.1 Notwithstanding anything to the contrary set forth in the Licence Agreement, the grant of all rights to the Licensee in respect of the Film (including, without limitation, the copyright interests therein) pursuant to the Licence Agreement or any security agreements or copyright assignments executed in connection therewith shall be subject in all events to the Licensee's indefeasible and irrevocable payment in full of the Licence Fee in accordance with the terms hereof, and the Licensee hereby acknowledges that payment of the Licence Fee in full hereunder is a condition precedent to the grant of rights to the Licensee in respect of the Film. Notwithstanding the foregoing, prior to the effectiveness of the grant of rights pursuant to the foregoing sentence, the Licensee may take such actions in respect of the Film, including, without limitation, promotion and marketing activities, as are customarily undertaken by the Licensees prior to the vesting of their rights, subject in all events to this Agreement.

5.2 Licensee hereby acknowledges and confirms that:

a. The Producer has granted to the Bank a first priority security interest in and to the Collateral including, but not limited to all of its right, title and interest in and to the Film and in, to and under the Licence Agreement. Until such time as the Licensee has paid the Licence Fee to the Bank, the Bank shall not exercise its rights as a secured party in a manner adversely affecting the rights of the Licensee under the Licence Agreement so long as the Licensee is not in material default of its obligations thereunder and hereunder and provided further that nothing herein shall be deemed to preclude the Bank from exercising its rights as against the Producer at any time. At such time as the Licence Fee is indefeasibly and irrevocably paid in full, the rights of the Bank in respect of the Film shall be subject and subordinate to the fully vested rights of the Licensee in respect of the Film in the Territory under the Licence Agreement, and thereafter notwithstanding any foreclosure or other action by the Bank against the Collateral, the Licensee shall be entitled to quiet enjoyment of its rights in and to the Film in the Territory under the Licence Agreement, subject to Paragraph 2 hereof:

b. Pursuant to the Producer's Agreement, the Producer has granted to the Completion Guarantor a security interest in and to the Film, including, without limitation, all of its right, title and interest under the Licence Agreement, which security interest is subject and subordinate to the Bank's rights and security interest hereunder and under and pursuant to the Loan Agreement and the Security; and

c. The security interests granted to the Licensee pursuant to the Licence Agreement shall, until the indefeasible payment of the Licence Fee in full to the Bank, be fully subordinate and junior to the liens of the Bank in and to the Collateral, and the Licensee shall execute subordinations and similar documents as the Bank may reasonably request to evidence such subordination.

The establishment of a delivery date (and an outside delivery date in the event of delays) is settled for the benefit of all parties. The elements which will constitute delivery for the purposes of the payment of the Licence Fee are also set out, notwithstanding the terms of the delivery requirements in the Licence Agreement. This provision and the schedule setting out the delivery items are usually settled between the Completion Guarantor and the Licensee with the Completion Guarantor attempting to dispense with as many non-essential items as possible. Banks will typically only finance production receivables contingent on delivery where all delivery items necessary for payment are bonded by the Completion Guarantor.

6. Delivery

6.1 Notwithstanding anything to the contrary in the Licence Agreement, the Licensee shall have the right to refuse to pay the Bank the Licence Fee only in the event that the Producer or the Completion Guarantor fail to make delivery to the Licensee on or before [ ], ('Delivery Date') (as same may be extended in the event of force majeure but in no event beyond [ ], (the 'Outside Delivery Date') of the items ('Mandatory Delivery Items') referred to in the Delivery Schedule attached hereto as Schedule '1'. For the purposes hereof, Mandatory Delivery shall be deemed to have occurred when the Mandatory Delivery Items have been delivered to the Licensee.

6.2 Notwithstanding anything contained in the Licence Agreement to the contrary it is understood and agreed that the Film as delivered to the Licensee may include such minor variations from the approved screenplay as may be required by or as a result of on-set dialogue changes and/or production exigencies and/or such other minor changes, provided that none of the foregoing shall materially alter the story or characters. The Completion Guarantor expressly acknowledges and agrees for the Bank's benefit that Mandatory Delivery hereunder (and 'Completion and Delivery', as such term is defined in the Completion Guarantee) includes delivery of the Mandatory Delivery Items and delivery of the Film conforming to the approved screenplay, with only such minor changes as are contemplated by the foregoing.

These provisions assure quick resolution of any dispute between the parties to the Licence Agreement, including disputes concerning delivery and acceptance. The onus is on the Licensee to specify in detail why delivery is rejected and on the Producer and the Completion Guarantor to remedy any defects about which complaints have been made. If the parties continue to disagree, the issue is submitted to arbitration. The arbitrator must then decide if, in fact, delivery has occurred and whether and by whom funds are owing. Banks typically require quick resolutions to avoid the costly delays of litigation. These provisions will require alteration depending on the governing jurisdiction and the laws pertinent to arbitration in such jurisdiction.

7. Arbitration

7.1 Notwithstanding anything to the contrary in the Licence Agreement or elsewhere, the Licensee, the Producer and the Completion Guarantor and the Bank hereby agree that in the event any dispute, claim or controversy arises between any of the parties hereto with respect to this Agreement, whether in contract, tort, equity or otherwise or as to whether Mandatory Delivery has been made or whether any sums are owing pursuant to the Licence Agreement or the Completion Guarantee, the parties agree to submit such dispute for resolution by mandatory binding arbitration under the Arbitration Rules (the 'Arbitration Rules'). Any of the parties may initiate such arbitration proceeding pursuant to the Arbitration Rules. The arbitration shall be held in [name of city]. The parties shall appoint a single arbitrator with expertise in the film industry and failing such agreement, the single arbitrator shall be determined in accordance with the Arbitration Rules. Each of the parties hereto agree that each will abide by any decision rendered in such arbitration and no right of appeal shall lie therefrom. Each of the parties further agrees that, in the event of a dispute relating to Mandatory Delivery, recourse shall not be had to the arbitration procedure herein until:

a. The Licensee has first given written notice to the Producer, the Bank, and the Completion Guarantor specifying with particularity and in detail the alleged defect or insufficiency in the delivery of the Film or the Mandatory Delivery Items; and
b. The Producer or the Completion Guarantor shall have had 10 business days after receipt of such written notice to cure the alleged defect or insufficiency complained of pursuant to Sub-Clause (a) above.

In the event that the Licensee does not provide such written notice as aforesaid, within 10 business days of receipt of the Mandatory Delivery Items, or in the event that the Licensee does not provide written notice specifying any alleged defect or insufficiency in the delivery of the Film or the Mandatory Delivery Items which have been re-delivered by the Producer or the Completion Guarantor within 5 business days of receipt of such re-delivery, then the Licensee shall be deemed, for all purposes, to have accepted delivery of the Film and shall be immediately responsible to pay the Licence Fee to the Bank.

7.2 The cost of the arbitration proceeding and any proceeding in court to confirm or to vacate any arbitration award, as applicable (including, without limitation, attorney's fees and costs), shall be borne by the unsuccessful party or at the discretion of the arbitrator, may be prorated between the parties in such proportion as the arbitrator determines to be equitable and shall be awarded as part of the award or judgment.

7.3 The parties agree that the arbitration as set forth above shall be the sole means of resolving any disputes, claims and controversies among them arising out of this Agreement.

7.4 Unless the issue(s) before the arbitrator do not include whether or not Mandatory Delivery was effected, the arbitration must result in either a finding that Mandatory Delivery has been effected or a finding that Mandatory Delivery has not been effected and the arbitrator shall promptly notify the Licensee, the Producer, the Completion Guarantor and the Bank in writing of the finding made. If it is found that Mandatory Delivery has been effected, the arbitrator shall issue an award against the Licensee requiring the immediate payment of the Licence Fee to the Bank. On the other hand, if it is found that Mandatory Delivery has not been effected, then the arbitrator shall issue an award against the Completion Guarantor requiring the Completion Guarantor to immediately pay the Bank an amount equal to the Licence Fee with accrued interest thereon. The Licensee shall immediately return to the Completion Guarantor, if the Completion Guarantor has paid the Bank, at the Completion Guarantor's expense, or the Bank, if the Completion Guarantor has not so paid the Bank, at the Producer's expense, all delivery items theretofore delivered to the Licensee.

8. Notices

8.1 All notices and copies thereof required to be given hereunder must be in writing and delivered by hand, by certified mail, return receipt requested, by telecopy, provided that a hard copy is mailed immediately thereafter and shall be deemed to have been given when received by the party to which sent. The address for notices to the Licensee, the Producer, the Completion Guarantor and the Bank are:

To the Licensee:
To the Producer:
To the Completion Guarantor:
To the Bank:

9. Waiver

9.1 Any waiver (whether express or implied) by any party hereto of any breach of any of the provisions hereof shall not be construed as a continuing waiver or consent to any subsequent breach on the part of any of the parties.

10. Further assurances

10.1 The parties hereto mutually agree and undertake to do and execute all such further acts, deeds and documents as may be reasonably required to give full further effect to the provisions of this Agreement.

11. Severability

11.1 If at any time any one or more of the provisions of this Agreement becomes invalid, illegal or unenforceable in any respect under any law, the validity legality and enforceability of the remaining provisions hereof shall not in any way be affected or impaired thereby.

12. Validity of licence agreement

12.1 The terms of the Licence Agreement, except as modified by this Agreement, shall remain in full force and effect.

This provision ensures that the Licence Agreement is superseded by the terms of the Interparty Agreement, with the Licensee reserving all of its rights as against the Producer under the Licence Agreement.

13. Complete Agreement

13.1 The terms of this Agreement (and the exhibits hereto) constitute the entire agreement between the parties with respect to the matters contained herein and supersede any prior understandings or representations by the parties with respect to the terms hereof. This Agreement may be modified only by an agreement in writing by all the parties hereto. As among the Bank, the Completion Guarantor, and the Licensee, but not as between the Producer and the Licensee, in the event of any inconsistency between this Agreement and the Licence Agreement, the terms of this Agreement shall prevail and govern. Without limiting the generality of the foregoing, as between the Bank and the Completion Guarantor, in the event of any inconsistency between this Agreement and the Completion Guarantee, the terms of this Agreement shall govern.

14. Counterparts

14.1 This Agreement may be executed in one or more counterparts, all of which together shall constitute one and the same original.

Banks and Completion Guarantors usually require the interparty agreement to be governed by the laws of their own jurisdiction and not the jurisdiction of the Licensee, whereas the underlying Licence Agreements are often governed by the laws of the Licensee's jurisdiction. An example of such a clause is set out below.

Governing law

This Agreement shall be governed by the laws of [ ]. The parties hereto each hereby submit to the jurisdiction of the courts of [ ]. Notwithstanding the foregoing, the Bank may, at its option, bring suit or institute other judicial proceedings against the Producer or any of its assets in any state or federal court of the United States or any Province of Canada or in the United Kingdom of any country or place where the Producer or the Licensee or such assets may be found.

IN WITNESS WHEREOF, the parties hereto have entered into this Agreement as of the date first above written.

6 The Completion Guarantee

After we deliver, it's your problem mate!
Completion guarantor to sales agent

Completion Guarantees

A completion guarantee is a particular type of contract of insurance required by financiers and distributors of films to protect the investment they have made until such time as the film is delivered to them for exploitation. Completion guarantors are specialist companies who offer a form of insurance coverage against certain events that could prevent a film production from being completed.

Contributors to the financing of a production would lose their investment, without a hope of return, if a film was not completed for a particular reason. There are many reasons why a film may not complete. Running out of money usually tops the list.

Therefore, most banks or financiers of a production require a completion guarantee or a completion bond (a 'bond' or 'guarantee') that will either:

- guarantee that the film is completed and delivered on time and on budget; or
- guarantee to repay the financier its investment if the film cannot be completed.

A feature film production will require a bond almost without exception. Financiers are unwilling to provide an open chequebook to a production. They need certainty that if and when the sum that they have agreed to provide runs out, additional funds will be available to finish the production. The fee charged by completion guarantors for providing a guarantee is approximately 5–6 per cent of the production budget of the film. However, guarantors commonly give refunds, referred to as the 'guarantee fee rebate' if the guarantee is not called upon.

Under their agreement with the producer and as an obligation to the bank or financier to whom the guarantee is given, guarantors have the right to monitor a film from the first day of principal photography of production. This means that a completion guarantee company needs extensive knowledge of the production process. Monitoring the production gives the guarantor the ability to stop any potential problems or overruns either by stepping in and taking over production or by exercising some lesser form of control over the production. The guarantor's objective, as with all insurers, will be to minimize the extent of its financial liability.

Application Requirements

In order for the completion guarantor to assess the viability of a project they will require the following:

- a copy of the screenplay;
- a budget;
- a production schedule.

Most completion guarantors prefer that these documents are initially approved by the intended financiers and distributors for the film.

Once the completion guarantor has reviewed these documents, they may wish to meet with certain key personnel such as the line producer, director, production accountant, production supervisor, stunt co-ordinator or anyone else that the company feels is relevant for the film.

The completion guarantor will ensure that the experience of those involved is sufficient to complete the Film within the budget and schedule. If the completion guarantor feels uncomfortable with any personnel then they will suggest another suitably qualified person.

Once the completion guarantor is satisfied with the various elements set out above, they will issue a letter of intent. (See end of chapter for sample letter.)

Documentation

Once the producer has signed off on the letter of intent, the completion guarantor will issue long form documents. The documents used by the completion guarantor include:

- the guarantee between the guarantor and the bank/ financier(s);
- the completion agreement – between the guarantor and the producer.

The completion agreement will give the guarantor the right to monitor the production and, if necessary, assume control of it.

The Guarantee

Most film financings involve a bank. The bank will cash flow certain agreements that the producer has with film distributors who agree to pay the producer for rights in the film, if and when the film is delivered to those distributors. This is known as discounting a distribution advance.

The risk to the financier is that the distributor may refuse to pay the advance, because the film is not delivered, or the film does not meet the contractual specifications set out in the distribution agreement. For example, if the distribution contract stipulates who the lead actors of the film are and the producer makes a film with two different lead actors then this would give the distributor a reason to refuse delivery and payment of the film. A distributor can also refuse delivery for various technical reasons and therefore it is essential that the guarantor agrees to guarantee to the financier the delivery of substantially what the distributor is agreeing to pay for. This will include the attachments (actors, directors) to the film and technical quality.

Liability of the Completion Guarantor

Under a completion guarantee, the guarantor is not liable for any payments under the guarantee until certain condition precedents have been satisfied. In the completion guarantee there are certain conditions whereby the completion guarantor is under no obligation to make any payments until an amount called the 'Strike Price' has been paid into the production bank account. The Strike Price is the total amount of contributions by the financing parties of a production that the guarantor will agree to protect. From a financier's or bank's perspective they will want the Strike Price to be the same amount of money that they are providing in relation to the film. In circumstances where there is more than one financier, the completion guarantor will not accept any financial responsibility until the entire budget of the film has been funded. Under a completion guarantee, one of the condition precedents is that the fee payable to the guarantor is paid either at the start of principal photography or upon signature of the agreement.

Completion guarantees usually have a schedule that sets out specific completion and delivery issues in relation to the film. These usually make reference to various agreements of broadcasters and distributors or others that are liable for payment upon delivery.

Payments under the Guarantee

If the completion guarantor needs to pay for completion of a film, then it will be entitled to recoup its contribution to the production costs from the first proceeds of exploitation of the film. Once the completion guarantor has paid back the bank or primary financier of the film, then it will be in a position to recoup any monies (including interest) advanced by it.

If the completion guarantor takes over the production it is entitled to an assignment of all the agreements relating to the film. This will include amongst others the production bank account and any distribution agreements.

In a completion guarantee there are certain exclusions that the completion guarantor will not be obligated to pay for. These will include:

- the cost of certain delivery items which are not mandatory under the delivery schedule or set out in the definition of Delivery Materials of the guarantee;
- the cost of legal fees, interest and other finance fees that are not specifically stated;
- in some circumstances the completion guarantee will only cover those costs that are required to actually finish and deliver the film to a specific distributor. For example, it will not be responsible for certain distribution expenses such as censorship or exhibitor requirements or perhaps making a foreign language version of a film, which would include dubbing or

sub-titling. If the completion guarantor decides not to deliver the film, then its liability will be limited to the amount set out as the Strike Price.

Completion guarantees are also drafted so that the guarantor will not have certain responsibilities. Matters that are excluded include the following:

- defects in the chain of title. The completion guarantor will require an Errors and Omissions Policy to cover any potential problems with the underlying rights, copyright or screenplay for the film;
- the artistic quality of the film;
- for extra costs, such as obtaining a certificate from the British Board of Film Classification or the Motion Picture Association of America;
- the cost of cutting, re-editing, re-recording or perhaps making cover shots for a television version of the film;
- additional delivery items.

Force Majeure

One of the major issues for consideration in the completion guarantee is the force majeure clause. This means 'superior force' and it refers to certain events beyond the control of the completion guarantor that may force suspension of the agreement. The actual clause in a completion guarantee may look like this:

> *The term 'Force Majeure' shall refer to any production exigency, including but not limited to prevention or interruption of the production of the film because of an accident; fire; explosion; casualty; epidemic; act of God; earthquake; flood; torrential rain; strike; walkout; picketing; labour controversy and other disputes; civil disturbances; terrorist acts; embargo; riot; act of a public enemy; war or armed conflict; unavailability of any essential materials and supplies; equipment, transportation; power or other commodity; failure or delay of any transportation agency; laboratory or any furnisher of essential supplies; equipment or other facilities; enactment of any law; any judicial or executive order or decree; the action of any legally constituted authority under death, incapacity or unavailability or default of the director or any principal cast member or other event or cause of the nature of force majeure beyond the control of the*

producer or Guarantor which causes any interruption or suspension of, or materially hampers, interferes with or delays the commencement of the production or delivery of the film to the distributors.

As you can see, this list is quite substantial and if one of these events restricts the completion guarantor from delivering the film, then under the force majeure clause the agreement will be under suspension. This will enable the completion guarantor to postpone the agreed delivery date for a specific period, which is usually equal to the duration of the force majeure plus an additional period of time to enable the completion guarantor to resume production. In most cases there is an outside delivery date which is between 30 and 60 days from the original delivery date under the agreement.

Abandonment

In some circumstances the completion guarantor will have the right to abandonment, which means that it can repay the bank or financier in full rather than complete the film. In these circumstances, the completion guarantor will make a commercial decision that the production is not capable of completion and it is cheaper to abandon it.

Cut Through

If the completion guarantor is not part of a large insurance company, then it will obtain re-insurance from a third party insurance broker such as Lloyds of London. The re-insurance is a way for the completion guarantor to spread its risk on a production. A bank participating in financing of a film will require that they are insured directly with the insurance company rather than the third party broker. In these circumstances, the completion guarantor will arrange a 'cut through letter', which will enable the financier or bank to go directly to the re-insurer for payment if the completion guarantor fails to pay for any over-cost, abandonment or if the guarantor goes bankrupt. The terms 'Loss Payee Endorsement' or 'Cut Through Letter' are used in most financing documents.

The Completion Agreement

The completion guarantor will enter into a separate agreement with the producer that gives the guarantor certain rights of control in relation to the production so that it can perform its obligations to the financier or bank. The completion agreement ensures that the producer undertakes to deliver the film on budget and on time and according to the specifications of all the various financiers and/or distributors. The main focus of the completion agreement is that the completion guarantor will, if required, have the right to step in and take over the production of the film from the producer.

Under the completion agreement the producer will agree with the completion guarantor the following:

- to produce and deliver the film on time and on budget and in accordance with the various production and financing agreements, and any of the agreements relating to a distributor who has pre-bought the rights in the film;
- to make the film in accordance with the budget, the script, the production schedule, engage only those actors and production personnel that are approved prior to shooting by the completion guarantor;
- to give the completion guarantor the right to inspect the production records and obtain weekly production cost reports;
- to allow any representative of the completion guarantor access to any location or studio where the film is being shot which also includes any post-production activities such as cutting and editing.

Completion guarantors usually make it clear that they want to work with the producer in a constructive way rather than in an acrimonious or meddling manner. From a producer's perspective they may wish to limit the amount of control that a completion guarantor may have. Usually this is done by the producer providing daily cost and production reports that are in accordance with the budget and cash flow for the film. They will also ask the completion guarantor to pre-approve various production personnel and actors.

Under the completion agreement the completion guarantor will usually have the right to suspend, dismiss or replace artists or production personnel, provided that this does not compromise or breach any existing distribution or talent agreements. In many film financings, there are essential elements that cannot be replaced. If there are essential elements in a film (such as a lead actor or director), prior to closing the financing, the film company will suggest a list of approved replacements for them. However, in some circumstances, there may be a requirement for essential element insurance. From a practical perspective, it is best not to agree any essential elements in a production.

Essential element insurance covers a situation where a financier or distributor makes it a condition of their financing or pre-sale that a specific element such as an actor or director must be involved in that film. If the actor dies or cannot finish the film for any reason then this insurance will cover the cost of abandoning production of the film.

In some circumstances, the completion guarantor will have the right to take over the production of the film. This is very rare and most completion guarantors have no interest in doing this. If the completion guarantor exercises its right to take over control of the film, then the completion guarantor will be deemed to have been irrevocably appointed as the manager and agent of the producer to complete the film. The completion guarantor must give the producer, the bank, the distributor and any other financiers notice in writing of this decision to take over control of the production. Once this happens, the completion guarantor will assume responsibility for all aspects of the production, which include the bank accounts, the use of production funds, all personnel, facilities and equipment being used or to be used in relation to the film, and any other aspect that the completion guarantor requires to finish the film. The completion guarantor will have the right to deal directly with the film laboratory or post-production house. In relation to the production bank account, the bank, who will most likely have a charge over the production account, will then have to comply with the completion guarantor's instruction so that they can make payments on behalf of the producer. From a bank's perspective, the completion guarantor will take a charge over the film and the related assets of the producer. This charge, however, will rank in second place in order of priority to the bank or financier.

The completion guarantor will also have the right to take over from the producer if the producer or his/her company becomes bankrupt, goes into receivership, liquidation or makes an arrangement with his creditors. Generally, any insolvency proceedings against the producer will give the completion guarantor the right to take over the production.

The completion guarantor will, in most cases, require specific types of insurance before signing off on the completion guarantee and completion agreement. These include:

- cast and crew insurance;
- employees and public liability insurance;
- personal accident insurance;
- errors and omissions insurance;
- faulty stock, camera, editing, negative, videotape and processing insurance;
- political risk insurance (e.g., if shooting in Iraq!).

Completion Guarantors

The following is a list of completion guarantors in the UK:

i. Film Finances – James Shirras, Director, Film Finances Ltd, 15 Conduit Street, London W1S 2XJ – Tel +44 207 629 6557.
ii. International Film Guarantors – Luke Randolph, Managing Director, IFG (International Film Group), 25 Maddox Street, London W1S 2QT – Tel +44 207 493 4686.

How to Find Sample Completion Guarantor's Documents

1. See Film Finances Inc.'s website, http://www.ffi.com for a sample Completion Guarantee and Sample Completion Agreement.
2. See International Film Guarantors Inc.'s website, http://www.ifgbonds.com for a sample Completion Guarantee Agreement and Producers Completion Agreement.

Completion Bond Letter of Commitment

From: [Name of Completion Guarantor]

Re: [Name of Film]

Dear [Producer],

We are pleased to inform you that we approve, in principle, the issuance of a guarantee of completion on the above motion picture production, subject to our review and approval of the screenplay, final budget and schedule, and approval of our legal counsel of the underlying documentation.

Yours faithfully
For and on behalf of

[Bond Company]

Film Finances' Sample Completion Guarantee

Film Finances, Inc.

9000 Sunset Boulevard, Suite 1400

Los Angeles, California 90069

As of [ ], 200[ ]

[ ]

(the 'Financier')

[ ]

[ ]

Attn: [ ]

Re: '[ ]' (the 'Film')

Gentlemen:

We have been informed by [ ] (referred to herein as 'Producer') that you have agreed to advance $[ ] to Producer to pay for the production costs of the Film upon the terms and conditions of that certain agreement between yourselves and [ ] ('Producer') dated as of [ ], 200[ ] (the 'Financing Agreement'). The Producer has also informed us that as a condition to your advancing the funds, you have required the Producer to procure for you a guaranty of completion of the production and delivery of the Film. The Producer has applied to us to provide such guaranty, and we have agreed to do so subject to, and in consideration of, the payment to us of the fee hereinbelow referred to.

In consideration of the foregoing premises and of your lending the referenced funds to the Producer, we have agreed with you as follows:

1. Guaranty. Subject to the provisions of this agreement we:
   a. guaranty the Completion and Delivery of the Film (as that term is defined in Schedule I attached hereto);
   b. agree to procure or provide the Completion Funds, if any are needed, to Complete and Deliver the Film, as aforesaid, if the Producer shall fail to do so; and if Producer fails to

Complete and Deliver the Film, we shall Complete and Deliver the Film as aforesaid; and

c. if we fail to Complete and Deliver the Film as aforesaid, we shall make the payments specified in paragraph 7(a) hereof.

2. Definitions. The terms defined herein shall have the meaning set forth in Schedule II attached hereto.

3. Fee. Our obligations hereunder are conditioned upon the payment to us of our fee of $[ ] in full, as follows: [ ] ('Fee').

4. Production Controls: pursuant to the Completion Agreement (the terms of which you need not be concerned) we shall have the right to Complete and Deliver the Film in accordance with this Completion Guaranty, or to procure the Completion and Delivery of the Film by any other person or company in accordance with the terms of the Completion Agreement.

5. Conditions of Guaranty: we shall be under no obligation hereunder:

a. Until the Strike Price has been made available to the Producer or us in full, as and when required by the Producer or us, as provided in the Financing Agreement, whether or not an event of default has occurred thereunder. Notwithstanding anything to the contrary contained herein, you shall not be obligated to supervise or administer to the application of the Strike Price to be made by you to Producer or us as aforesaid, it being agreed that your obligation shall only be to advance such sums in accordance with the terms of the Financing Agreement and this Completion Guaranty;

b. To obtain any seal, certificate or rating of the Motion Picture Association of America, Inc. ('MPAA'), except as required to Complete and Deliver the Film;

c. To deliver any materials other than the Delivery Materials prior to the Delivery Date or to deliver the Delivery Materials to any locations other than the locations, if any, designated in Schedule I attached hereto;

d. For the quality of the Film or the Delivery Materials, other than the technical quality thereof necessary to Complete and Deliver the Film;

e. In respect of any defect in the copyright of the Screenplay, the Underlying Literary Property, if any, or the Film, or in the rights acquired for the Film in the Screenplay or in the Underlying Literary Property, if any, or in the title of the

Film, or in the music of the Film (except for the rights in such music that are acquired by us in the event we take over the production of the Film and then acquire rights in and to music which is used in the Film);

f. With respect to any claim or liability arising out of any tort or any breach of contract committed by the Producer, except to the extent necessary to Complete and Deliver the Film;

g. With respect to any of the Excluded Risks (as defined in Schedule II); and

h. Any Over-Budget Costs arising as a result of currency fluctuations.

6. Excluded Costs: notwithstanding any provisions of this Completion Guaranty to the contrary, the Guarantor shall not be obligated to provide funds for the payment of the following costs except to the extent such costs are (i) specified in the Budget, (ii) required to Complete and Deliver the Film, (iii) required to correct technical defects in the Film, or (iv) conform the Film to contractual specifications for which we are responsible under this Completion Guaranty;

a. The cost of delivery items which are not Delivery Materials;

b. The cost of legal, interest and finance fees and expenses, except as provided for in paragraph 7(a) hereof;

c. Any distribution expenses, including costs incurred in meeting censorship or exhibitor requirements, or to make foreign language versions of the Film (dubbed, subtitled or otherwise) or any other versions except the original version in the language specified in the Screenplay; advertising and publicity costs, including costs incurred for previews;

d. Any costs incurred to photograph, record or include in the Film 'cover shots' for television or other purposes or other substitute or additional material; provided, however, that if 'cover shots' are required to Complete and Deliver the Film, we will be obligated to deliver such 'cover shots'; and,

e. Any costs incurred after the Completion and Delivery of the Film or incurred in connection with recutting, reediting, retakes (other than retakes done by the director during the ordinary course of production in accordance with the Production Schedule) and changes.

7. Failure to Complete and Deliver the Film; Insurance:

a. In the event that we fail to Complete and Deliver the Film, our liability hereunder shall be limited (except as otherwise provided herein) to (i) the payment to you of, and we shall pay to you upon demand, an amount equal to the Obligations (as defined in Schedule II) less so much thereof as may have been refunded to and retained by you by insurance or otherwise indefeasibly paid to you in connection with the Film, and (ii) the payment of any additional costs or expenses of the Film that we are required to pay pursuant to this Completion Guaranty. The payment referred to in paragraph 7(a)(i) hereof shall be made to you without reduction or set-off and notwithstanding any Completion Funds advanced by us to Producer or expended by us directly to Complete and Deliver the Film in accordance with the terms of this Completion Guaranty. Upon our payment to you provided in paragraph 7(a)(i) hereof, we shall be automatically subrogated to all of your rights, claims, causes of action and security interests in relation to the Film. You agree to execute such assignments and other instruments as we may reasonably require to evidence and effectuate such subrogation at our sole cost and expense.

b. If any claim covered by production/indemnity insurance should arise in relation to the Film, the insurance recovery (unless paid to a third party, such as in relation to a personal injury or property damage claim) shall be paid and disbursed as provided as an Insurance Recovery specified in Schedule II attached hereto.

8. Rights of Financier: so long as you do not interfere with our ability to Complete and Deliver the Film pursuant to this Completion Guaranty, you may at all times, without prejudice to this Completion Guaranty and without discharging or in any way increasing our liability hereunder, make further advances to the Producer or grant to the Producer any time or indulgence, or deal with, exchange, release, modify or abstain from perfecting or enforcing any security interest or other guaranty or rights which you may have from or against the Producer or with any other person or guarantor, provided that such action shall not materially prejudice our rights or obligations under this Completion Guaranty. In any event, you agree that, without our prior written consent, which consent shall not be unreasonably withheld, you will not agree to any amendment to the Financing Agreement or any agreements ancillary thereto or take any other action (including interference with our access to the physical elements of the

Film) which in any way materially prejudices our rights or obligations under this Completion Guaranty. If the Financing Agreement provides that you have the right to take over control of the production of the Film you acknowledge that such right is subject to our rights under this Completion Guaranty. You shall not be obligated to see to the application of the funds provided by you pursuant to the Financing Agreement.

9. Subordination: we hereby subordinate any rights and claims which we may have against the Producer, and its principals and affiliates (whether by way of subrogation or otherwise) and any security interest which we may have in any collateral of the Film in which you have or may have a security interest pursuant to the Financing Agreement or other agreements furnished to us by yourselves, to the repayment to you of the Obligations in full and to all of your rights and security interests and claims under the Financing Agreement or otherwise in connection with the Film.

10. Assignment: you shall have the right to assign the benefit of this Completion Guaranty, in whole or in part, to any third party who succeeds to the Financier's rights in the Film or the Financing Agreement. Any other assignment to any other person or company shall be null and void.

11. Notices: any notice given hereunder shall be conclusively deemed to have been received by the addressee and to be effective on the day on which it is personally delivered to such party at the address set forth below (or at such other address as such party shall specify to the other party in writing) or, if sent by registered or certified mail, on the fifth business day after the date on which it is mailed, postage pre-paid, addressed to such party at such address, or if sent by cable, telegram, telex or telecopier on the third business day after the day on which it is wired or telexed, charges pre-paid or provided for, addressed to such party at such address:

a. If to you, at [ ], with a copy to [ ];

b. If to us, at its offices at 9000 Sunset Boulevard, Suite 1400, Los Angeles, California 90069, with simultaneous copies to Ballantyne, McKean & Sullivan, Ltd., Latham House, 16 Minories, London EC3N 1AX, Attn: Roy Martin, Esq. and to Sedgwick, Detert, Moran & Arnold, One Embarcadero Center, Sixteenth Floor, San Francisco, California 94111, Attn: David Bordon, Esq.

12. Miscellaneous Provisions: this Completion Guaranty has been executed in [ ], and shall in all respects be interpreted, enforced and governed by the laws of [ ]. The language of this Completion Guaranty shall be construed as a whole according to its fair meaning and not strictly for or against either of the parties. If any one or more of the provisions of this Completion Guaranty shall be held to be illegal or unenforceable in any respect, the legality and enforceability of the remaining provisions shall not in any way be affected or impaired thereby. NO MODIFICATION OR WAIVER OF ANY PROVISION OF THIS COMPLETION GUARANTY OR WAIVER OF ANY DEFAULT HEREUNDER SHALL BE EFFECTIVE UNLESS IN WRITING AND SIGNED BY AN OFFICER OF BOTH YOU AND US (IN THE CASE OF A MODIFICATION) OR BY THE WAIVING PARTY (IN THE CASE OF A WAIVER) AND SUCH WRITING EXPRESSLY STATES THAT SUCH WRITING IS A MODIFICATION OR WAIVER (AS APPLICABLE) OF THIS COMPLETION GUARANTY.

13. Corporate Action: we warrant that we are not required to obtain any authorizations, approvals or consents from any governmental bodies or regulatory authorities for the execution and delivery by us of this Completion Guaranty and the performance thereof; provided, however, if any such authorizations, approvals or consents are hereafter required, Guarantor shall comply with such requirements. We further warrant that the execution, delivery and performance of all of the terms and provisions hereof have been duly authorized by proper corporate or other action under the laws of the State of California and that no consent of any third party to the execution, delivery and performance hereof is otherwise required.

14. Remedies: in the event of a dispute hereunder, the provisions for arbitration specified in Schedule III attached hereto shall apply. Each and all of the several rights and remedies provided for in this Completion Guaranty or at law or in equity shall be cumulative and no one of them shall be exclusive of any other right or remedy. The exercise of any one or more of such rights or remedies shall not be deemed to be a waiver of or an election not to exercise any other such right or remedy. The obligations of the Producer and us are several, not joint. You may proceed against us without having first instituted proceedings or made demand upon or against

Producer. If action, suit or other proceeding is brought for the enforcement of this Completion Guaranty, to declare rights or obligations hereunder, or as a result of an alleged breach, default or misrepresentation by either party, the prevailing party shall be entitled to recover its reasonable attorneys' fees and other costs, in addition to any other relief to which that party may be entitled.

15. Amendments: any amendments to this Completion Guaranty must be in writing, and if any such amendments are agreed to concurrently with the execution hereof, the same shall be those specified in Schedule IV attached hereto.

16. Counterparts: this Completion Guaranty may be signed in counterparts and each such counterpart shall constitute an original document and each such counterpart, taken together, shall constitute one and the same instrument.

17. Miscellaneous: the captions used herein are for convenience only and have no other significance. The term 'we', 'us' or 'our' as used herein shall mean Guarantor and the term 'you' or 'your' as used herein shall mean Financier.
Please sign below to indicate your approval to the terms hereof, including the Schedules attached hereto, which are incorporated herein by reference.

Very truly yours,

Film Finances, Inc.

By: [ ]

Its: [ ]

Agreed:

[ ]

('Financier')

By: [ ]

Its: [ ]

Schedule I: Completion and Delivery of Film

1. The term 'Completion and Delivery of the Film' or 'Complete and Deliver the Film' as used in this Completion Guaranty shall have the following meaning:

a. The production of the Film in accordance with the Budget and the Production Schedule, and the Film as produced shall: (i) be based upon the Screenplay; (ii) qualify for an MPAA rating of not more than [ ]; (iii) be [ ] to [ ] minutes in length, including main and end titles; (iv) be shot in color [ ] black and white [ ] in 35 mm; (v) be of technical first class quality; and have the following elements, all of which are subject to the approval by the Guarantor:

Principal Cast:

[ ] in the role of [ ]

[ ] in the role of [ ]

[ ] in the role of [ ]

Director: [ ]

Producer: [ ]

b. the delivery to [ ] by the Delivery Date of the film and soundtrack materials specified in Exhibit 'A' attached hereto (the 'Delivery Materials').

2. The term 'Delivery Date' shall mean [ ], subject to postponements due to the occurrence of events of force majeure which extend the delivery date and any periods of notice, cure and arbitration as provided in Schedule III attached hereto.

3. The term 'Distribution Agreements' shall mean the following agreements:

[ ]

[ ]

4. The term 'Distributors' shall mean the following:

[ ]

5. The term 'Production Bank Account' shall mean account [ ] located at [ ], in the name of the Producer, where all advances by Financier shall be made unless otherwise agreed to in writing by Guarantor.

   You hereby acknowledge that if you receive written notice from us that we are entitled to assume control of the production funds of the Film, you will provide your consent that the only authorized signatories on the Production Bank Account be a signatory or signatories designated by us.

   In the event you exercise any rights of offset against the Production Bank Account, whether arising out of a security interest or otherwise, our obligations under paragraph 7(a) of the Principal Agreement of this Completion Guaranty shall not be modified or altered as a result thereof, and you shall still be responsible (as far as we are concerned) to advance the Strike Price (as hereinafter defined) in full.
6. The term 'Strike Price' shall mean the aggregate sum of U.S. [ ], including the Fee.

Schedule II: Definitions

Budget: the final budget of the Film dated [ ], 200[ ], which has been approved in writing by the Producer, the Guarantor and, if required, the Distributor(s) and Financier. Guarantor hereby acknowledges its receipt and approval of the Budget.

Budget Costs: the projected production costs of the Film as set forth in the Budget.

Budget Funds: the monies needed to pay the Budget Costs.

Complete and Deliver the Film: the term 'Complete and Deliver the Film' shall have the meaning specified in Schedule I.

Completion Agreement: the agreement between the Producer and the Guarantor.

Completion and Delivery of the Film: the term 'Completion and Delivery of the Film' shall have the meaning specified in Schedule I.

Completion Funds: the monies needed to pay Over-Budget Costs, if any.

Completion Guaranty: this agreement consisting of the Principal Agreement and the attached Schedules.

Delivery Date: the term 'Delivery Date' shall have the meaning specified in Schedule I.

Delivery Materials: the term 'Delivery Materials' shall have the meaning specified in Schedule I.

Distribution Agreement(s): the term 'Distribution Agreement(s)' shall have the meaning specified in Schedule I.

Distributor(s): the term 'Distributor(s)' shall have the meaning specified in Schedule I.

Excluded Costs: those costs of the Film which are not Guarantor's responsibility under paragraph 6 of the Principal Agreement.

Excluded Risks: the term 'Excluded Risks' shall mean any loss based upon, arising out of, directly or indirectly resulting from or in consequence of or in any way involving:

1. loss or destruction of or damage to any property whatsoever or any loss or expense whatsoever resulting or arising therefrom

or any consequential loss and any legal liability of whatsoever nature directly or indirectly caused by or resulting or arising from a) ionizing radiations or contamination by radioactivity from any nuclear fuel or from any nuclear waste from the combustion of nuclear fuel, b) the radioactive, toxic, explosive or other hazardous properties of any explosive nuclear assembly or nuclear component thereof, or (c) any actual or alleged seepage, pollution or contamination of any kind;

2. insolvency and/or financial default of the Financier;
3. war, whether declared or not, civil war or insurrection;
4. the failure to obtain or maintain various insurance for the Film required by Guarantor including but not limited to Producers' Indemnity Insurance, (i.e., cast insurance, negative insurance, props, sets, wardrobe and miscellaneous equipment insurance) or with respect to any loss actually paid or reimbursed under any such insurance policies.

Fee: the term 'Fee' shall have the meaning specified in paragraph 3 of the Principal Agreement.

Film: the motion picture designated as the Film in the Principal Agreement.

Financier: the guaranteed party under this Completion Guaranty which shall be [ ].

Financing Agreement: the agreement referred to in the first grammatical paragraph of the Principal Agreement.

Guarantor: Film Finances, Inc.

Including: means including but not limited to.

Insurance Recovery: all insurance recoveries in relation to the production of the Film shall be paid as follows: (i) if paid prior to Guarantor's having advanced any funds, or prior to Guarantor's having taken over production of the Film, they shall be deposited in the Production Bank Account and they shall be made available to pay production costs of the Film before Guarantor is called upon to provide funds toward the completion of the Film ('Completion Sums'); (ii) if paid after Guarantor has advanced any Completion Sums or after Guarantor has taken over production of the Film, they shall be paid to Guarantor, and shall be used to reimburse Guarantor for any Completion Sums advanced by Guarantor and thereafter to pay production costs of the Film before Guarantor is required to advance additional (or any) Completion Sums; (iii) any surplus remaining after such receipts have been applied pursuant to the foregoing shall be paid to Producer or Financier as their respective interest may appear. Notwithstanding the foregoing, if an insured event occurs which results in Guarantor's election to abandon production of the Film, the insurance recovery shall be paid first to Financier until Financier has been fully repaid all Obligations pursuant to the Financing Agreement, and thereafter to Guarantor until Guarantor's has recovered an amount equal to any Completion Sums advanced by Guarantor. Any surplus shall be paid to Producer or Distributor as their interests may appear.

MPAA: Motion Picture Association of America, Inc.

Non-Budget Costs: costs which the Guarantor is not obligated to fund pursuant to the Principal Agreement, including the Excluded Costs.

Obligations: the term 'Obligations' shall mean (i) all sums advanced by Financier under the Financing Agreement, including, without limitation, the principal amount of all advances made by Financier under the Financing Agreement, and (ii) interest on said advances payable to Financier under the Financing Agreement and all costs and expenses payable to Financier thereunder.

Over-Budget Costs: those costs of Completing and Delivering the Film which are in excess of the Strike Price.

Principal Agreement: the agreement (to which this Schedule is annexed) between the Financier and the Guarantor whereby the Guarantor undertakes this Completion Guaranty.

Producer: the company designated in the Principal Agreement as the Producer which shall be [ ].

Production Bank Account: the term 'Production Bank Account' shall have the meaning set forth in Schedule I.

Production Schedule: the final production schedule of the Film (including the pre-production and production schedules) dated [ ], 200[ ], which has been approved in writing by the Producer, the Guarantor and, if required, the Distributor(s) and the Financier.

Screenplay: the final screenplay on which the Film is to be based, dated as of [ ], 200[ ], written by [ ], and which has been approved in writing by the Producer, the Guarantor and, if required, the Distributor(s) and the Financier.

Secured Sums: all monies, if any, expended by the Guarantor in relation to the production and delivery of the Film, pursuant to the Completion Agreement or pursuant to this Completion Guaranty, including Completion Funds and, if Completion Funds have been advanced, all out-of-pocket costs, expenses, losses and liabilities reasonably paid to third parties (other than lawyers) by the Guarantor directly in relation to or arising out of the performance of the Completion Agreement or this Completion Guaranty, less any refunds received and retained by the Guarantor from insurance or otherwise; provided, however, that Secured Sums shall not include any costs or expenses incurred by the Guarantor in monitoring the production of the Film prior to such time, if ever, that the Guarantor takes over control of the production of the Film, or (irrespective of whether Guarantor has taken over control of the production of the Film) any costs, salaries or expenses attributable to the Guarantor's general overhead (including any costs or expenses incurred by the Guarantor in connection with the preparation and negotiation of this Completion Guaranty and all agreements ancillary thereto).

Underlying Literary Property: the underlying literary material, if any, upon which the Screenplay is based.

Schedule III: Notice Cure and Arbitration Agreement

1. With respect to any dispute relating to the delivery of the Film the following provisions will apply:

a. Distributor shall issue a notice ('Objection Notice') specifying the defects in the Completion and Delivery of the Film as defined in the Completion Guaranty to which this Schedule III is attached (hereafter 'Delivery');

b. The Objection Notice shall specify (with particularity and in detail) the purported defects in Delivery of the Film, and all items that must be corrected, delivered or otherwise modified in order to complete same; provided that if within three (3) business days after receiving the Objection Notice, Producer or Guarantor request additional information which they believe in good faith is necessary in order to determine whether Delivery has been effected notwithstanding such Objection Notice, or how any defect in Delivery can be cured, then Distributor shall have three (3) business days after its receipt of such request to respond in good faith thereto (the 'Response'). Following the receipt of the Objection Notice or Response, whichever is applicable, Guarantor shall have the following alternatives:

i. Effect Delivery in accordance with the specifications of the Objection Notice and (if applicable) the Response, but in no event later than thirty (30) business days after receiving the Objection Notice or Response, whichever is later to occur, and give such party notice thereof ('Cure Notice'); or,

ii. Give Distributor written notice ('Arbitration Notice') within five (5) business days after receiving the Objection Notice or Response, whichever is later to occur, that Delivery has been effected notwithstanding the Objection Notice and that Guarantor has elected to submit the issue of whether Delivery has been effected for expedited arbitration in accordance with paragraph 3(a) hereof; provided that if there are any items referred to in the Objection Notice which the Guarantor elects to correct, deliver or modify to enable Guarantor to serve a Cure Notice, the time allowed for serving an Arbitration Notice in respect of any items which the Guarantor does not so intend to correct deliver or modify shall be extended so that it is co-terminous with the period allowed for the service of the Cure Notice.

2. Distributor, Producer and Guarantor hereby agree that in the event any dispute arises between any of the parties hereto as to whether or not Delivery has been effected such dispute will be submitted to binding arbitration as hereinafter provided.

3. If a Cure Notice is given as aforesaid, then Distributor shall have five (5) business days from and after its receipt of same within which to verify that Delivery has been effected in accordance with the specifications of the Objection Notice and (if applicable) the Response and to notify Guarantor, Financier, Distributor and Producer that either:

i. Delivery has been effected as aforesaid (and such notice shall constitute an Acceptance Notice for all purposes hereunder); or,

ii. Delivery has not been effected and Distributor has elected to submit the issue of whether Delivery has been effected (and such issue only) for expedited arbitration in accordance with paragraph 3(a) below ('Arbitration Notice').

a. In the event Distributor or Guarantor elects to submit the issue of whether Delivery has been effected to arbitration pursuant to this agreement, the following shall apply:

i. the arbitration shall be submitted to three (3) arbitrators who shall be selected as follows:

A. Upon receipt of notice ('Arbitration Notice') from Guarantor or Distributor ('First Party') that it has elected to submit such dispute to arbitration, the party ('Second Party') receiving notice and the party serving notice shall each appoint one arbitrator with knowledge and experience in the United States motion picture industry and the technical delivery issues relating to motion pictures, and said arbitrators so selected shall then appoint a third arbitrator and shall give written notice thereof to both parties within two (2) days of such appointment; provided, however, that if either Distributor or Guarantor shall fail to appoint its respective arbitrator within five (5) business days after receipt of the Arbitration Notice, then the arbitrator appointed by the other party shall have full authority to act as the sole arbitrator of such arbitration; the two party-appointed arbitrators shall appoint the third arbitrator within ten (10) days of the appointment of the later of the two (2) to be appointed, failing which, at the request of either party, the then President of the American Arbitration Association, or his/her replacement in the event the President is unavailable, shall be requested to appoint the third arbitrator within ten (10) days of the application.

ii. The arbitration shall commence at a location in Los Angeles, within twenty (20) business days after the selection of the three (3) arbitrators ('Arbitrators'), and such arbitration shall continue on each consecutive business day therefrom until fully concluded, unless continued by the Arbitrators for good cause shown. Except as expressly provided for herein, such arbitration shall be conducted in accordance with the commercial rules and procedures of the American Arbitration Association then in effect.

iii. There shall be made available to the Arbitrators all relevant documents and the delivery materials. The parties shall participate in an exchange of information before the hearing. The parties acknowledge and agree that each party shall be entitled to reasonable discovery for the purposes of any such arbitration, including (without limitation) document production and the taking of depositions. The party desiring such discovery may apply to the Arbitrators at the outset of the arbitration for particular discovery requests. The parties will make themselves and all documents as may be required available so as to enable full and complete discovery in a timely fashion. The Arbitrators may deny only such discovery as is unreasonable or is intended unduly to delay the prompt conclusion of the arbitration.

iv. The Arbitrators must determine whether Delivery has been effected or has not been effected, and shall promptly notify the parties in writing of the finding made.

v. The Arbitrators' award shall provide for payment by the losing party or parties of the Arbitrators' and any court reporter's fees, as well as the reasonable attorneys' fees incurred by the prevailing party in the arbitration.

Schedule IV

The following provisions shall amend the Completion Guaranty to which this Schedule IV is appended:

[ ]

[ ]

Film Finances' Sample Completion Agreement

AGREEMENT made as of the [ ] day of [ ], between [ ], a [ ] corporation ('Producer') of [ ] [ ] FILM FINANCES, INC., a California corporation (herein 'Guarantor'), of 9000 Sunset Boulevard, Suite 1400, Los Angeles, California 90069.

WITNESSETH:

1. **Representations of Producer:** the Producer represents that it intends to produce a motion picture (the 'Film') having the following elements:
   a. Present title: '[ ]'
   b. Based upon:
      i. Underlying literary property: None
      ii. Screenplay: entitled '[ ]', written by [ ] dated [ ];
   c. Producer: [ ];
   d. Director: [ ];
   e. Executive Producer: [ ];
   f. Principal members of the cast.
      [ ] in the role of '[ ]',
      [ ] in the role of '[ ]';
      Subject to Guarantor's approval.
   g. Budget (dated [ ]) consisting of:

Direct Costs	$[ ].00
Contingency Allowance	$[ ].00
Guarantor's Fee	$[ ].00
	========
Total	$[ ].00

   h. Production Schedule dated: [ ];
   i. Location agreements: To be approved by Guarantor if requested.
   j. Delivery Date: [ ]
2. **Financing:** the Producer further represents that the financing for all of the Budget Costs, and the interest and other financing charges in connection therewith, will be provided pursuant to that certain agreement ('Financing Agreement') dated as of [ ] between [ ] and Producer.

3. **Distribution:** producer further represents that the following distribution rights in the Film have been granted to the following distributors:
   i. Pursuant to that certain agreement ('[ ] Agreement') dated as of [ ] as amended [ ], between Producer and [ ] ('[ ]'). Producer has granted to [ ] certain rights in and to the Film in the territories specified in the [ ] Agreement;
   ii. Pursuant to that certain agreement ('[ ] Agreement') dated as of [ ] between Producer and [ ] ('[ ]'), Producer has granted to [ ] certain rights in and to the Film in the territories specified in the [ ] Agreement. [ ] are collectively referred to herein as the Distributors and the [ ] Agreement and the [ ] Agreement are collectively referred to herein as the Distribution Agreements.
4. **Guarantor's Rights:** the Producer further represents that if the Guarantor expends any Secured Sums, and if such Secured Sums are not otherwise repaid to the Guarantor in full, the Guarantor shall have the right to recoup the unpaid balance of such Secured Sums from the Gross Receipts of the Film. Such right of recoupment shall be subject to the Prior Rights, which for the proposes of this Completion Agreement consist of:
   a. The rights and security interests of Financier pursuant to the Financing Agreement;
   b. The rights and security interests, if any, of the Distributors pursuant to the Distribution Agreements; and
   c. A Screen Actors Guild security interest, if any (provided that said guild executes a subordination agreement in form and substance satisfactory to Guarantor) and laboratory liens in relation to the production of the Film (provided that each such laboratory executes a laboratory pledgeholder agreement (or similar instrument) in form and substance reasonably satisfactory to Guarantor).

   In this regard, to secure the repayment of the Secured Sums to Guarantor Producer hereby assigns to Guarantor the Gross Receipts of the Film which are payable to Producer, and Producer hereby agrees to execute all such documents and instruments reasonably acceptable to Producer which are required to evidence the aforementioned assignment, but said security interest shall be deemed terminated for all purposes whether or not Guarantor executes such documents and/or instruments. At such time, if ever, that Guarantor has recouped the Secured Sums, Guarantor's security interest in the Collateral (including the Gross Receipts) shall terminate and Guarantor shall execute and deliver to Producer such documents and instruments as Producer may deem to be reasonably necessary to evidence or effectuate such termination.

Notwithstanding anything contained herein to the contrary, Guarantor acknowledges that the Secured Sums and the repayment thereof shall be without recourse to Producer and shall be paid to Guarantor from the Gross Receipts of the Film, but Guarantor reserves all rights and remedies which it may have at law or in equity as a result of any material breach of this Completion Agreement or (to the extent such breach gives rise to any liability to Guarantor) the Financing Agreement.

5. **Application for Guaranty:** the Producer has applied to the Guarantor to issue its guaranty of completion of production of the Film to the Financier.
6. **Agreement of the Parties:** in consideration of the Producer's representations set forth above, and of the Producer's warranties and agreements hereunder, and subject to the payment by the Producer to the Guarantor of the referenced Guarantor's Fee of $[ ].00, upon the execution hereof, the Guarantor agrees to issue its Completion Guaranty to the Financier, in form mutually approved by the Guarantor and the Financier, and upon the terms and conditions set forth in the Guarantor's Standard Terms attached hereto and made a part of this agreement by this reference. By executing this Completion Agreement, the parties hereto agree that they will, respectively, fully perform their respective obligations and agreements under this Completion Agreement, and under the agreements which are ancillary hereto.
7. **Notices:**

a. Copies of all notices to the Producer shall be sent to:

[ ]

[ ]

[ ]

[ ]

IN WITNESS WHEREOF, the parties hereto have executed this Completion Agreement on the day and year first above written.

[ ]

('Producer')

By [ ]

Its [ ]

FILM FINANCES, INC.

('Guarantor')

By [ ]

Its [ ]

Completion Agreement: Standard Terms

1. **Definitions.** The words and phrases defined in this paragraph 1 are used in the Principal Agreement and in these Standard Terms as so defined:

   Budget: the final budget of the Film, as described in paragraph 1(g) of the Principal Agreement, and which has been approved in writing by the Producer, the Guarantor, and, if required, the Distributors and the Financier.

   Budget Costs: the projected production costs of the Film as set forth in the Budget.

   Budget Funds: the monies needed to pay the Budget Costs.

   Collateral: see paragraph 8(a) of these Standard Terms.

   Completion Agreement: the agreement between the Producer and the Guarantor consisting of the Principal Agreement and these Standard Terms.

   Completion Funds: the monies needed to pay Over-Budget Costs, if any.

   Completion Guaranty: the agreement between Financier and Guarantor.

   Distribution Agreements: the agreements identified as the Distribution Agreements in paragraph 3 of the Principal Agreement.

   Distributors: the distributing companies identified as such in paragraph 3 of the Principal Agreement.

   Employees: persons engaged to perform services in relation to the production of the Film, whether as employees, or under loanout agreements, or as independent contractors or otherwise.

   Employment Agreements: the agreements whereby personnel are employed to perform services in relation to the production of the Film, whether such agreements are employment agreements, loanout agreement or other types of agreements, and whether such agreements are oral or in writing, or are formal agreements, memorandum agreements, deal memoranda or otherwise.

   Film: the motion picture designated as the Film in the Principal Agreement.

Financier: the company identified as 'Financier' in paragraph 2 of the Principal Agreement.

Financing Agreement: the agreement whereby the Financier agrees to provide the funds for payment of Budget Costs.

Gross Receipts: all of those gross receipts of the Film derived by and actually payable to Producer from the distribution, exhibition and other exploitation of the Film.

Guarantor: Film Finances, Inc.

Including: means including but not limited to.

Location Agreement: an agreement for the use of a location for the production of the Film.

Music: includes background music and songs (including the music, lyrics and titles of such songs) used in the Film.

Non-Budget Costs: costs which the Guarantor is not obligated to fund, pursuant to paragraphs 4.1 and 4.2 of these Standard Terms.

Over-Budget Costs: those production costs, if any, of the Film which are in excess of the Budget Costs.

Principal Agreement: the agreement between the Producer and the Guarantor to which these Standard Terms are annexed.

Prior Rights: the rights identified as such in paragraph 4 of the Principal Agreement, to which the Guarantor's recoupment rights and the Guarantor's security interest securing such recoupment rights, are subject and subordinate.

Producer: the company designated in the Principal Agreement as the Producer.

Production Bank Account: the term 'Production Bank Account' shall mean account [ ] in the name of the Producer located at [ ] where all advances by Financier shall be made unless otherwise agreed to in writing by Guarantor.

Production Schedule: the final production schedule of the Film (including the pre-production and post-production schedules), identified in paragraph 1(h) of the Principal Agreement.

Screenplay: the final screenplay on which the Film is to be based, identified in paragraph 1(b)(ii) of the Principal Agreement, and which has been approved in writing by the

Producer, the Guarantor and, if required, the Distributors and the Financier.

Secured Sums: all monies, if any, expended by the Guarantor in relation to the production and delivery of the Film, pursuant to this Principal Agreement or pursuant to the Completion Guaranty, including Completion Funds and all out-of-pocket costs, expenses, losses and liabilities reasonably incurred by the Guarantor directly in relation to or arising out of the performance of this Completion Agreement or the Completion Guaranty, less any refunds received and retained by the Guarantor from insurance or otherwise; provided, however, that Secured Sums will not include any costs or expenses incurred by the Guarantor in monitoring the production of the Film prior to such time, if ever, that Guarantor takes over control of the production of the Film, or any costs, salaries or expenses attributable to Guarantor's general overhead (including any costs or expenses incurred by Guarantor in connection with the preparation and negotiation of this Completion Agreement and all agreements ancillary thereto).

Underlying Literary Property: the literary property or other work, if any, upon which the Screenplay is based.

2. **Warranties, Representations and Agreements of the Producer.** the Producer hereby warrants, represents and agrees that:
   a. The Screenplay, Production Schedule and Budget have been approved by the Producer and, if required, the Distributors and Financier. For the purposes of this agreement, a copy of the Screenplay, Production Schedule and Budget shall be initialled by the Producer, the Financier and the Distributors, and shall be delivered to and initialled by the Guarantor concurrently with the execution of this Completion Agreement.
   b. The producers, executive producers, if any, director and principal members of the cast of the Film (as identified in paragraph 1 of the Principal Agreement) have been approved by the Producer, the Financier and, if required, the Distributors. If any such person is not identified in the Principal Agreement, the person engaged to perform such services shall be subject to the Guarantor's approval. Such approval shall not be based on artistic or creative

considerations, but only on matters which, in the Guarantor's reasonable judgment, might increase Budget Costs or adversely affect the Guarantor's obligations under this Completion Agreement or the Completion Guaranty. The Producer has entered into or will use its best efforts (prior to the commencement of services of the respective Employee) to enter into written Employment Agreements with the persons identified in paragraph 1 of the Principal Agreement, and (if not so identified) with the persons engaged to perform the services referred to in said paragraph. All such written agreements shall be subject to the Guarantor's approval, which approval shall not be unreasonably withheld. In any case in which the use of a specific location for filming is an important element of the production of the Film, the Location Agreement shall also be in writing and shall be subject to the Guarantor's approval, which shall not be unreasonably withheld. Written notice of approval or disapproval shall be given within ten (10) business days after the respective agreement is submitted for approval, and shall not be deemed to have been given unless given in writing (or not responded to within said period). If the Guarantor disapproves of any agreement so submitted, the reason(s) for the disapproval shall be given in the notice. Disapproval because an agreement includes a 'stop date' or because it does not include 'pay or play' provisions (as those terms are understood in the entertainment industry) shall be deemed to be reasonable.

c. The Financing Agreement and the Distribution Agreements have been executed, have been approved by the Guarantor, and are in full force and effect, and no default exists thereunder.
d. Subject to the provisions of the Distribution Agreements and the Financing Agreement, the Producer owns, solely and exclusively, all such rights in the Screenplay and in the Underlying Literary Property, if any, and owns or, prior to the completion of production and delivery of the Film, will own (or will have obtained licenses for) all such rights in the music used in the Film, and in all results and proceeds of all services performed in relation to the production of the Film, and in all other content of the Film, as are and will be necessary to permit (without violating

any rights of third parties) the production of the Film; and such rights are and will be free and clear of all adverse rights, claims and security interests whatsoever, except for the Prior Rights.

e. The Producer will be the producer of the Film.
f. Except as otherwise provided in the Financing Agreement or the Distribution Agreements, the copyright of the Film and all rights to market and exploit the Film will be owned solely and exclusively by the Producer throughout the production of and upon the completion of production of the Film.
g. Subject only to the Prior Rights, all of the Gross Receipts will be available for the recoupment of the Secured Sums, if any.
h. All proceeds received by Producer under the Financing Agreement shall be applied by Producer in payment of budgeted production costs of the Film in accordance with the Financing Agreement, the Distribution Agreements, the Budget and this Completion Agreement.

3. **Insurance.** The Producer represents, warrants and agrees that:
   a. The Producer has obtained or will obtain that insurance in relation to the Film which is listed in Schedule 1 of this Completion Agreement. Said insurance shall be maintained in force throughout the production and until the delivery of the Film; provided that the so-called Errors and Omissions Insurance shall be maintained in force for a period of not less than three years from the date of commencement of production of the Film, or for such shorter period of time as the Guarantor may approve in writing. The Guarantor and its various underwriters under Policy #930222A and any renewals thereof shall be named as additional insureds and as loss payees of all such insurance, as their interests may appear. The insurer and the policies of insurance shall be subject to the Guarantor's reasonable approval. The Guarantor hereby approves the standard forms used by Truman Van Dyke, Lloyds of London, Fireman's Fund and Pacific Indemnity for the coverage listed in Schedule 1. Among other things, such insurance shall (i) provide that at least ten days' prior written notice of cancellation thereof must be served upon the Guarantor, if any such insurance is cancelled, and (ii) include a notice to the insurer of the Guarantor's rights pursuant to subparagraphs (c) and (e) of this paragraph 3. Copies of the insurance policies and of

receipts for premiums paid shall be delivered to the Guarantor on demand.

b. The Producer shall from time to time during the production of the Film, if any material conditions change substantially and Guarantor determines in the exercise of its good faith sound business judgment that such change results in the need for additional insurance, obtain such additional insurance for such amounts as the Guarantor may reasonably specify, and shall immediately replace any cancelled insurance so as to maintain full insurance in effect at all times until the completion of the production and delivery of the Film. The Producer shall inform the Guarantor of all additional insurance, modifications, extensions or substitutions effected as aforesaid and shall deliver to the Guarantor on demand the additional policies of insurance or endorsements to existing policies and the receipts for premiums paid (which premiums shall be included in the cost of production of the Film). If Budget Funds or funds from other sources are not available for such premiums, the Guarantor shall advance the necessary funds to pay such premiums as Completion Funds.
c. The Producer shall not knowingly do or permit or suffer to be done any act or thing whereby any such policy of insurance may become in whole or in part void or voidable. If an insured event has occurred which results or contributes to the cost of the Film being over-budget, or which in the Guarantor's good faith sound business judgment may have such result, the insurance claim shall not be settled without the Guarantor's prior written approval.
d. If the Producer shall fail to obtain any such insurance or to maintain it in force, the Guarantor may obtain such insurance, and in that event any premiums paid by the Guarantor for such insurance shall forthwith be repaid to it by the Producer from the Budget Funds, or if such funds are not available, such payments shall be deemed to be Completion Funds advanced by the Guarantor.
e. If an insurance loss has occurred, the insurance recovery (unless paid to a third party, such as in relation to a personal injury or property damage claim) shall be paid and disbursed as follows:
   i. If the recovery is paid after all costs of production have been paid, and if at the time of receipt of the recovery

the cost of the Film is over-budget, the insured loss has caused or contributed to the over-budget condition and the Guarantor has expended or will become obligated to expend Secured Sums, the insurance recovery shall first be used to reimburse the Guarantor for such Secured Sums advanced by the Guarantor. The Guarantor shall not be concerned with the disposition of any surplus; such surplus shall be disbursed in accordance with the Producer's other contractual obligations. Likewise, if the Guarantor has not expended and will not become obligated to advance Secured Sums, the entire recovery shall, so far as the Guarantor is concerned, be disbursed in accordance with the Producer's directions.

ii. If the recovery is paid before all costs of production and delivery of the Film have been paid, such recovery shall be paid into the Production Account of the Film, and shall first be used to pay production and delivery costs of the Film. Any surplus of such funds remaining after all production and delivery costs of the Film have been paid shall then be used to reimburse the Guarantor for Secured Sums, if any. The Guarantor shall not be concerned with the disposition of any surplus thereafter remaining (or of any surplus in the Production Account, if there were no Secured Sums), and so far as the Guarantor is concerned, such funds shall be disbursed in accordance with the Producer's directions.

iii. Notwithstanding the foregoing, if an insured event occurs which results in the production of the Film being abandoned or which results in the Producer or Guarantor being unable to complete the production and deliver the Film, the insurance recovery shall be paid as follows: first, to Financier until the indebtedness under the Financing Agreement is repaid in full; second, to the Guarantor until the Secured Sums, if any, are repaid in full; and third, any surplus thereafter remaining shall be disbursed in accordance with the Producer's directions.

f. If any costs are incurred by the Producer which ought to have been covered by insurance pursuant to this paragraph 3, but which are not insured, or are not insured for at least the minimum amounts specified in Schedule 1, the Producer shall pay the Guarantor on demand such sums as would have been received from the insurer had such costs been insured in full or (as the case may be) had been insured for at least the minimum amounts specified in Schedule 1, but not exceeding (with sums paid to the Guarantor pursuant to subparagraph (e) of this paragraph 3) any unreimbursed Secured Sums. If the Producer has in force all of the insurance provided for in Schedule 1, and any other insurance required by the Guarantor pursuant to subparagraph (b) of this paragraph 3, the Producer shall be deemed to have satisfied the requirements of this subparagraph (f). Nothing contained herein shall be deemed to render the Producer liable to the Guarantor for any breach of contract by the Film's insurers.

g. If the Film goes over-budget, in whole or in part, because of acts of omission or commission by third parties which are not covered, or are only partially covered, by insurance obtained hereunder, the Guarantor shall be subrogated to all of the Producer's rights and remedies against and recoveries from such third party or its insurers, to the extent of the Secured Sums, if any, resulting from such over-budget condition. Any surplus of such recoveries over the amount of such Secured Sums shall be paid to the Producer, the Financier or other party, as their respective interests may appear. The Producer agrees to execute and deliver to the Guarantor such instruments as may be reasonably necessary or desirable to evidence or effectuate such subrogation, and otherwise to cooperate with the Guarantor for this purpose. Subject to the terms of the Completion Guaranty, the Guarantor shall control all actions taken to recover such loss, including all settlement negotiations, and the Producer agrees to do nothing which would prejudice these rights. The cost of obtaining such recoveries, if and to the extent paid by the Guarantor, shall be Secured Sums. The Guarantor will consult with the Producer with respect to all actions taken by the Guarantor to recover any such loss and all settlement negotiations relating thereto. In any event, the Guarantor's rights pursuant to this subparagraph shall be subject to the rights of the Producer's insurers in the case of a partially insured loss.

4.1 Non-Budget Costs. The Guarantor shall not be obligated to advance Completion Funds for any of the following costs:

a. legal fees in excess of the amount allowed in the Budget;
b. the cost of delivery items not provided for in the Budget;
c. advertising and publicity costs in excess of the amounts allowed in the Budget;
d. except to the extent required by the Completion Guaranty, interest and finance charges;
e. any costs incurred in obtaining for the Film the seal, certificate or rating of the Motion Picture Association of America, Inc., or arising from the Film not conforming to the standards and requirements of production set forth in the Production Code of said association, other than the fee of said association for such seal, certificate or rating, if provided for in the Budget; provided, however, that the Guarantor will not itself photograph or record any material which would result in a rating of said association more restrictive than 'R' and further provided that the Film as delivered by the Guarantor will qualify for that rating which is necessary to Complete and Deliver the Film (as that term is defined in the Completion Guaranty);
f. any costs incurred to photograph, record or include in the Film 'cover shots' for television or other purposes or other substitute or additional material except and only to the extent provided for in the Budget;
g. except to the extent provided for in the Budget, the cost of previews;
h. except to the extent provided for in the Budget, any costs incurred in connection with recutting, reediting, retakes and changes required for reasons other than (1) correction of technical defects or (2) conforming the Film to the contractual specifications for which the Guarantor is responsible pursuant to the Completion Guaranty;
i. except to the extent provided for in the Budget, guild and union deferred or contingent payments;
j. any payments pursuant to tax indemnity obligations;
k. scenes or other material not included in the Screenplay;
l. except to the extent provided for in the Budget, any costs incurred as a result of the violation by the Producer of any collective bargaining agreement, or of any law or governmental regulations;

m. any production costs incurred after the completion and delivery of the Film, except such production costs, if any, for which the Guarantor is responsible under the Completion Guaranty;
n. any distribution expenses, including costs incurred in meeting censorship or exhibitor requirements, or to make foreign language versions of the Film (dubbed, subtitled or otherwise) or any other versions other than the original English language version (unless included in the Budget). The Producer agrees not to expend Budget Funds or Completion Funds for the payment of Non-Budget Costs, and to pay all such Non-Budget costs from other funds.

4.2 Certain Costs in Excess of Budget. Producer hereby agrees that

a. the rates of compensation (including minimum guarantees) which the Producer has agreed and shall agree to pay personnel engaged to perform services in relation to the Film, and the number of persons employed in each classification (including but not limited to performers, extras, stand-ins and crowds) will not exceed the rates and allowances provided therefor in the Budget;
b. the rates upon which the expense allowances provided for in the Budget are computed will not be exceeded; and
c. the cost of obtaining and recording the music and lyrics contained in the Film, including all worldwide clearances with respect thereto, will not exceed the allowances provided therefor in the Budget. If any of the limitations provided for above in this paragraph are exceeded, the resulting excess costs ('Excess Costs') shall not be Guarantor's responsibility, and Producer shall provide or cause to be provided any additional monies needed to finance such Excess Costs, on demand. No Budget Funds will be expended for the payment of such Excess Costs. Notwithstanding the foregoing, if the production and delivery of the Film are completed within the Budget, so that the Guarantor is not called upon to provide Completion Funds, the Excess Costs may be paid for from the unused excess of the Budget Funds, or if any such Excess Costs are incurred, but are offset by savings in any of the costs referred to in this paragraph, such savings of costs may be used to pay such Excess Costs.

5. **Guarantor's Rights Concerning Production.**
   a. The Producer shall, until the Guarantor shall be released from the Completion Guaranty, promptly inform the Guarantor of all matters substantially and adversely affecting the Producer's credit and financial condition, including any proceedings threatened or commenced against the Producer, the progress of such proceedings, and any judgments obtained against the Producer.
   b. The Producer shall produce the Film in all respects in accordance with the provisions of the Distribution Agreements, the Financing Agreement, the Screenplay, the Production Schedule and the Budget, and shall not without the prior written consent of the Guarantor vary from or make or agree to make any modification therein or in the personnel or other details of production approved by the Guarantor other than minor variations or modifications arising as a result of the normal exigencies of film production and/or minor discretionary changes customarily made by the director which do not result in an increase in the cost of production of the Film or in a violation of the Distribution Agreements or the Financing Agreement. In this regard, and without limiting the generality of the foregoing, the Producer will not enhance the Film in any manner without the prior written consent of the Guarantor. In the event the Producer enhances the Film, the Producer shall provide (or shall cause to be provided) such sums as are necessary to pay for the cost of such enhancement, and the cost of any such enhancements shall in no way be the responsibility of Guarantor; provided, however, if the production and delivery of the Film are completed within the Budget, so that the Guarantor is not called upon to provide Completion Funds and the Film is enhanced but the cost of the enhancement is affected by savings of cost in other categories of the Budget, the Producer's obligations under this paragraph 5(b) shall be limited to provided the funds needed to pay the amount not affected, if any. The term 'enhance' means adding to or changing any elements of the Film which result in increasing the cost of production of the Film.
   c. During the production of the Film the Producer shall keep the Guarantor informed about the progress of production and the plans for continuing and completing the production

and delivery of the Film, shall telephone or telex to the Guarantor daily production progress reports, shall prepare and promptly deliver to the Guarantor weekly itemized production cost statements (including item by item good faith estimates of cost to complete), and shall promptly submit to the Guarantor any estimates of future expenditures or statements of costs incurred or other production reports which the Producer is required to submit to the Distributors, or the Financier or which the Guarantor may reasonably require from time to time. The Guarantor or its representatives shall be entitled at any reasonable times and without interfering with the production and delivery of the Film until it shall be released from the Completion Guaranty to attend at the studios or locations where the Film is being produced to watch the production of the Film, to see rushes or rough cuts and to inspect the production accounts, books and records of the Producer in relation to the Film and take extracts therefrom.

d. The Guarantor shall have the right to demand from the Producer an explanation of any matter relating to the production of the Film, whether or not arising from anything disclosed in the documents and accounts made available to the Guarantor as aforesaid, if it seems to the Guarantor in the exercise of its good faith sound business judgment that such matter is likely to involve the Guarantor in the risk of incurring liability under the Completion Guaranty. The Producer shall give such explanations as may be required without delay and (if required by the Guarantor) shall attend one or more meetings at which the producer, director or any other person concerned with the production, whose presence the Guarantor shall request, shall be present to discuss the matter with the Guarantor's representatives (provided always that no such meetings shall by reason of their place, time or frequency interfere with the production of the Film) and shall give full consideration to the views and proposals put forward by the Guarantor regarding the steps to be taken to avoid or reduce such risk.

e. If:
   i. after such explanations or meeting(s) the Guarantor shall not be satisfied, in the exercise of its good faith sound business judgment, that the likelihood of such

risk arising will be avoided or adequately reduced by the steps proposed to be taken by the Producer, or

ii. at any time it seems to the Guarantor, in the exercise of its good faith sound business judgment, that the production is likely to involve the Guarantor in a risk of incurring liability under the Completion Guaranty, or

iii. the Producer shall at any time fail, refuse or neglect to comply with any of the terms of this Completion Agreement, the Distribution Agreements, or of the Financing Agreement, and the Guarantor determines in the exercise of its good faith sound business judgment that such failure, refusal or neglect is likely to involve The Guarantor in a risk of incurring liability under this Completion Agreement or the Completion Guaranty, the Producer shall (1) forthwith and thereafter faithfully comply with all instructions given by the Guarantor with respect to the production of the Film for the purpose of avoiding or reducing such risk or remedying such failure, refusal or neglect, including but not limited to the dismissal of any person(s) engaged in the production of the Film, provided that no such instruction shall be contrary to the provisions of the Distribution Agreements, or of the Financing Agreement, or any other contractual obligations of the Producer in respect of the Film previously approved by the Guarantor, except with the consent of the third person concerned, and (2) if requested by the Guarantor, place at the disposal of the Guarantor the production bank accounts and all other production funds in relation to the Film, but the Guarantor shall expend such funds only for the production and delivery of the Film.

f. If:

i. the Producer shall be in default in the performance of any of its material obligations under any of the provisions of this Completion Agreement, and shall fail to remedy such default within two (2) business days after service of written notice thereof by the Guarantor upon the Producer and the Financier, or

ii. at any time it seems to the Guarantor, in the exercise of its good faith sound business judgment, that the production is likely to involve the Guarantor in a risk of incurring liability under the Completion Guaranty, and the Producer fails within two (2) business days after service of written notice thereof by the Guarantor, as aforesaid, to cure the situation which is of concern to the Guarantor, to the Guarantor's satisfaction, or to carry out immediately and faithfully any instructions given by the Guarantor pursuant to the provisions of this paragraph 5, the Guarantor shall have the right to take over control, and to complete, the production and delivery of the Film, subject to the provisions of the Completion Guaranty. Where reference is made above to two (2) business days, and the instructions to cure given by the Guarantor are of such nature that they cannot be completed within two (2) business days, the Guarantor may, in its sole discretion, but need not, allow the Producer such additional time to remedy the default or to cure the situation as the Guarantor shall deem to be sufficient to do so, provided that the Producer immediately initiates the required action and diligently carries it to completion, and provided that the situation does not worsen, in the Guarantor's good faith sound business judgment. If the Guarantor exercises its right to take over control of the production of the Film, the Guarantor shall be deemed to have been irrevocably appointed the manager and agent of the Producer for such purpose. The Guarantor shall give the Producer, Distributors and Financier written notice of its decision to take over control of the production of the Film, as aforesaid, and forthwith upon service of such notice the Producer shall place at the disposal and under the control of the Guarantor the production bank account(s) and all other production funds, and all persons, facilities and equipment employed and used and to be employed and used by the Producer for the production of the Film, and shall in all other respects required by the Guarantor cooperate with the Guarantor so that all necessary personnel, facilities and equipment will be available to the Guarantor, as manager and agent for the Producer, as would have been available to the Producer had the Producer remained in control of production of the Film. The Guarantor shall incur no liability to the Producer from such appointment as manager and agent for the Producer, and from the performance by the Guarantor of its functions in those capacities, but in the performance of such functions the Guarantor agrees to observe the contractual obligations of the Producer to third parties relating to the production of the Film, provided that they have been made known to the Guarantor and (to the extent required to be approved under this Completion Agreement) approved by the Guarantor, and are consistent with the provisions of this Completion Agreement, the Distribution Agreements, the Financing Agreement, the Budget and Production Schedule. The Guarantor shall fully indemnify Producer against all costs, claims, demands, losses and liability incurred by the Producer because of or arising out of any default by the Guarantor under the immediately preceding sentence of these Standard Terms, if and only to the extent, if any, that the Producer has been prejudiced by the occurrence of any such default. The Guarantor reserves all of its rights and remedies against the Producer, at law or in equity, in the event of any material or substantial breach of this Completion Agreement by the Producer. The exercise of the rights granted to the Guarantor under subparagraphs (e) and (f) of this paragraph 5 shall terminate if (x) the Producer shall raise such additional funds or take such other steps as shall in the Guarantor's good faith judgment adequately protect the Guarantor from incurring liability under the Completion Guaranty (including immediate repayment of any Secured Sums), but without prejudice to the right of the Guarantor subsequently to exercise any of its rights under said subparagraphs (e) and (f), if the Guarantor should again conclude that its position under the Guaranty is at risk, or (y) each of Financier, Distributors and Producer release Guarantor from any and all of its obligations under this Completion Agreement, the Completion Guaranty and any other agreement which the Guarantor enters into in connection with the Film, and immediately repay the Secured Sums, if any, to the Guarantor. If the Guarantor takes over control of production of the Film, the Guarantor shall keep true and accurate records of its expenditures in relation to the Film, and shall retain all such records, and any other documents which it may obtain in relation to its production of the Film, for not less than one year. Thereafter, if it desires to dispose of such records and documents, it shall first offer them to the Producer and Distributors, who in the meanwhile shall have access thereto at reasonable times for auditing purposes. If the Producer or Distributors fail to take possession of such records and documents within thirty (30) days after they are offered to the Producer or Distributors, the Guarantor shall have the right to destroy them.

6. **Recoupment.** To the extent that the Producer has or will have any control of or interest in the worldwide Gross Receipts and the gross income from the sale or exploitation of the other Collateral referred to in paragraph 8 hereof, the Producer shall pay or cause to be paid to the Guarantor out of said Gross Receipts and other income an amount equal to the Secured Sums, if any, subject only to the Prior Rights.

7. **Insolvency and Adverse Proceedings.** The Secured Sums, if any, shall become immediately due and payable to the Guarantor by the Producer if the Producer is adjudicated a bankrupt, or if a petition for or consent to any relief under any bankruptcy, receivership, liquidation, compromise, arrangement or moratorium statute is filed against the Producer, or if a petition for the appointment of a receiver, liquidator, trustee or custodian for all or a substantial part of the Producer's assets is filed, or if a receiver, liquidator, trustee or custodian for all or a substantial part of the Producer's assets is appointed, or if any judgment is obtained against the Producer which substantially and adversely affects its credit and financial standing, and such judgment is not discharged or stayed within fourteen days after such judgment is obtained, or if an attachment or execution is levied upon any of the Producer's property needed for the production of the Film and such attachment or execution adversely affects the production of the Film, or if proceedings are initiated to wind up or liquidate the Producer (except winding up for the purposes of consolidation or other corporate reorganization), or if the Producer shall cease or threaten to cease to carry on its business. The occurrence of any such event shall permit the Guarantor to immediately

exercise its rights under paragraphs 8 and 9 of these Standard Terms.

8. Security Interest.

a. To the extent, if any, that the Producer owns any right, title or interest in the Collateral, the Producer hereby grants to the Guarantor a security interest in the Collateral to secure repayment of the Secured Sums, if any. Said security interest shall be subject to the Prior Rights, but shall have priority over any other rights or security interests of any other person, company or entity in or with respect to the Collateral, including deferments and gross receipts or net profit participations. The Collateral, as that term is used in this Completion Agreement, consists of: (i) all positive and negative film, all sound tracks and all other physical properties of or relating to the Film, whether now or hereafter in existence and wherever located; (ii) all literary property and ancillary rights in relation to the Film, including without limitation the Screenplay, the Underlying Literary Property, if any, and the copyrights thereof, (iii) the copyright or copyrights of the Film; (iv) the music of the Film; (v) all rights to distribute, lease, license, sell, exhibit, broadcast or otherwise deal with the Film by all methods and means and in all media throughout the universe; (vi) all contracts and contract rights, accounts, inventories and general intangibles of the Producer relating to the Film or to any literary property and ancillary rights and any other elements of the Film referred to in this subparagraph; (vii) the Gross Receipts and all other financial proceeds of the Collateral, including all income and receipts derived and to be derived from the marketing, distribution, licensing, sale, exhibition, broadcasting and other exploitation of the Film and of the other elements of the Collateral, and (subject to paragraph 3 of these Standard Terms) all proceeds of insurance relating to the Film; (viii) the Reserved Rights.

b. With respect to its security interest, the Guarantor, its successors and assigns, are hereby granted all of the rights, powers and privileges of a secured party under the California Uniform Commercial Code in force and effect from time to time.

c. The Producer agrees to execute and deliver to the Guarantor, when requested by the Guarantor from time to time, UCC Financing Statements and a Mortgage of Copyright in form satisfactory to the Guarantor for recording purposes, confirming and evidencing the Guarantor's security interest in and to the Collateral. The Guarantor is hereby irrevocably appointed the Producer's attorney-in-fact to execute such instruments in the name and stead of the Producer, should the Producer fail to do so upon request, and to file or record them as deemed necessary or advisable by the Guarantor.

d. The Producer shall not (i) grant any rights or security interests (other than the Prior Rights) ranking in priority to or pari passu with the security interest hereby granted; (ii) while any monies are due to the Guarantor hereunder, agree to market or exploit any of the Collateral, other than pursuant to the Distribution Agreements, and the Financing Agreement, without the prior written consent of the Guarantor.

e. The security interest hereby granted shall terminate: (i) if and when it is finally determined that the Guarantor will incur no liability under the Completion Guaranty; or (ii) (if such liability has been incurred) if and when the Guarantor has received payment in full of the Secured Sums. When and if said security interest terminates, the Guarantor shall execute such instruments as may be necessary to evidence the release and termination of its security interest.

f. In the event that, pursuant to the Completion Guaranty, the Guarantor repays any financing provided by the Financier, then, in addition to its security interest hereunder, the Guarantor shall automatically be subrogated to the security interests of the Financier in relation to such financing, and shall in all respects succeed to the position of the Financier under the Financing Agreement and under all instruments ancillary thereto.

9. **Additional Remedies.** As an additional remedy, but subject to and so as not to adversely affect the rights of the Distributors pursuant to the Distribution Agreements, and of the Financier pursuant to the Financing Agreement, or any other Prior Rights, if the Guarantor expends or advances any Secured Sums the Guarantor shall, after consulting with the Producer, have all or any of the following rights (either itself or by appointment of an agent, on such terms as to the

compensation of such agent and otherwise as the Guarantor shall reasonably determine):

a. To take possession of the Collateral or any part thereof;
b. To manage and control, or to supervise the management and control, of the business of the Producer in relation to the Film, and for this purpose to raise or borrow monies upon the security of the Collateral or any part thereof, and to engage such personnel or such other companies as it shall consider necessary;
c. To enter into distribution, exhibition, sales and leasing agreements in relation to the Film or any of the Collateral for any media and for any territories, and to make any settlements, arrangements and compromises, and to do such other acts and things in relation to the Film as the Producer would itself have the right to do.

All such acts of the Guarantor shall be such as in its good faith judgment it considers to be in the best interests of the Guarantor, the Distributors, the Financier and the Producer. If called upon by the Guarantor, the Producer shall, without compensation, render such assistance to the Guarantor in connection with such action by the Guarantor or its appointee as the Guarantor may reasonably require from time to time. The Producer irrevocably appoints the Guarantor its attorney-in-fact, with power to appoint other persons as attorney-in-fact, to execute such instruments in the name and stead of the Producer as they may consider necessary and proper in acting pursuant to this paragraph 9. The powers and authority of the Guarantor pursuant to this paragraph 9 shall cease when the Guarantor has recouped the Secured Sums, without prejudice however to any acts done by the Guarantor or its appointee and the continued effectiveness of all instruments executed by them or either of them pursuant to this paragraph. Subject to the Prior Rights, all monies received by the Guarantor or its appointee pursuant to the exercise of the Guarantor's powers and authority under this paragraph, which remain after payment or recoupment of all costs, charges and expenses incidental to the exercise of such powers and authority, and after payment of the Secured Sums, shall be paid to the Producer or other party entitled thereto.

10. Statements. If and as long as there are any unrecouped Secured Sums, the Producer shall deliver or cause to be delivered to the Guarantor, concurrently with or immediately following delivery thereof to the Producer, copies of all statements and reports which the Producer receives from the Distributors and other third parties in relation to the marketing and exploitation of the Film, or any of the other Collateral.

11. **The Completion Guaranty.** The Producer hereby acknowledges and confirms that it is not entitled to nor does it have any interest in the benefit of the Completion Guaranty, and the Producer hereby waives and releases all interest and benefit in the Completion Guaranty, present or future.

12. **Miscellaneous Provisions.** This Completion Agreement has been executed in the State of California, and shall in all respects be interpreted, enforced and governed by the laws of that State. The language of this Completion Agreement shall be construed as a whole according to its fair meaning and not strictly for or against either of the parties. If the Producer consists of more than one company, this agreement shall be binding jointly and severally upon such companies and each of them. Any term used in this Completion Agreement in the singular shall be deemed to be used in the plural wherever appropriate. The Producer acknowledges that the Guarantor has entered into agreements with certain insurers who insure certain of the Guarantor's obligations in relation to the Film. Pursuant to those arrangements, such insurers shall have the right to assume the Guarantor's obligations and rights under this Completion Agreement, subject to the terms hereof. If any one or more of the provisions of this Completion Agreement shall be held to be illegal or unenforceable in any respect, the legality and enforceability of the remaining provisions shall not in any way be affected or impaired thereby. No modification or waiver of any provision of this Completion Agreement or waiver of any default hereunder shall be effective, unless in writing and signed by the parties hereto (in the case of a modification) or by the waiving party (in the case of a waiver), and any such waiver shall apply only to the specific matter waived.

13. **Notices.** Notices may be served by either party hereto on the other by mail, telecopy or telegram, and shall be deemed to have been served at the expiration of one business day after the date of mailing, postage pre-paid, or the date of

dispatching the telecopy or telegram, charges pre-paid or otherwise provided for. In proving such service it shall be sufficient to show (by affidavit of the person who sent the notice) that the telecopy, telegram or letter was dispatched or posted as aforesaid. The respective addresses of the parties shall be as stated at the beginning of the Principal Agreement, but either party may change its address from time to time by written notice to the other party.

END OF STANDARD TERMS

Schedule 1: Insurance

a. Cast Insurance in an amount equal to at least 100 per cent of the amount of the Budget to cover, among other things, extra expense necessary to complete the principal photography of the Film due to the death, injury or sickness of any principal performer or the director.
b. Negative Insurance in an amount equal to at least 100 per cent of the amount of the Budget to cover, among other things, all risks of direct physical loss, damage or destruction of raw film stock, exposed film, whether developed or undeveloped, and sound tracks.
c. Faulty Stock, Camera and Processing Insurance to cover, among other things, loss, damage or destruction of raw film stock, exposed film, whether developed or undeveloped, and sound tracks caused by or resulting from fogging or the use of faulty sound equipment, faulty developing, faulty editing and faulty processing.
d. Props, Sets and Wardrobe Insurance to cover, among other things, all risks of direct physical loss, damage or destruction of props, sets and wardrobe during production of the Film.
e. Extra Expense Insurance to cover, among other things, any extra expense necessary to complete the principal photography of the Film due to the damage or destruction of property, including, without limitation, facilities, props, sets or equipment used in connection with the Film, including loss due to faulty generators.
f. Miscellaneous Equipment Insurance to cover, among other things, all risks of direct physical loss, damage or destruction to cameras, camera equipment, sound, lighting (including breakage of globes) and grip equipment, and mobile equipment, vans or studio location units or other such similar units owned by, or rented to, the producer of the Film.
g. Property Damage Liability Insurance covering, among other things, the damage to or destruction of the property of others, including, without limitation, the loss of use of that property while such property is in the care, custody or control of the Producer of the Film.
h. Errors and Omissions Insurance covering, among other things, the legal liability and defense of the producer of the Film against lawsuits alleging the unauthorized use of title, format, ideas, characters, plots, plagiarism, unfair competition and

breach of implied or quasi-contract. Such insurance shall also protect against alleged libel, slander, defamation of character and invasion of privacy. The Errors and Omission Insurance shall be in the minimum amount of $1,000,000 U.S. per occurrence and $3,000,000 U.S. in the aggregate with a deductible of $10,000 U.S. and a period of coverage of not less than three years from delivery of the Film (plus such longer periods as coverage is required to be in effect pursuant to contracts for the exhibition or distribution of the Film).

i. Comprehensive Liability Insurance covering the producer of the Film against, among other things, all claims for bodily injury, personal injury or property damage which arise in connection with the Film, with minimum liability limits of $1,000,000 U.S.
j. Worker's Compensation Insurance as required by the various jurisdictions in which any services are rendered in connection with the Film covering, among other things, all temporary or permanent cast or production crew members.
k. Any insurance coverage required by applicable collective bargaining agreements. Coverage is to be blanket and the limits of liability must be sufficient so as to meet all requirements of such collective bargaining agreements.
l. Broad Form Monies and Securities Insurance covering, among other things, the loss of money or other securities through disappearance, destruction or wrongful abstraction at any location site any place in the world in an amount equal to the greater of $25,000 or the amount of the highest estimated weekly cash payroll for the Film.

7 Collection Agreements

If you can count your money, you don't have a billion dollars.
J. Paul Getty

Collection Agreements

In the world of multiparty film financing, investors, or those entitled to a share of revenues arising from the exploitation of a film, always have an interest in getting their money back or seeing a net profit.

Collection Account Management Agreements have become an important aspect of a film financing transaction. Before the widespread use of collection accounts and the engagement of collection management companies, revenues from the sale of a film to international distributors were usually administered by the sales agents. Those entitled to receive revenues from sales would sometimes find it difficult to get statements or payments to which they were entitled from the sales agent. Many sales agents would mix funds with the sales from other films and, in some cases, charge exorbitant costs on top of their already expensive sales commissions. When challenged by an investor or the producer, certain sales agents would make it very difficult to provide proper reports. In many cases, a sales agent would go bankrupt and therefore any funds that the investor or producer were entitled to would be virtually impossible to collect.

Now that film financing transactions have in some circumstances become so complex, those with a financial interest in the production will make it a condition of their financing that a collection account manager is appointed to the film in order to receive, administer and disburse any revenues that are collected.

The involvement of a collection management company forces all parties in a film financing transaction to focus on specific details about the allocation of potential revenues for the film at an early stage. It also ensures that the recoupment schedule for a film is completed prior to the closing of all financial contributions to the film. The collection account manager acts as an independent third party looking after the interests of all investors and financiers. The collection account manager will charge a fee for providing their services that will be collected first, before it disburses any funds to investors. In some cases, a collection account manager will charge a minimum fee up front and then take a smaller fee based on a percentage later on. A standard collection account manager's fee would be 1 per cent of the revenues collected. However, in some cases this may be higher or lower depending on the specific deal and amount of work involved.

Those with a financial interest in a film include: co-producers, financiers, investors, film funds, sales agents, completion guarantors and talent.

The collection account manager will open a collection account at a designated bank in a designated country. In some circumstances, the location of the bank account can have certain tax implications. For example, a sale to some territories will result in withholding tax. Withholding tax is a type of tax whereby a distributor purchasing the rights to a film will have to hold back a certain percentage of that sale in their home territory. Therefore, structuring the sales through the collection account manager in a certain jurisdiction will result in greater net income from the sale to that territory that would otherwise be subject to withholding tax.

The sales agent will be a party to the Collection Account Management Agreement, which requires the sales agent to instruct local distributors who purchase the film for their home territory to pay all minimum guarantees into the collection account.

The collection account manager will be the sole signatory to the collection account and will receive, administer, allocate and disburse all revenues in accordance with the recoupment schedule, which is usually annexed to the Collection Account Management Agreement. The collection account manager will provide all parties to the agreement with reports that reflect all sales made in relation to the film. The report will also show actual payments received in the collection account and who has been allocated any sums under the recoupment schedule.

By utilizing an independent third party, all financial parties involved in a film financing can closely monitor the revenue streams and allocation of funds.

The following is a Collection Account Management Agreement used by a well-known collection management company, Freeway Entertainment Group BV. Their details are as follows:

Freeway Entertainment Group BV
Andrassy ut 12
1061 Budapest
Hungary
Tel: +36 14734300
Fax: +36 14734301
E-mail: gadi.wildstrom@freeway-entertainment.com
cecile.huberts@freeway-entertainment.com
martijn.meerstadt@freeway-entertainment.com

Sample Agreement

DATED AS OF THE [ ] DAY OF [ ], 2004

FREEWAY CAM BV
– and –
STICHTING FREEWAY CUSTODY
– and –
THOSE PERSONS, FIRMS OR OTHER ENTITIES SPECIFIED IN SCHEDULE 1

COLLECTION ACCOUNT MANAGEMENT AGREEMENT

Collection Account Management Agreement

RE: ['*FILM TITLE*']

AGREEMENT dated as of the [ ] day of [ ], 2004

BETWEEN:

1. **FREEWAY CAM B.V.** (a company registered under the laws of The Netherlands) c/o Andrássy út 12, 1061 Budapest, Hungary ('**FCAM**');
2. **STICHTING FREEWAY CUSTODY** (a foundation registered under the laws of The Netherlands) c/o Andrássy út 12, 1061 Budapest, Hungary ('**FCustody**'); and
3. **THOSE PERSONS, FIRMS OR OTHER ENTITIES SPECIFIED IN SCHEDULE 1 HERETO** (together '**Parties**' and individually '**Party**' which expressions shall include each of the Parties successors in title and assigns).

IT IS HEREBY AGREED that the Parties jointly appoint FCustody to open the Collection Account and that FCustody accepts such appointment.

Furthermore, it is hereby agreed that the Parties jointly appoint FCAM to administer the collection and distribution of Collected Gross Receipts on behalf of the Parties in accordance with the provisions of the Schedules hereto and FCAM's Standard Terms of Agreement and that, in consideration of FCAM's Remuneration, FCAM accepts such appointment.

Schedule 1: Names and Addresses of the Parties

[To include the 'Completion Guarantor', 'Producer' and 'Distributor']

Schedule 2: Definitions

In this Agreement the following words and expressions shall have the meanings hereby ascribed to them which meanings shall apply to this Agreement and the Schedules hereto:

'Accounting Currency'	[please advise];
'Beneficiary (ies)'	those persons, firms or entities specified in Schedule 4;
'Business Day'	any day excluding Saturdays, Sundays and any days which are public holidays in the country in which any of the Parties has its principal place of business;
'Collection Account'	a designated bank account held in the name of FCustody and referring to the name of the film into which all Gross Receipts are paid, established with; Account Name: '[title film]' Account No: [123456789] SWIFT address: [ ];
'Collected Gross Receipts'	all Gross Receipts actually received in the Collection Account and interest thereon;
'Completion Guarantee'	the agreement dated [ ] and made between the Completion Guarantor and [ ] relating to the Film;
'Completion Guarantor'	[ ];
'Delivery Date'	the date upon which the Film is delivered in accordance with the provisions of the Completion Guarantee;
'Distribution Agreement'	the agreement dated [ ] and made between the Producer and the Distributor relating to the exploitation of the Film and any additional or replacement agreement;

'Distributor'	[ ] and any additional or replacement agent duly appointed by the Producer;
'Entitlement(s)'	that part of the Collected Gross Receipts payable to a Beneficiary pursuant to the terms of this Agreement;
'FCAM Expenses'	all expenses incurred by FCAM as provided for in this Agreement;
'FCAM's Remuneration'	the sum of [ ] ( ) to be paid from the first Collected Gross Receipts together with [ ] % of all Gross Receipts;
'Film'	the [feature film/television programme] a brief specification of which is set out in Schedule 3;
'Gross Receipts'	all monies or any other proceeds derived from Sub-Distribution Agreements or from any other source of exploitation relating to the Film or the Rights received by any Party directly or indirectly;
'Net Profit Participants'	the persons, firms or entities specified in Schedule 6;
'Net Profits'	as specified in Schedule 5;
'Person'	means any of the Parties or the Beneficiaries or any other individual, corporate entity or partnership;
'Producer'	[ ];
'Residuals'	any sums of money payable to any person, firm or entity providing services, facilities and/or rights for the purposes of the production of the Film (other than monies included in the budgeted cost of the Film or which are payable by any of the Parties) which become payable pursuant to any union or guild agreement relating to the production of the Film by

	reference to the manner or place or means by which the Film is exploited and which have been notified to FCAM in writing;
'Rights'	all copyright and similar rights in and to the Film and all ancillary or associated rights thereto or in the underlying rights thereof the proceeds from the exploitation of which are intended by the Parties to be collected and distributed pursuant to the terms hereof;
'Statement'	a statement by FCAM specifying the sources from which Collected Gross Receipts have been derived and their allocation;
'Sub-Distribution Agreement(s)'	all agreements with Sub-Distributors for the exploitation of the Film and the Rights throughout the Territory;
'Sub-Distributors'	those persons, firms or other entities who enter into Sub-Distribution Agreements;
'Territory'	[the world].

1.1 Where the context so admits, words importing the singular shall include the plural and vice versa and words importing the neuter gender shall include the masculine or feminine gender and words importing persons shall include firms and corporations.

1.2 References to paragraphs and Schedules shall, save where otherwise expressly stated, be construed as references to the paragraphs of and Schedules to this Agreement.

1.3 Any reference in this Agreement to an Act of Parliament shall include every statutory amendment and re-enactment thereof and every regulation and order made thereunder or under any Act replacing the same.

Schedule 3: Film Specification

Film Title:	[ ]
Writer:	[ ]
Director:	[ ]
Individual Producer:	[ ]
Principal Artists:	[ ]
Delivery Date:	[ ]
Budgeted Cost:	[ ]

Schedule 4: Beneficiaries

[Including the Parties]

Schedule 5: Distribution of Collected Gross Receipts

1. To FCAM in payment of FCAM's Remuneration and the FCAM Expenses; and thereafter
2. any Residuals as notified to FCAM; and thereafter
3. the Completion Guarantor in respect of monies paid out (if any) pursuant to the terms of the Completion Guarantee; and thereafter
4. the Distributor in respect of such fees, commissions and expenses as shall have been notified to FCAM pursuant to Clause 5.5 of FCAM's Standard Terms of Agreement; and thereafter
5. pari passu the deferees as follows:
   a. [Name] as to USD [ ]
   b. [Name] as to USD [ ]
   c. [Name] as to USD [ ];
   and thereafter
6. the balance remaining after the payment of all the sums referred to above shall form the 'Net Profits' of the Film and shall be paid to the Net Profit Participants as set out in Schedule 6.

(NB any other beneficiaries due to be paid from the Collected Gross Receipts and who are not Net Profit Participants to be inserted in this Schedule at the appropriate position)

Schedule 6: Net Profit Participants

a. [Name] as to [ ]%
b. [Name] as to [ ]%
c. [Name] as to [ ]%

to be paid pro-rata in accordance with their percentage entitlement.

FCAM'S Standard Terms of Agreement

1. Gross Receipts

1.1 Any Party owning or controlling any Rights hereby undertakes with FCAM and the other Parties hereto to issue irrevocable instructions to Sub-Distributors in a form approved in writing by FCAM to pay all Gross Receipts directly into the Collection Account.

1.2 The Producer hereby undertakes to procure that the Distributor or, if no Distributor is appointed, the Producer itself will promptly notify FCAM of delivery of the Film to the respective Sub-Distributor(s) and, to the extent known, the respective release dates of the Film.

1.3 If any Party shall receive Gross Receipts itself, that Party will promptly inform FCAM of such receipt and transfer such Gross Receipts into the Collection Account without deduction (other than bank charges).

2. FCustody's and FCAM's Obligations

FCustody shall:

2.1 hold all Collected Gross Receipts upon trust for the benefit of the Beneficiaries to the extent of the Beneficiaries' respective interests as specified in this Agreement;

FCAM shall:

2.2 pay into the Collection Account any Gross Receipts directly received by FCAM from Sub-Distributors, Distributor or any other person;

2.3 provided FCAM shall have been given a copy of the relevant completed Sub-Distribution Agreement(s), monitor the dates upon which payments of Gross Receipts fall due to be paid to the Collection Account;

2.4 use reasonable endeavours to ensure the Collected Gross Receipts earn interest at the most favourable rate available at the CA Bank for similar accounts and amounts;

2.5 use reasonable endeavours to advise upon request of any of the Parties who are parties to a Sub-Distribution Agreement if payments of Gross Receipts due under the said Sub-Distribution Agreement have not been received;

2.6 convert Collected Gross Receipts received in a currency other than the Accounting Currency into the Accounting Currency at the exchange rate prevailing on the day of such conversion;
2.7 calculate the amount of Collected Gross Receipts payable to each Net Profit Participant and pay and distribute Collected Gross Receipts to all Beneficiaries in the manner, amounts and order set out in Schedules 5 and 6;
2.8 on written request provide any Party with copies of statements and/or accounts received by FCAM from the Distributor or Sub-Distributors.

3. Distribution of Gross Receipts

3.1 FCAM shall commence distribution of Collected Gross Receipts from the Collection Account from the later of the Delivery Date or the last date of the month during which Gross Receipts are first credited to the Collection Account and then monthly thereafter for the first year, quarterly for the following two years and annually thereafter.
3.2 FCAM shall not be obliged to remit Entitlements to any Beneficiary unless such Beneficiary is entitled to be paid not less than USD 500.00.
3.3 FCAM shall not be obliged to pay on behalf of the Producer or any other Party any withholding tax, income tax, corporation tax, value added tax or other sales tax or any similar payments when distributing Collected Gross Receipts unless agreed in writing between the relevant parties or unless FCAM is required so to do by law.
3.4 Residuals shall only be payable by FCAM upon written notification being received by FCAM from the Producer and/or the Distributor.
3.5 FCAM shall not be obliged to make any payment out of Collected Gross Receipts if the making of such payment would constitute a breach of any court order or would otherwise be unlawful.

4. Accounting

4.1 For the first twelve (12) months after the Delivery Date or the last date of the month during which Gross Receipts are first credited to the Collection Account, in respect of each calendar month during which Gross Receipts are credited to the Collection Account, FCAM shall provide the Parties with a Statement within twenty (20) Business Days of the end of each calendar month to which it relates.

4.2 From the thirteenth (13th) month after the Delivery Date or the last date of the month during which Gross Receipts are first credited to the Collection Account until thirty six (36) months thereafter, FCAM shall provide the Parties with a Statement on a quarterly basis, within twenty (20) Business Days of the end of each quarter to which it relates.

4.3 Thereafter, until termination of this Agreement, FCAM shall provide the Parties with Statements on an annual basis.

4.4 Unless specifically requested by the Parties in writing, no Statements shall be provided to Parties that have received their Entitlement in full. Any such Parties shall have no further rights pursuant to this Agreement after such receipt.

4.5 FCAM will pay the Entitlements simultaneously with or within five (5) Business Days from the issue of a Statement.

4.6 FCAM shall at all times keep at its principal place of business complete and accurate books of account and records relating to all monies received in and paid from the Collection Account.

4.7 Any Party hereto shall have the right on giving prior reasonable notice no more than once in any twelve (12) month period to audit the books and accounts of FCAM in relation to the Film at its office and such audit shall be at the expense of the requesting party unless such audit reveals an error of the greater of five per cent (5%) or USD 5,000.00 against the interests of the requesting party, in which case FCAM shall pay the reasonable costs of such audit which costs shall not form part of the FCAM Expenses for the purposes of this Agreement;

4.8 Provided FCAM distributes Collected Gross Receipts in accordance with the terms of this Agreement, no liability shall attach to FCAM on account of its application of any sums received by FCAM under this Agreement or for any other obligations on the part of FCAM under this Agreement save as provided for by Clause 4.7 above or in the event of gross negligence or wilful misconduct on the part of FCAM. FCAM will make good any underpayments on its part provided that a claim has been lodged in writing with FCAM within 20 Business Days after the date of payment to which such claim relates.

5. Obligations of the Parties

Each of the Parties agrees with FCAM, FCustody and with the other Parties:

5.1 that they will not during the term of this Agreement authorize or permit any third party to collect or administer Gross Receipts nor will any Party interfere with, frustrate or take any action contrary to the terms of this Agreement;

5.2 to provide FCAM promptly with copies of all Sub-Distribution Agreements, other relevant agreements, irrevocable instructions or other information FCAM may reasonably request in order to perform its obligations under this Agreement;

5.3 that if any Party receives a sum in excess of their Entitlement or if withholding tax on Gross Receipts has to be refunded, the relevant Party shall immediately repay such amount into the Collection Account. If any such sum is not repaid by the relevant Party within 5 Business Days of written notification by FCAM, FCAM shall not be obliged to make any further payments to such Party until the amount due has been either deducted from the next Entitlement (if any) of the Party concerned or repaid in full plus interest (calculated from the date of receipt of such excess or request to refund withholding tax) at the rate of LIBOR plus 1% p.a.;

5.4 that FCAM shall not be required to incur any expense under this Agreement on its account nor to make any payment to any Beneficiary save from Collected Gross Receipts;

5.5 to provide FCAM prior to the Delivery Date with the following information and such further information as FCAM may require in order to discharge its obligations under this Agreement:

5.5.1 names and address of all Beneficiaries;

5.5.2 fees, commissions and incurred expenses of the Distributor;

5.5.3 procedure for approval of Distributor's expenses and of expenses payable to any other person; and

5.5.4 names and addresses of persons entitled to Residuals with details of the amounts to be paid.

5.6 that the Parties shall jointly and severally indemnify FCAM and agree to hold FCAM safe, harmless, defended and indemnified against any liabilities, losses, damages, costs or expenses (including legal fees and costs and arbitration fees and costs) by reason of any claim, action or proceeding arising out of or in connection with FCAM's acceptance of or performance under this Agreement (including third party claims and the costs of any legal advice taken by FCAM pursuant to Clause 7);

5.7 that they shall not put or attempt to put any lien, charge or any similar legal instrument over the Collection Account or the Collected Gross Receipts or any other monies standing to the credit of the Collection Account.

6. General

6.1 In the performance of its duties and exercise of its powers under this Agreement, FCAM will be entitled to rely upon any document reasonably believed by FCAM to be genuine and to have been sent or signed by the person by whom it purports to have been sent or signed and the opinion and statements of any professional advisor selected by FCAM in connection herewith and shall not be liable to any Party for any consequence of any such assumption, action or reliance.

6.2 FCAM and FCustody shall have no duties or obligations pursuant to this Agreement save as expressly set forth herein.

6.3 If FCAM is unable for reasons outside its control to carry out any of the provisions hereof, FCAM shall incur no liability as a consequence thereof for so long as the relevant situation continues and during such period FCAM shall have no responsibility for its inability to carry out or perform the relevant provisions hereof.

6.4 If FCAM is unable at any time to make payments out of Collected Gross Receipts by reason of the failure of the Parties to provide any information required by FCAM, FCAM shall not be obliged to make any further payments to any Beneficiary until such time as any Party hereto shall have provided sufficient information to FCAM in order to make such payments.

6.5 FCAM shall have no obligation to protect the copyright or any similar rights in or to the Film in any part of the world whether by registration or otherwise.

6.6 Notwithstanding anything to the contrary of the provisions contained in Clause 6.11, if claims conflicting with the interpretation of the terms of this Agreement are notified to FCAM by any Party relating to the Collection Account or the Collected Gross Receipts, or if any third party should assert claims in respect thereof, FCAM shall be entitled, at FCAM's discretion, to:

6.6.1 notwithstanding any other provision herein contained, suspend the distribution of Collected Gross Receipts without liability to any Party until any conflict is in the opinion of FCAM resolved; and/or

6.6.2 invoke the arbitration procedure referred to in Clause 8 hereof.

6.7 FCAM shall not be obliged to take any action under this Agreement which may in FCAM's opinion involve any expense or liability on FCAM's part unless FCAM shall have first been furnished with an indemnity from the Parties in a form acceptable to FCAM. Any such expense incurred by FCAM pursuant to this Clause 6.7 shall be deemed FCAM Expenses for the purposes of this Agreement.

6.8 FCAM shall be entitled without liability to engage in its normal and customary business with any Party or any affiliate or associate of any Party provided that nothing in this sub-paragraph shall affect the right of the Parties to receive their Entitlements.

6.9 If any payment by FCAM is subject to the approval of one or more of the Parties, and such approval has not been received in writing by FCAM within seven (7) Business Days after a request for the same in writing, such Party shall be deemed to have given its approval to the relevant act or payment and FCAM shall be entitled to make the relevant payment or otherwise act in accordance with the terms and conditions of this Agreement.

6.10 This Agreement shall be deemed to be the sole document relating to the distribution of the Collected Gross Receipts.

6.11 In the event of any conflict between the provisions of this Agreement and the provisions of any other agreement relating to the Film with respect to the disbursement of receipts from the Film, the provisions of this Agreement shall prevail.

6.12 The Parties agree that FCAM shall be entitled to a credit on all copies of the Film in the form 'World revenues collected and distributed by Freeway CAM B.V.'.

6.13 The Parties, FCAM and FCustody jointly and severally agree with each of the others that the terms of Schedules 5 and 6 of this Agreement are confidential to the Parties, FCAM and FCustody and shall not be disclosed to any third party, save that any Party, FCAM and FCustody shall be entitled to reveal such terms to its professional advisors and to any Beneficiary in relation to matters which affect such Beneficiary.

6.14 The parties hereto agree and declare that the provisions of the United Kingdom Contracts (Rights of Third Parties) Act 1999 (or any similar provision in any other relevant jurisdiction) shall not apply to this Agreement and that no term or condition of this Agreement shall confer or be construed as conferring any right on any third party.

6.15 The clause and paragraph headings in this Agreement are provided for convenience only and shall not affect the construction, interpretation or effect of this Agreement.

6.16 The Distributor shall provide FCAM with one VHS (PAL) video cassette or one DVD and one poster of the Film as soon as these become available.

6.17 Nothing herein shall constitute a partnership or joint venture between the parties hereto or any two or more of them.

7. Legal Advice

7.1 FCAM may at any time and in its absolute discretion (but after having consulted with each of the Parties) seek independent legal advice with regard to any non-payment of Gross Receipts by any Sub-Distributor or to any other matter relating to or affecting the performance of FCAM's duties or powers set out in this Agreement and each Party hereby undertakes to assist FCAM to obtain as fully informed and accurate legal advice as possible by:

7.1.1 providing FCAM with copies of any relevant document in the possession of that Party;

7.1.2 taking all reasonable steps to procure that copies of any relevant documents that have been but are no longer in that Party's possession are provided to FCAM; and

7.1.3 informing FCAM of any relevant information in the knowledge of that Party or (if appropriate) in the knowledge of its officers, servants and/or agents.

7.2 FCAM shall provide to each of the Parties a copy of any legal advice so obtained.

7.3 The Parties jointly and severally indemnify FCAM against all costs, charges and expenses connected with or arising out of obtaining any such legal advice and such costs, charges and expenses shall be deemed to be FCAM's Expenses for which FCAM is entitled to be reimbursed in accordance with Schedule 5. If at any time FCAM shall determine that the amount of Collected Gross Receipts then standing credited to the Collection Account is not sufficient to discharge such costs, charges and expenses as are to be or have been incurred by FCAM the Parties (excepting FCAM) shall forthwith pay to FCAM the amount of any such shortfall or the estimated amount thereof and shall be jointly and severally responsible therefore.

7.4 Any sums paid by the Parties to FCAM pursuant to Clause 3 shall (notwithstanding the provisions of Schedule 5) be repaid to the Parties in first position out of Collected Gross Receipts.

8. Arbitration

8.1 Should any dispute arise between any two or more of the Parties or between any of the Parties and FCAM, the dispute shall be resolved by arbitration in [London] under the Rules then in force for International Arbitration of the American Film Marketing Association subject to the provisions of this Clause 8.

8.2 FCAM shall provide the Parties with a written notice summarizing the dispute and the relevant Parties shall within ten (10) Business Days after such notification mutually appoint at their own expense an AFMA approved arbitrator. If the Parties fail to agree upon the appointment of an arbitrator within such period, the Arbitral Agent of AFMA will then appoint an arbitrator as soon as possible after such application. The Parties shall provide the arbitrator with all relevant information and documentation within thirty (30) days of the appointment and the arbitration shall commence at a location in [London] as expeditiously as possible and in any event within thirty (30) business days after the appointment of the arbitrator.

8.3 Forthwith after a decision by the arbitrator, the Parties shall forthwith comply with that decision in accordance with the terms thereof.

8.4 All costs, charges and expenses incurred by FCAM in relation to the resolution of the dispute, inclusive of time spent by FCAM executives at a reasonably hourly rate, shall be deemed FCAM Expenses, provided that if FCAM itself is a party to the arbitration proceedings, the payment of any costs incurred by FCAM shall be subject to any award of costs made by the arbitrator.

9. Termination

9.1 FCAM and FCustody may at any time terminate this Agreement upon thirty (30) Business Days by written notice to all of the Parties provided that FCAM's and FCustody's notice shall specify the arrangements proposed to be made by FCAM and FCustody to pay Entitlements which, apart from such termination, would then have been payable to Beneficiaries under the provisions hereof and FCAM and FCustody shall give good faith consideration to any representations made to FCAM and FCustody concerning such proposed arrangements as any Beneficiary may provide to FCAM and FCustody within fourteen (14) Business Days thereafter.

9.2 All the Parties and Beneficiaries shall have the right to terminate this Agreement by unanimous written notice to FCAM and FCustody at any time subject to FCAM's right to FCAM's Remuneration and FCAM Expenses unpaid at that date.

9.3 This Agreement may be terminated by the Parties without notice if FCAM either commits a material breach of the terms of this Agreement which is not remedied within twenty one (21) Business Days of written notice given by a majority of the Parties, of which the Producer must be one, or if FCAM shall enter into liquidation (except for the purpose of a scheme for amalgamation or reconstruction) or if any winding-up petition is issued against FCAM and remains undischarged for a period of twenty eight (28) Business Days.

9.4 Upon termination pursuant to this Clause 9, the Parties shall within twenty one (21) Business Days instruct FCAM and FCustody in writing to transfer the administration of Collected Gross Receipts less FCAM Remuneration and FCAM Expenses up to and including the termination date to a successor collection account manager.

9.5 As from the date of termination pursuant to this paragraph, FCAM and FCustody shall have no further obligation to perform its obligations hereunder and shall be fully released and discharged therefrom, without prejudice to any accrued rights and obligations in respect of the period prior to such termination.

10. Notices

10.1 Any notice required or permitted to be given under this Agreement shall be in writing and sent by hand, first-class recorded letter or facsimile addressed to the relevant Party at the Party's address given in this Agreement or such other address as may be notified to by that Party to the other hereto.

10.2 Any such notice sent by first-class recorded letter shall be deemed to have been received five (5) Business Days after posting; any such notice sent by facsimile shall be deemed to have been received at the time of despatch if during the recipient's business hours and otherwise at the commencement of the next Business Day of the recipient provided always that the sender shall have received a successful transmission report; any such notice sent by hand shall be deemed to have been received at the time of delivery.

11. Execution

11.1 This Agreement may be executed in any number of counterparts (each of which shall be deemed an original) and all of which, taken together, shall constitute one and the same agreement and any party may enter into this Agreement by executing a counterpart.

11.2 If one or more parties do not execute this Agreement, it shall nevertheless be in full force and effect as between the Parties that have executed this Agreement and FCAM and FCustody. The Entitlement(s) of any Parties who do not sign the Agreement will be retained in the Collection Account for thirty six (36) months after the Delivery Date or until such Parties duly execute the Agreement and FCAM has received the same, whichever first occurs. FCustody shall be released from any obligations pursuant to Clause 2.1 above in respect of any Party failing to execute this Agreement within thirty six (36) months after the Delivery Date whereupon any such Party's Entitlement will be allocated to the other Beneficiaries in accordance with the terms hereof.

12. Governing Law

This Agreement shall be construed and performed in all respects in accordance with and shall be governed by [English] Law and the parties irrevocably submit to the arbitration procedure contained in Clause 8.

AS WITNESS the hands of the parties hereto the day and year first above written.

EXECUTED and unconditionally

delivered as its Agreement by

FREEWAY CAM B.V.

[ ]

EXECUTED and unconditionally

delivered as its Agreement by

STICHTING FREEWAY CUSTODY

[ ]

EXECUTED and unconditionally

delivered as its Agreement by

[ ]

EXECUTED and unconditionally
delivered as its Agreement by

[ ]

EXECUTED and unconditionally
delivered as its Agreement by

[ ]

8 Recoupment – Net Profits

The safest way to double your money is to fold it over and put it in your pocket.
Kim Hubbard

Net Profits

As a general rule of thumb, a film producer should try to retain 50 per cent of net profits for himself and use the other 50 per cent to pay investors in the film. Producers will be required to pay talent, such as writers, actors and the director, a share of the net profits as part of their overall payment. The balance retained by the producer is sometimes known as 'Producer's Net Profits'.

During the deal-making process, it is important to define what the producer is actually offering. Those negotiating with the producer should enquire whether the percentage offered is the entire net profits of the film or only from the producer's share of net profits. There can be a noticeable difference between 5 per cent of 100 per cent of net profits and 5 per cent of 50 per cent of net profits.

Generally, net profits would be those revenues from the sales and exploitation of the film after deductions of:

1. the distributor or sales agents commissions;
2. the distribution or sales agents expenses;
3. the actual cost of production;
4. any deferments.

Producer's net profits would be all of the revenues from the exploitation of the film after the above deductions and any share of 'net profits' payable to third party investors and not retained by the producer for his or her own benefit.

However, it should be stressed that this is only a general rule and, depending on the circumstances of the transaction, a financier's or producer's lawyer will make specific variations.

Gross Receipts

The Recoupment Schedule set out below reflects a sales agency agreement between a sales agent and a producer in relation to an advance of funds to the producer for certain rights in a film. The term 'Advance' will also be defined in the agreement with the producer. Other terms such as: 'Deferred Fees', 'Sales Agent Costs', 'Excluding Sales Agent Costs', 'Gross Receipts', 'Net Receipts', 'Film', 'Producer' and others will also be defined within the agreement.

The example below reflects an agreement where the sales agent is first entitled to recoup part of the advance made to the producer. In most cases the sales agent will recoup their advance first and the other participants will follow. This example shows that there are certain equity investors who have put up cash and therefore are entitled to a specific corridor for recoupment.

Second, the sales agent is entitled to deduct their costs in relation to sales. In this case, the costs are capped at 5 per cent of the total revenue payable to the sales agent. If there is no cap placed on the costs, then the sales agent can allocate or 'cross' costs from other films against the sale of this specific film. This is also known as cross-collateralization.

Third, the sales agent will then pay himself a fee for selling the film so well! However, in this agreement, part of the fee is deferred until a certain revenue from amount of sales are made.

Fourth, the producer's equity investors (i.e., private individuals putting up cash or perhaps a film fund) will now have a corridor for recoupment in the same position as the sales agent. This example assumes that the sales agent has still not recouped the entire advance but enough of it so that further revenues can be shared with the producer's investors.

Fifth, at this stage of recoupment, the sales agent's advance has been paid off and the producer and investor can now both be repaid.

Sixth, at this stage of the recoupment schedule the producer's equity investors have recouped in full and any further income will be shared between the sales agent (who has in this case deferred some of their sales agent fees) and the producer who may also have deferred some of his or her fees.

Finally, in seventh position, will be those sums left over that, in this example, are defined as 'Net Receipts'. One should note that this definition is not a rule of thumb and is sometimes referred to as 'net profits' or 'producer's net profits'. In many circumstances, the producer will deduct certain costs from net receipts for himself and then will pay those participants who are entitled to certain payments after these deductions. In this case, these participants will be entitled to 'Producer's Net Profits' (i.e., those profits after deductions by the producer from net receipts).

One should note that this is only a guide and each definition is different depending on the transaction. Recoupment is an area for which expert legal advice should be obtained.

Sample Recoupment Schedule

1. **Sales Agent Fee.** Sales Agent shall be entitled to deduct and retain a Deferred Sales Agent Fee in respect of the first Gross Receipts received up to £[ ] in accordance with paragraph 2. Sales Agent shall be entitled to deduct and retain the Sales Agent Fee from Gross Receipts received beyond the first £[ ] as set forth in the paragraph 2(c), such fee being inclusive of all sub-Sales Agent fees and any Sales Agent or similar fees (whether or not paid to affiliates, subsidiaries or other companies related to Sales Agent) with respect to the exploitation and Sales Agent of the Film.

2. **Allocation of Sales Agent's Gross Receipts.** Sales Agent agrees that Gross Receipts derived from the Territory shall be applied as follows:
   a. First, to Sales Agent until Sales Agent has received £[ ] to be applied by Sales Agent in reduction of the Advance;
   b. Second, on an ongoing basis, to the payment to Sales Agent of its Sales Agent Costs it being understood that Sales Agent Costs incurred by Sales Agent will be capped at five per cent (5%) of gross revenues payable to Sales Agent and, in addition, its Excluded Sales Agent Costs;
   c. Third, on an ongoing basis, to the payment to Sales Agent of the Sales Agent Fee;
   d. Fourth, of the next £[ ] of Gross Receipts (after deduction of the fees and expenses permitted under subparagraphs (b) and (c)), on a pro rata pari passu basis, £[ ] shall be paid to Sales Agent in reduction of its Advance and £[ ] shall be paid to the Producer to be applied to recoup the contributions of the Producer's investors in the Film (less any amounts paid to the Sales Agent on account of permitted fees and expenses);
   e. Fifth, the next £[ ] of Gross Receipts (after deduction of the fees and expenses permitted under subparagraphs (b) and (c)), shall be paid to the Producer to be applied to recoup the contributions of the Producer's investors in the Film;
   f. Sixth, Gross Receipts (after deduction of the fees and expenses permitted under subparagraphs (b) and (c)), shall thereafter be allocated between Sales Agent and the Producer on a pro rata pari passu basis until the Sales

Agent has received its Deferred Sales Agent Fee of £[ ] and the Producer has received £[ ];

g. Seventh, the balance (**'Net Receipts'**), to the Producer is accordance with below:
   i. First, the Producer in relation to all unrecouped development costs for the film;
   ii. Second, the Producer in relation to all unrecouped overheads costs relating to the film;
   iii. The balance (Producer's net profits) to those set out below;
   iv. Producer: 50%
       Director: 10%
       Writer: 5%
       Talent Pool: 10%
       Equity Investors: 25%

9 Gap Financing

If you think gap financing is to fix your kids' teeth, think again.
Lewis Horowitz, well-known film financier and banker

Gap financing, is a form of lending whereby a bank lends money against the value of unsold rights to a film. For example, if the budget for a film is three million pounds (£3 m) and two million pounds (£2 m) of the budget is already covered by pre-sales, tax funds, public subsidies and other collateral, the remaining one million pounds (£1 m) that is not covered by any collateral, is considered the 'gap'.

In a traditional film financing transaction, a bank will only lend against existing pre-sales and those agreements that ensure some form of secure repayment. A bank in this case needs proper collateral as it will not lend against speculative pre-sales. Banks generally do not take risks and need to know exactly when they will be repaid.

When the United States domestic and international pre-sale market began to dry up in the early 1990s, many banks that traditionally only lent money against existing pre-sales looked to gap financing as an alternative means of earning fees. Certain banks who had specialist film financing divisions realized that unsold territories still had value, only that their value could not be determined until the film was completed. Therefore, these banks who had relationships with reliable sales agents, felt comfortable making loans based on sales estimates for unsold distribution rights. From the banks' perspective, they were not investing in the film but were lending against collateral that was not as strong as an existing pre-sale. Therefore, they would add a premium to the cost of such a loan.

Criteria for Gap Financing

The banks that are now involved in the gap financing business usually have certain requirements before approving a loan. Banks, typically, will gap finance between 10 and 40 per cent of a film's budget. However, most gap financiers tend to gap only 20 per cent of a film's budget. In general, banks will not gap finance a film unless there are already several major pre-sales in place. Having a pre-sale in place shows that there is a market for this type of film and that the sale estimates given by a sales agent are accurate.

One of the most important factors in a gap deal is the sales agent; the bank will need to be comfortable with who they are. They will look at how long they have been in business, their reputation and whether they have worked on previous gap deals.

The actual sales estimates for unsold rights are also a vital factor in considering whether to proceed with a transaction. Depending on which bank is involved, they will require that at least 1.5–2 times the amount of the sales estimates will cover the gap. This means that if the gap is one million pounds (£1 m) then the sales estimates must be at least one and a half to two million pounds (£1.5 m–£2 m). The next step is for the bank to analyse all sales estimates and decide whether they are comfortable proceeding with the deal. Most banks prefer lending not only the gap portion of the budget but the entire production loan, including existing pre-sales and other forms of collateral such as tax credits and public subsidies.

Financing the gap portion of a Film's budget can also be very expensive. Banks can charge anywhere between 7 and 15 per cent of the amount of the gap being financed, plus interest charges. This means that a bank who is financing the entire production will earn fees and interest on the traditional part of the financing and much larger fees and interest on the gap portion of the transaction.

Producers who are involved with a gap financing deal should be aware that, in such a transaction, the Bank will require a larger interest reserve than in traditional production financing. This is because there is an ongoing interest charge associated with sales being made after the film has finished. In a traditional banking deal, once the film is delivered, the distributors pay the amount owing to the Bank and interest stops accruing because the loan has been extinguished. In a gap financing deal the Bank will give the producer a period of twelve (12) to twenty-four (24) months to make the sales necessary to pay off the loan. Therefore, a bank will calculate an interest reserve to cover this additional period after completion of the film.

Gap financing a film can sometimes be very advantageous to an independent producer. In a typical film financing, the gap for unsold territories is usually financed by a sales agent who puts up an advance against sales. When a sales agent puts up an advance, they will charge a commission (25–40 per cent) on any sales made, plus costs and in most cases interest on the amount of the advance. In a gap financing deal, the sales agent will not advance any funds and will only sell the film on behalf of the producer and gap financier. In these circumstances, the sales agent is usually only entitled to a small commission (5–15 per cent) and limited costs. If the sales agent eventually sells enough of the film's distribution rights to repay the gap to the bank they will be entitled to a larger commission.

In many cases, a gap financing deal, even with higher bank fees, may result in a higher share of revenue for the producer.

The examples below highlight the savings to a producer.

Example 1 – Sales Agent Advance Against Sales

Budget – £3 m

i. Available finance (pre-sales × 2, tax funds, other government subsidies) – £2 m
ii. Gap – £1 m
iii. Cost of sales agent's advance £1 m
iv. Sales agent commission 30 per cent
v. Cost of sales (capped) 5 per cent
vi. Interest on advance 5 per cent
[ ]
Off the top of all Sales = 40 per cent

Therefore – sales agent must sell approximately £1,667,000 before covering the advance against sales.

Example 2 – Gap Financing Deal (No Sales Agent Advance)

Budget £3 m

i. Available finance – £2 m
ii. Gap – £1 m
iii. Assume bank gap fee of 10 per cent – £100 k
iv. Sales agent will charge 12.5 per cent commission
v. Capped costs of £25 k

Sales agent needs to sell approximately £1,280,000 before recouping the gap costs and fees.

Sample Sales Estimates

Used in a Gap Deal (UK/France/Germany Co-production)

ASK PRICES (US$)

Territory	*Ask*	*Minimum*
Latin America		
Argen/Para/Urug	100,000	40,000
Brazil	180,000	100,000
Central America	25,000	15,000
Chile	15,000	10,000
Colombia	30,000	20,000
Mexico	160,000	100,000
Peru/Bol/Ecuador	20,000	12,000
Venezuela/Ar/Cu	20,000	12,000
Pan Latin American Sat.		
EUROPE		
Benelux	175,000	100,000
France		NA
Germany/Austria		NA
Greece/Cyprus	30,000	20,000
Italy	600,000	400,000
Portugal/Mozamb	30,000	15,000
Spain	700,000	450,000
Iceland	10,000	5,000
Scandinavia	200,000	125,000
Switzerland	75,000	50,000 theatrical only
FAR EAST		
China		
Hong Kong/Macao	30,000	20,000
Indonesia	20,000	12,000

Territory	*Ask*	*Minimum*
Japan/Okinawa	900,000	650,000
Korea	120,000	65,000
Malaysia	20,000	10,000
Sing/Brun	20,000	10,000
Philippines	30,000	15,000
Taiwan	130,000	60,000
Thailand/Burma	75,000	35,000
Pan Asia Satellite		
ENGLISH SPEAKING		
Australia/New Zeal	400,000	300,000
UK and Eire		NA
S. Africa	60,000	30,000
W. Indies	8,000	4,000
USA	3,000,000	1,500,000
OTHER		
India	15,000	10,000
Israel	30,000	15,000
Middle East	35,000	20,000
Pakistan		
Turkey	80,000	40,000
Sri Lanka	2,000	1,000
Canada	200,000	175,000
EASTERN EUROPE		
Bulgaria	8,000	4,000
Czech & Slovak Republics		NA
Hungry	25,000	10,000
Poland		NA
Romania	8,000	4,000
CIS	55,000	25,000
Ex Yugoslavia	12,000	8,000
AIRLINES	300,000	200,000
TOTALS	**$7,753,000**	**$4,522,000**

The foregoing projections are estimates only. No representation is being made that the projections will be realized. Actual results may vary materially from the projections for numerous reasons including, but not limited to, the final cast and creative elements of the picture.

10 Alternative Financing

If we don't succeed, we run the risk of failure.
Dan Quayle

Enterprise Investment Schemes (EIS)

Overview

EIS schemes encourage small, higher risk, unquoted trading companies to raise finance by issuing full risk ordinary shares to investors who are resident and ordinarily resident for tax purposes in the UK. They can provide a much needed and valuable source of equity to UK film production companies.

Finance is sourced by the issue of a prospectus to the public and the sale of new, ordinary shares to investors in a 'qualifying' public limited company. The production of feature films is classed as a 'qualifying' trade.

Investors

1. The investor must hold shares in the EIS investment scheme for at least 3 years.
2. EIS schemes provide a convenient means of tax relief. Individuals previously unconnected with the company in which they invest may:
   a. obtain income tax relief (currently at 20 per cent) in any one tax year on the maximum investment of (currently) £200,000 in any one tax year;
   b. defer capital gains tax in conjunction with the income tax relief at 1(a) above in respect of any chargeable gain arising from the disposal of assets after 28 November 1994 on reinvestment to the value of the amount of the gain in the shares of a qualifying EIS company;

c. obtain exemption from capital gains tax on disposal of the shares in the EIS investment if the shares are disposed at least 3 years after their issue; and
d. set any losses on an EIS investment against income or gains at the taxpayer's highest rate of tax.

Film production companies

3. EIS investment offers film production companies an alternative method of raising finance for the development and production of feature films to the more established:
   a. film partnerships providing equity investment in the production costs of a film (these schemes afford high net worth investors a 40 per cent tax break on the cost of production but normally have a very high threshold for minimum investment in the scheme);
   b. sale and leaseback funds (which may be prevented from being combined with the equity investment under paragraph 3(a) above as so-called 'double-dipping'); or equity investment in the budget of the film or the film production company by so-called 'angel investors' (a high risk investment with no guarantee of any return or profits if the film fails at the box office).
4. EIS investment can be in an individual film or slate of films or in the film production company itself.
5. It is also possible to set up:
   a. a so-called 'seed funding' company that sources EIS investment in order to develop a film or a slate of films to the production stage (for example by purchasing options, preparing budgets, paying scriptwriters, casting and sourcing distribution agreements and pre-sales); and
   b. a production funding company which uses EIS sourced funds to purchase the fully developed film or films from the 'seed funding' company and funds the production costs of the film.
6. EIS investments funds may be safely combined with sale and leaseback funds.
7. EIS investment does not require negotiations between the investor, the production company and any other investor (such as a distributor or provider of government subsidy) in respect of recoupment corridors and distribution of profits.

Additional benefits to investors

A further incentive to participation in an EIS scheme is involvement in the production of the feature film or slate of films. Investors may be entitled to:

a. visit the set during principal photography;
b. meet the cast and crew;
c. attend the premiere of the film or films; and/or
d. a screen credit.

Pitfalls

The following points are of note:

a. any dividends are taxable;
b. during the minimum investment period of 3 years investors may not hold any rights that protect them from the risk of investment such as the right to redeem the shares;
c. investors may lose their entire investment (although the losses may be set against income or gains at the taxpayer's highest rate of tax under paragraph 2(d) above);
d. the 'qualifying' company must be public, thereby exposing it to regulatory and statutory obligations;
e. if the minimum amount is not raised within 40 days of the issue of the prospectus, all funds must be returned to investors; and
f. the benefits of an EIS scheme are geographically limited to people who are resident and ordinarily resident in the UK for tax purposes.

Please also note that this is only a summary and potential investors must obtain independent specialist investment advice before investing in an EIS scheme.

Limited Liability Partnerships

Since April 2001 it has been possible to structure film production and sale and lease back partnerships as a Limited Liability Partnership ('LLP'). Although LLPs were originally conceived to be used for professional partnerships, such as architects and accountants, they have become the vehicle of choice for anyone seeking to set up a film fund.

An LLP is a hybrid between a limited company and a partnership combining the limited liability of a company with the flexibility and tax transparency of a partnership and can therefore be a highly attractive vehicle for film investors.

To understand why LLPs have superseded the previously more common Limited Partnerships (LPs) as the preferred fund vehicle, we will look more closely at the LLP structure, highlighting, where relevant, their advantages over LPs.

Limited liability

An LP generally offers limited liability for investors. However, one partner must still act as a general partner (GP) with unlimited liability. In practice, a special purpose vehicle without assets is usually set up as the GP to try to 'ring fence' any potential liability. In an LLP all the partners (or 'members' as they are more commonly known) enjoy limited liability and their position is largely analogous with that of shareholders in a limited company in that, subject to certain limited exceptions, the liability of any member of an LLP is limited to his or her capital contributions made to the LLP. An LLP also exists as a separate 'body corporate' with its own distinct legal personality separate from that of its members and, unlike an LP, will contract in its own name.

Tax transparency

Both LPs and LLPs are tax transparent vehicles, that is to say that each of the investing members is considered to be undertaking a pro-rated part of the partnership trade with a view to a profit (this last requirement excludes charities from being set up as LLPs or other forms of partnership). However, this may cause some timing difficulties in terms of a member's individual tax liability in that, if a profit accrues to the LLP, the member will be liable to pay tax on such profit when it accrues without necessarily receiving the requisite distribution from the partnership itself.

Designated members

Unlike an LP, an LLP is required to have a minimum of two 'designated members' who are responsible for undertaking certain statutory functions on behalf of the partnership as required by the Limited Liability Partnerships Act 2000 (the 'LLP Act'). These include notifying the Registrar of Companies of certain changes to the Partnership and ensuring that an annual return and accounts are filed with the Registrar of Companies. Unless certain members are notified to the Registrar as being the designated members of the LLP then each and every member of the partnership will be treated as a designated member.

Confidentiality

Like a limited partnership, the main document that governs the relationship of the members in an LLP, i.e., the Members' Agreement (see below), is confidential and need not be filed with the Companies Registrar. However, unlike limited partnerships, LLPs are required to have their accounts audited and, once filed with the Registrar, these accounts will be publicly available from Companies House.

Insolvency

Members of LLPs are subject to a statutory 'clawback' provision that provides that any amount withdrawn by members in the two years before the commencement of a winding-up of the LLP may be required to be repaid to the LLP or 'clawed back' if the person making the withdrawal knew or could have reasonably concluded that after the withdrawal there was no reasonable prospect that the LLP would avoid an insolvent liquidation.

Incorporation of the LLP

Much like limited companies, LLPs are incorporated by registration at Companies House and the incorporation document (Form LLP2) must be submitted by the initial members of the LLP. The Form LLP2 will set out the name of the LLP, the registered office address, details of the initial members and will identify which of those members are to be the designated members, together with a statement that the LLP complies with the LLP Act.

On incorporation, the Registrar of Companies will issue the LLP with a Certificate of Incorporation, stating the registered number of the LLP together with its date of incorporation, and the Registrar will also issue to each of the designated members a unique designated member number.

The name of the LLP, as is the case for limited companies and business names, will only be registered if it does not contravene one of the many restrictions in relation to the use of certain words. In addition, it will not be possible to register an LLP with the same name as that of an existing limited company.

Members' agreement

An LLP does not have a Memorandum or Articles of Association as a limited company would have, nor does it have a specified management structure. Therefore, it is up to the members to agree amongst themselves how they should run and regulate the LLP. It is important that a properly drafted Members' Agreement is prepared to set out the terms of the partnership, especially as partnership law cannot be expressly implied in relation to those terms.

The Members' Agreement should cover, amongst other matters, the following:

- the capital contributions made by members and how these may be increased or transferred;
- the profit sharing ratio;
- how decisions of the LLP are made;
- the procedure for admitting new members;
- the identity of the designated members and the scope of their designated authority, if any, over and above their statutory duties;
- the intended lifetime of the LLP and how it can be wound-up;
- how the Members' Agreement can be amended and the procedures for meetings of members.

Financial Services Regime

Many LLPs, utilized as film fund vehicles will, unless the members have had the responsibility for the 'day to day' running of the LLP (which recent case law states must be actual involvement as opposed to the right to be consulted over the more material matters of the business of the LLP), constitute an unregulated 'collective investment scheme' (CIS) for purposes of the Financial Services and Markets Acts 2000 (FSMA) and the Financial Services Authority (FSA).

The implications of an LLP being a CIS are that the LLP will be required to appoint an FSA-authorized 'operator' to the scheme to undertake the regulated activities of the scheme, such as admitting new members to the Partnership. Whilst the sponsor of any film partnership need not in themselves be a regulated person, care must be taken to ensure that anything that does constitute a regulated activity under FSMA is undertaken by the operator or another third party with the requisite level of authorization and permissions granted by the FSA.

As an unregulated CIS, investments in the LLP may not be promoted to the general public and may only be promoted to certain categories of investor, who are able to invest in the fund under the financial services legislation, e.g., investors who have been certified as being sufficiently sophisticated to understand the risks involved in such an investment. In addition, as an unregulated scheme, compensation under the FSA's compensation scheme is unlikely to be available.

The LLP fund will usually be promoted using a document called an Information Memorandum, which sets out the parties involved in the fund, the investment strategy of the LLP, the costs of the LLP and a statement of the likely taxation consequences and returns of an investment in the fund. This, together with the members' agreement and any agreements with any promoters and operators of the fund, will constitute the 'scheme documentation'.

Conclusion

The LLP was the vehicle of choice for most film schemes incorporated since 2001 because of the added flexibility created by the LLP's structure, the existence of limited liability to all members and the tax transparent structure. In addition, and unlike an LP, an LLP permits its members other than the general partner to actively participate in the running of the business of the partnership. However, as word of caution, the way in which investments in an LLP and the running of an LLP are treated for tax purposes by the Inland Revenue is constantly evolving, so that it is always advisable to receive up to date legal and taxation advice on the latest developments in setting up such schemes. In 2004 the Inland Revenue made substantial changes to the rules relating to Film schemes. Therefore, producers should seek professional advice to determine if this type of scheme is appropriate.

Sale and Leaseback Transactions

Although sale and leaseback transactions will come to a close in July 2005, it is worthwhile looking at the scheme because of its importance over the last few years to the British film industry. At the time of writing this book, the scheme will be replaced with a transferable tax credit system. Some feel that this type of transferable tax credit system will be similar to the one used in Luxembourg. Check the Department for Culture, Media and Sports (DCMS) website for further details.

Sale and Leaseback

The current UK tax legislation allows for a 100 per cent write off of film production costs for a qualifying British Film in the year of completion or acquisition of the film. The Government's stated objective when introducing such tax deductions was to offer producers a means to reduce the cost of their film production and thus promote production activity in UK.

In order to take advantage of this tax deduction it has become common practice for film producers to enter into a transaction in the form of a sale and leaseback of the film. Several companies in the UK facilitate sale and leaseback transactions, which by virtue of the tax deduction available enable grouping individuals to purchase the film through a partnership.

In order to receive the benefits of a sale and leaseback transaction, a production must be certified as a British Film by the Department for Culture, Media and Sports (DCMS).

In order to access the UK sale and leaseback benefits you will require a UK co-producer if the production is set up as an international co-production.

What is the applicable legislation?

The UK tax write-off is found in Section 48 of the Finance (No. 2) Act 1997. This was added to by the Finance (No. 2) Act 1999 which extended the relief by a further 3 years until 1 July 2005.

There are three conditions to be met before Section 48 applies:

1. the expenditure must be incurred after 2 July 1997 and before 1 July 2005;
2. the total production expenditure on the film must be £15 million or less;
3. the film must be 'completed' after 2 July 1997.

The government issues detailed Statements of Practice which should be consulted for any changes.

How are sale and leaseback transactions structured?

The leasing structure developed in the UK enables a qualifying film to be sold by a producer to a partnership. That partnership is a see-through vehicle for tax purposes and enables tax losses to be passed on to the individual partners in that partnership. The partnership then enters into a finance lease, usually for a period of 15 years, leasing back the distribution rights to either the original producer or a third party.

As far as the producer is concerned, the distribution rights will be exploited in the normal way. The only change that has occurred is that the original 'freehold interest' that the producer once enjoyed has now been turned into a leasehold interest under a 15-year lease. The figure shows the way in which the structure operates.

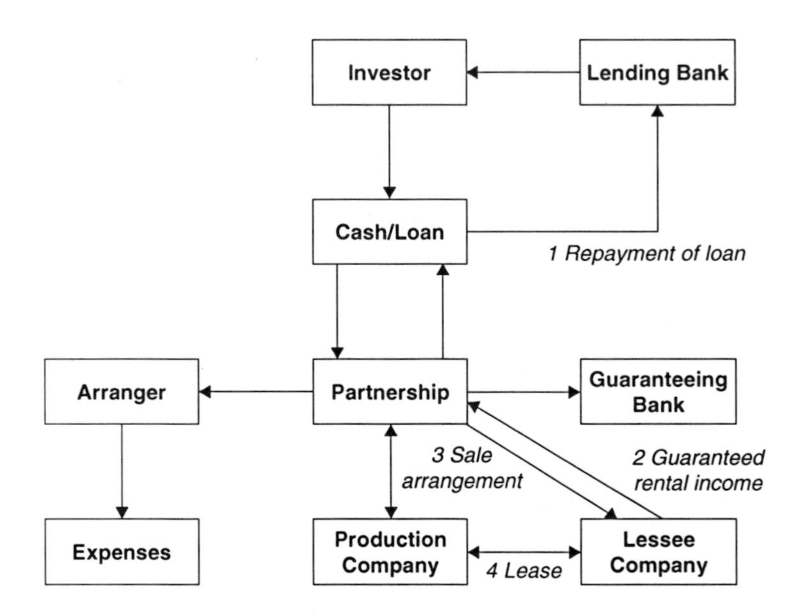

The first issue in the figure to note (see *1* on the figure) is that an investor leverages up his investment in a partnership by taking a loan from a bank. The bank will make a full recourse loan to the investor who must make a capital contribution into the partnership consisting of both the loan element (usually approximately 82 per cent of the investment) plus a cash element of 18 per cent.

The lending bank will be concerned that it has sufficient security in order for its loan to be repaid. You will see in the figure

(*2*) that guaranteed rental payments are paid from the producer/lessee to the partnership over a 15-year period. The sale price of, say, £1 million will be paid by the partnership to the producer (*3*). From the producer's perspective it would be wonderful if that were the end of the story, as he would then be re-financing 100 per cent of his film cost. What happens is that approximately 88 per cent of the £1 million, i.e., £880,000 will be placed in an account at the guarantee bank in the name of the producer but subject to a security interest in favour of the bank. In other words, the £880,000 is in a locked box account. That money will stay there over the 15-year lease term to act as collateral for the 15 annual rental payments made each year by the production company to the partnership.

Under the terms of the lease (*4* in the figure) the guarantee itself and the right to receive the rental income is assigned to the lending bank that exactly covers the principal and interest owed by each investor/partner to the bank under each individual loan. The lessee must pay the rent under the lease. In the event of default by the lessee, then the guaranteeing bank becomes liable under its guarantee to make up any shortfall or, indeed, to pay all future rentals as they fall due.

Now, the good news for the producer is that there is still an amount of free cash available once the transaction goes through. In our hypothetical case, 88 per cent has been placed in the locked box account but there is 12 per cent available for distribution to the producer. This is the producer's gross benefit.

What are the costs of the transaction?

From the gross benefit, there are three areas of expenditure the producer must take into account and for which he is responsible:

i. Payment of the guarantee fee to the guarantee bank (referred to in the business as the defeasance bank). Rates that are independently negotiated by the producer are approximately 0.4–0.5 per cent depending on which bank the producer selects. Again, it is a highly important tax principle that the producer must arrange and negotiate the terms of his own guarantee.
ii. The producer's own legal fees. These fees have come down over the last couple of years as documents have become more standardized.

iii. Certification fees. In order to obtain a British Film Certificate, which is required for a qualifying film and which is issued by the Department for Culture, Media and Sport (DCMS), an external audit must be carried out by an auditor who must produce a cost statement that is submitted to the DCMS. For British films the cost of this is approximately £5,000 but may be considerably more expensive in relation to a complicated co-production between various countries.

How is the sale and leaseback provider remunerated?

The sale and leaseback (S&L) provider takes its fees by charging the investor in relation to its management services. This does not affect the producer's benefit.

What is the definition of a British film?

To qualify as a British Film, a film must be certified as such by the DCMS under the Films Act 1985 (as amended). There is presently no method available to obtain certification prior to completion of a film. In certain circumstances, the acquisition of film rights by the partnership may take place prior to certification being issued if, either: (i) satisfactory evidence has been provided that the film will clearly qualify as a British Film; or (ii) security, in the form of a policy of insurance issued by a completion bond company covering such risk, is obtained in favour of the partnership to be held pending final determination by the DCMS that the film qualifies as a British Film. In general terms, a British Film is a film where:

- the producer was, throughout the time that the film was being made, a person ordinarily resident in or a company registered and centrally managed and controlled in a state of European Economic Area which is a member of the EU (EU member countries are Austria, Belgium, Cyprus, Czech Republic, Denmark, Estonia, Finland, France, Germany, Greece, Hungary, Ireland, Italy, Latvia, Lithuania, Luxembourg, Malta, Poland, Portugal, Slovakia, Slovenia, Spain, Sweden, The Netherlands and UK) or the EEA (European Economic Area – Iceland, Liechtenstein and Norway) or with which the EC has signed an association agreement (Bulgaria and Romania have associated agreements with the EC); and

- at least 70 per cent of the total expenditure incurred in the production of a film was spent on film production activity carried out in the UK; and
- the requisite amount of labour costs represent payments in respect of the labour or services of Commonwealth or European Union citizens, or persons ordinarily resident in a country in the Commonwealth or the European Union (the Isle of Man and the Channel Islands are not part of the UK or part of the EU/EEA for the purposes of Schedule 1. They are part of the Commonwealth. Their citizens are EU nationals; persons ordinarily resident there are ordinarily resident in the Commonwealth).

The percentage of labour costs paid, or payable, to citizens or ordinary residents of a Commonwealth country or member state must be the lesser of:

- at least 70 per cent of the total labour costs after deducting the cost of one non-Commonwealth/member state citizen or ordinary resident; or at least 75 per cent of the total labour cost after deducting the cost of two non-Commonwealth/ member state citizens or ordinary residents, one of whom must be an actor in the film.

Also eligible for relief are films produced under the terms of an official co-production treaty between the UK and another country or under the European Convention on Cinematographic Co-Production (ETS No. 147). Films produced under such treaties represent a growing proportion of British qualifying films.

What about films over £15 million?

Films with production expenditure exceeding £15 million also qualify for UK sale and leaseback benefits. However, the relevant section (S.42 Finance Act 1992) provides a 33 1/3 write-off. Benefits are at a lower level than under S.48.

What rights does a producer give away?

The producer sells the master negative and licenses worldwide distribution rights to the partnership. In order to achieve this, standard form documentation will include a laboratory pledgeholder letter that effectively passes on the ownership of the master negative to the partnership. That is the critical issue for the tax efficiency of this transaction combined with the licence of distribution rights. The licence transfers the worldwide exploitation rights to the partnership by way of licence. However, immediately subsequent to this agreement being entered into, the worldwide distribution rights are leased back to the production company. The way in which the documents are structured means that all of the distribution rights are transferred subject to the prior distribution rights that have already been entered into. However, to complete the documentation, a schedule containing details of each distribution contract entered into prior to the date of the sale and leaseback taking place is needed from the producer.

In addition the producer provides the partnership with a net profit participation. The partnership is in the business of leasing films not only for the rental entitlements under the lease but also to participate in net profit participations or other entitlements in the film. Therefore, on a case-by-case basis, the partnership will negotiate a profit participation with the producer in addition to the rental income. While the rental income is secured by bank guarantee, the profit participation is unsecured.

What costs are allowable in calculating production expenditure?

The UK does not have a formal accounting standard covering the film industry. However, production expenditure should, nevertheless, be identified by reference to normal accountancy principles, subject to the specific issues outlined below. It is not possible to list comprehensively what constitutes production expenditure. What follows is a guide.

- The cost of underlying rights used for a film;
- salaries, fees, benefits (and living expenses) and all associated costs (such as NIC and payroll taxes) of people involved in the making of the film, including payments to foreign nationals. This will include for example: all those employed in directing and producing, technical and industrial capacities, extras and miscellaneous staff; a relevant per cent of stills photographers and those engaged in processing and titling, etc., pro rata to the work done on the film;
- studio costs wherever they are situated and all studio labour costs, as they actually relate to the production of the film;
- cost of set construction and operations;
- wardrobe and all accessories;
- cost of sound synchronization;

- production overheads attributable to the film;
- location costs, including the rental of facilities on location and the costs of taking the unit to the location.

Certain costs are incurred during the final production phase and the release periods of films (sometimes termed exploitation costs) that are not related to the actual completion of the master negative. Examples of such costs are film prints, advertising, rents, salaries, and other distribution expenses. The Inland Revenue does not consider that these types of costs should be included as production expenditure.

Interest on money borrowed to finance production should be relieved for tax purposes in accordance with the normal rules for Case I/II of Schedule D (and via the loan relationship rules for companies), and should not be included as production expenditure. Similarly, any other costs connected with raising and servicing finance to make the film should not be included.

Both deferments (i.e., monetary amounts payable out of receipts from the film) and participations (i.e., percentage amounts payable out of receipts) are contractually due to producers, directors, actors, etc., but that are not paid in the course of production should normally be included as production expenditure, provided the deferment will be paid within 4 months of completion of the film. However, very strict rules exist regarding deferments and they need to be reviewed in detail.

Capital expenditure on the provision of assets such as film cameras, lights and sound recording equipment may be employed in the process of production, but which are not fully used up in that process, should not be regarded as production expenditure for the purposes of these provisions. In these circumstances the capital allowances rules may apply.

Sale and leaseback – a case study

Transaction

The Producer, a UK company, sells a film to a partnership for, say, £10 million and enters into a 15-year lease.

Invoicing

a. Producer issues an invoice to the partnership for £10 million + VAT @ 17.5 per cent (=£1,750,000).

b. The partnership invoices producer for all 15-year lease payments for, say, £13 million + VAT @ 17.5 per cent (=£2,275,000).

Treatment of VAT on above
VAT applies where the seller/lessee is a UK company. In the above example, the producer is therefore in a net VAT payable position to the partnership of £525,000 (=£2,275,000 less £1,750,000). If there is perceived to be a credit risk to the partnership, part of the benefit from the transaction payable to the producer may be escrowed until the VAT works its way through the system.

Cash movements
Purchase price: £10,000,000
Amount placed on deposit by producer at guarantor bank to guarantee lease rental payments: (£9,000,000)
Gross benefit to producer (12.0 per cent): £1,200,000
Guarantee cost (estimated at 0.45 per cent): (£45,000)
Legal: (£5,000)
Audit: (£5,000)

Net benefit: £1,145,000

What about a film that has already been released?

Paragraph 70 of the Statement of Practice states that 'where a film is sold prior to general public release for a sum equal to production expenditure ... the Revenue will not seek to challenge the price ... This also applies where there is a pre-release agreement and the sale takes place within three months of release'. So, in most cases, the S&L must take place prior to release. However, it is also open for a partnership/lessor to purchase a film on the basis of a valuation, i.e., without relying on the provisions of paragraph 70. A valuation may be carried out, i.e., valuing unsold territories over the period of the lease term (i.e., 15 years). Provided the film qualifies as a British film under the Films Act and the valuation is carried out by a professional valuer acceptable to the partnership, utilizing an appropriate methodology, catalogue material produced after 2 July 1997 could be re-financed in this way.

How do I get a British Film Certificate?

For a film to be certified as a qualifying British film by the Secretary of State for Culture, Media and Sport, it must fulfil either the conditions set out under Schedule 1 to the Films Act 1985 or the terms of an international co-production agreement to which the UK is party.

Films cannot be certified before they are completed.

Auditors' report

The Films Act requires a report to the Secretary of State verifying the particulars of salaries, wages and payments, prepared by an accountant who is a member of a body of accountants recognized under section 25 of the Companies Act 1989, who is not and was not at any time while the film was being made, a partner of, nor in the employment of, the maker of the film.

The auditors' report should include the following wording:

ACCOUNTANTS' REPORT TO THE SECRETARY OF STATE FOR CULTURE, MEDIA AND SPORT ON THE PRODUCTION AND LABOUR COSTS OF THE FILM [ ]

I/We have examined the books of the maker of the film referred to in the application dated 00/00/0000 in so far as they relate to the making of the film. The applicant is responsible for the preparation of the application. It is my/our responsibility to form an independent opinion, based on my/our examination, on those parts of the application referred to below and to report my/our opinion to you.

Basis of opinion

I/We have received all the information and documents necessary to enable me/us to ascertain the amount of production expenditure and the labour costs (as defined in paragraphs 4 and 6 respectively, of Schedule 1 to the Films Act 1985) of the film. This includes a proper and reasonable proportion of any annual salaries and fees to be attributed directly to the making of the film, and the allocation of these, in accordance with the requirement of paragraphs 4 and 7 of that Schedule regarding a film to be certified as a British film. My/Our work included examining, on a test basis, evidence relating to the amounts in the application and an assessment of the significant estimates and judgements, made by the applicant in preparation of the application.

On the basis of such examination, I/we report that in my/our opinion, not less than:

i. 70% of the production expenditure incurred in the production of the film was incurred on film production activity carried out in the United Kingdom; and
ii. either
   a. 70% of the total labour cost remaining [after deducting the cost of one person from the total labour cost – delete as applicable] represents payments paid or payable in respect of the labour of citizens of or persons ordinarily resident in the Commonwealth, a member State or a country with which the European Community has signed an association agreement; or
   b. 75% of the total labour cost, remaining after deducting the cost of two persons from the total labour cost, at least one of whom was engaged as an actor or actress and in no other capacity, represents payments paid or payable in respect of the labour of citizens of or persons ordinarily resident in the Commonwealth, a member State or a country with which the European Community has signed an association agreement.

The auditors' report should be addressed to:

The Secretary of State for Culture, Media and Sport
Department for Culture, Media and Sport
2–4 Cockspur Street
London SW1Y 5DH
UK

Appendix A: Glossary of Film Production and Finance Terms

Above the line: term denoting portion of a film's budget, usually including the writer, director, producer and main cast.
Access letter: a letter under which a laboratory undertakes to honour orders placed by a distributor, even though the laboratory may be owed money by the producer or, in relation to the film, by other persons. See also *Laboratory letter* and *Pledge holder agreement.*
Adjusted gross deal: a distribution agreement where the distributor deducts from gross receipts the costs of co-operative advertising and divides the balance, the adjusted gross, with the producer. The advantage for the producer is that he does not have to vet the distribution expenses. The disadvantage is that the distributor may cut back on distribution expenses, to the detriment of the commercial success of the film, if he does not think his share of adjusted gross receipts will cover his expenses.
Advance: see *Minimum guarantee*
Ancillary rights: rights that may be capable of commercial exploitation that accrue or are acquired as a result of or in the course of production of a film, as distinct from the exploitation of the film itself. They include merchandizing rights, television spin-off rights, sequel, prequel and remake, book publishing rights, computer game rights, soundtrack album rights and the music publishing rights in the score. These rights are sometimes referred to as secondary rights.
Angel: see *Private investor.*
Answer print: the composition print that emerges from the laboratory after the combination of the sound with the graded picture, optical effects and soundtrack. When the print is approved a computer tape is made which tells the printer what to duplicate and ensures that all subsequent copies are the same. Also known as the first trial print.

ASCAP: American Society of Composers, Authors and Publishers; one of a small number of American collecting societies, which act on behalf of composers and music publishers in the licensing and collection of license fees from public performances and broadcast of musical works. See also *BMI* and *SESAC*. ASCAP, One Lincoln Plaza New York, New York 10023, USA; 7920 Sunset Blvd Suite 300, Los Angeles CA 90046, USA; tel. +1 213 883 1000; fax +1 213 883 1047/ +1 212 595 3276; http://www.ascap.com.
Assignment by way of security: the method by which a financier takes a security interest in a film. The copyright in the film and the underlying rights (and the revenues) are assigned to the financier by way of security. Effectively they are mortgaged to the financier to secure the repayment of the financier's investment. The mortgage is registered at Companies House to establish its priority and appears on the production companies' register of charges, which is open to public inspection. See also *Priority agreement* and *Security agreement*. What is left of the revenue generated by a film after deduction of distribution fees and expenses, advances and minimum guarantees, recoupment of the financiers' investments, repayment of any sums advanced by the completion guarantor fees. Also known as net profit. See *Deferment* and *Producer's share of net profits*.
Basis points: one-hundredth of 1 per cent is typically used in the context of interest rates, for example, three basis points would be 0.03 per cent.
BBFC: the British Board of Film Classification is the body charged with viewing films and certifying their suitability for cinema audiences and for sale and rental of videos by reference to age groups. It is cheaper to certify a 16 mm print than a 35 mm print.
BECTU: Broadcasting Entertainment Cinematograph & Theatre Union. Trade union representing workers in film, television and theatre in the UK.
Below the line: term denoting portion of a film's budget excluding all elements that are considered above the line.
BFI: British Film Institute – the national body charged with fostering the development and understanding of the moving image as an element in British cultural life.

BMI: Broadcast Music Inc. – an American collecting society acting on behalf of composers and music publishers. See also *ASCAP* and *SESAC*.

Break costs or Funding breakage costs: the costs incurred by a bank as a result of receiving a pre-payment during the currency of an interest period or, in the case of a loan for a fixed term, prior to the term date or as a result of withholding a drawdown under the loan, having already funded it. The costs are calculated on the premise that, in order to fund a loan to its customer, the bank has taken deposits in the interbank market that it needs to liquidate or redeploy if its own borrower repays early or fails to draw down. Typically, on a pre-payment, the bank's break costs will represent the difference between the return that the bank would have earned on the pre-paid amount for the rest of the interest period if there had been no pre-payment and the return that the bank will derive in the interbank market on the pre-paid amount for the residue of the interest period.

British Actors Equity: Guild House, Upper St Martins Lane, London WC2H 9EG, UK; tel. +44 20 7379 6000; fax +44 20 7379 7001. See *Talent unions*.

British Film: any feature film that fulfils the criteria laid down under Schedule 1 of the Films Act 1985 and subsequent amendments.

Cap: an arrangement (unusually entered into separately from the underlying loan) between a bank and the borrower where, for a premium, an upper limit is set on the interest rate payable by the borrower on a floating rate loan. If the underlying interest rate rises above the upper limit, the provider of the cap reimburses the borrower for the excess above that limit.

Capital allowances: tax relief that may be claimed on the capital cost of acquiring a qualifying asset. It may be offset against a taxpayer's income liable to corporation tax or income tax. There are various forms of capital allowance and detailed rules governing the rates of capital allowances and how they are applied. They may be subject to clawback as a result of a balancing adjustment when the taxpayer disposes (or is deemed to dispose) of the relevant asset.

Cash flow: finance required to pay for the cost of physically producing a film.

Certification: the cost of production of a film, as certified by an independent firm of accountants.

Chain of title: the route by which the producer's right to use copyright material may be traced from the author to the producer through a 'chain' of assignments and transfers.
Co-operative advertising: advertising, the cost of which is shared between the distributor and exhibitors.
Co-production: a film produced through the co-operation of, and with substantial contributions from, two or more production companies.
Co-production treaty: an agreement between nations that may permit films made in or with resources from both nations to benefit from subsidies available from both.
Collecting society: an organization that acts on behalf of its members, who may for example be composers, music publishers, visual artists or record companies, to administer, collect and distribute sums to which the members are entitled from the commercial use of their works.
Collection agent: see *Collection agreement.*
Collection agreement: an agreement entered into by the producer and financiers of a film with a collection agent. The collection agent is appointed to collect the proceeds of the exploitation of the film and distribute them to the financiers, the producer and other beneficiaries, such as deferees and profit participants, in accordance with directions set out in the agreement. The collection agent would expect to receive a fee for this work, perhaps negotiated as a percentage of all sums collected by it. A collection agent is appointed because, whilst a production entity may have a continuing legal existence, it may not have a continuing physical existence in the sense of numbers of individuals who attend to its business on a daily basis. The collection agent offers physical continuity and is responsible for ensuring that distributors account for and pay the producer's share of the distribution revenues. The collection agent will hold revenues on trust and they are therefore intended to be secure from the collection agent's own creditors. The collection agent may also offer a degree of security, not only in the legal sense, but also because of its reputation and perceived permanence.
Completion guarantee: an agreement under which a completion guarantor guarantees to the financiers of a film, or a distributor who has advanced money prior to delivery, that the film will be completed and delivered by a given date to its principal distributors in accordance with the relevant distribution agreements.

Completion guarantor: a company that is in the business of providing completion guarantees for financiers.
Contingency: a final sum added to the budget for a film to cover unforeseen circumstances, usually 10 per cent of the budgeted cost excluding the completion guarantee fee.
Copyright search: a search in the US Copyright Office to see if any interest in the relevant work or film has been registered. No equivalent registry exists in the UK and accordingly no certain means of verifying the ownership of copyright interests exists.
Cost of funds: a bank's cost of lending money. This will depend on the nature of the loan – for example a bank's cost of funds on a sterling LIBOR loan will usually be LIBOR plus its MLA cost.
Costs off the top deal: a distribution agreement where distribution expenses are deducted from gross receipts and the balance is then divided between the distributor and the producer in agreed shares. Distributors' fees are usually calculated on gross receipts but in this case the distributor's share is effectively its fee, calculated on a lower base.
Cross collateralization: the application of revenues derived from one source, whether a territory or a means of exploitation, towards the recoupment of an advance irrespective of revenues arising from another territory or means of exploitation all falling within the same grant to a distributor or agent. This device is generally discouraged by the lawyers of independent filmmakers, but is widely encouraged by sales agents as a means of facilitating sales.
Debenture: technically a legal document evidencing indebtedness, but commonly used to mean a fixed and floating charge over the assets and undertaking of a company.
Deferment: a sum payable to a writer, performer, director, producer or someone else connected with a film out of revenues derived from the exploitation of the film, but after the deduction of distribution fees and expenses and, usually, after the financiers and the completion guarantor have recovered all of the sums they have advanced towards the cost of production and delivery of the film.
Deferred tax: an accounting entry that is included in, amongst other things, a company's financial statements, to reflect a potential liability to tax. Conventionally, deferred tax is established where reliefs and/or allowances (particularly capital allowances) have the effect of deferring liabilities to tax that would otherwise have crystallized. These are called 'timing differences'.

Deferee: a person to whom a deferment is payable.
Deficit: difference between the required budget of film and the amount of finance already raised. Also known as Gap.
Discount: to discount, for example, a distribution agreement means the assignment to a lender of the benefit of a distribution agreement under which advances are payable on delivery of the film in return for a loan, which can be used to meet the costs of production of the film as they are incurred. The agreement is 'discounted' because the sum made available by way of loan is less than the amount of the advance. The difference covers the lender's fees and legal expenses and the interest calculated to be payable on the loan during the period under the contracted repayment date.
Discounted cashflow or DCF: an investment appraisal technique that takes account of the time value of money by assessing the present value of future income and expenditure. It is often used in valuing an investment or to show the viability of a project. See *Internal rate of return.*
Distribution agreement: an agreement under which rights to exploit a film in one or more media are granted. The distributor grants rights as principal, not as agent. The agreement will provide either for a lump sum payment by the distributor or for a sharing of revenues.
Distributor: a party who organizes film distribution under a distribution agreement. See also *Sales agent.*
Domestic rights: the rights to distribute a film in North America. The world excluding North America is, just as confusingly for a non-American, often collectively referred to as 'foreign'.
Eady levy: a levy on the price of cinema admissions introduced in 1957, principally to provide money from film exhibition and distribution to support film production in the UK. Terminated in 1985.
Equity of redemption: the borrower's right to redeem (i.e., cancel) a mortgage on payment of the sums secured.
Errors and Omissions (E&O) insurance: insurance against claims arising out of infringements of copyright, defamation and unauthorized use of names, trade names, trademarks or characters. This insurance is usually taken out by the producer of a film, if the film is intended to be distributed in North America, on a film-by-film basis. Insurance will be with effect either from the first day of principal photography or from delivery. Cover will be forfeited if the claim arises out of an active failure to act that is

'wilful, wanton, intentional, malicious or conspiratorial' or if the production procedures laid down in the policy are not adhered to. The principal insured may be asked to have the financiers and distributors named as additional insureds.

European film: any feature film for which a European country – including the UK – was the prime source of ideas or cultural values portrayed.

Favoured nation: the most favourable terms accorded to any party to a transaction, including that no-one will get any better terms or if any improved terms are granted to a third party then the 'favoured nation' will be treated equally.

Feature film: a film with a running time of over 72 minutes made with the intention of securing a theatrical release.

Final cut: the final say on the editing of a film. This right will usually lie with the production company (subject to its obligations to financiers and distributors), unless the director is of sufficient stature to be able to insist on this right as a term of his agreement with the production company.

Financial covenants: the undertakings within loan documents requiring the borrower to maintain certain financial ratios, for example, current assets to current liabilities, or total debt to total equity, or to maintain a minimum net worth during the term of the loan. Such covenants would not be applicable where the business of the borrower consists only of the production of a single film.

Fine cut: the final edit of the film.

First trial print: see *Answer print.*

Floating charge: a charge that 'floats' above the assets subject to it (typically a company's debts and trading stock), allowing the company to deal in those assets in the ordinary course of the company's business until the occurrence of stated events of default. On any such event, the charge 'crystallizes' and becomes a fixed charge over the relevant assets then owned by the company.

Floating rate: interest at a rate that fluctuates, typically by reference to changes in LIBOR or the base lending rate of a specified bank.

Foreign rights: the converse of domestic rights, which are the rights to distribute a film outside North America.

Forward rate agreement or FRA: an agreement to fix a rate of interest for a future period where the borrower would otherwise be paying at a floating rate. Typically, on the date on which the fixed rate first becomes operative, the borrower or the bank will settle the discounted difference between the fixed rate for the period and the floating rate for the same period.

Four walling: the practice where a producer rents all the seats for all the shows for a week (usually at a discount) and then puts in his/her own film and collects the box office.

Free television: a television broadcast intended for reception by the public where no charge is made to the viewer other than any government licence fee or tax. See *Standard television.*

Fringes: social security and, in some cases, pension payments due to the cast and crew on top of wages shown in the below the line section of the budget. Fringes are often detailed in a separate schedule and summarized in a line in the final section of the budget top sheet.

Gap: difference between the required budget of film and the amount of finance already raised. Also known as deficit.

Gap financing: a speciality lending arrangement whereby a bank will lend the difference between production finance raised and the minimum expected from sales by a reputable sales agent.

Gearing: the relationship between a company's indebtedness and its equity capital – also referred to as a company's 'debt/equity ratio'.

Gross participation: an arrangement under which a participant in a film, usually a major artist, will share in gross, rather than net, receipts.

Grossing-up clause: a clause customarily found in loan documents which provides that, where withholding taxes are imposed on payments by the borrower to the lender, the borrower will pay an additional amount to the lender so that the lender receives what it would have received had there been no such taxes. The additional payment is referred to as a 'gross-up payment' and the requirement to pay as a requirement to 'gross up'.

Hedge: in a financing context, any technique to offset the impact of movements in interest rates or currency exchange rates. Typical examples of hedging instruments are swaps, options and forward rate agreements.

Holdback: a period during which a particular form of exploitation is not allowed. A videogram hold back, for example, means a period following theatrical release that must expire before videograms of the film can be released.

Hollywood Studios: certain US-based companies that own the physical locations and facilities for film development, pre-production, production and post-production. They also have subsidiaries responsible for film production, distribution and, in some cases, exhibition. The most well-known of these are; Columbia/Tri Star, MCA/Universal, MGM, Paramount, 20th Century Fox, Walt Disney and Warner Brothers.

Increased costs clause: customarily found in loan documents, this clause provides that if there is a change in regulatory requirements after the loan agreement is signed that raises the cost to the bank of making or maintaining a loan (or reduces its effective return), the borrower will compensate the lender. See also the MLA costs.

Independent film: a film made without the financial participation of the Hollywood Studios.

Interparty agreement: the interparty agreement regulates the relationship between various financing parties to a film.

Internal rate of return or IRR: an investment appraisal technique, also known as discounted cash flow yield, from which the profitability of a project or investment can be assessed. The IRR of an investment is the rate of return at which its anticipated future income and expenditure (cash flows) must be discounted to give a net present value of zero. If that IRR is greater than the anticipated cost of funding the project or investment, the project is likely to be profitable.

Internegative: when a film has been shot on colour reversal stock a duplicate stage (interpositive) is omitted by making a CRI (colour reversal internegative) from the camera negative. An internegative is made directly from this to produce a duplicate negative from which exhibition print copies of the film are made.

Interpositive: a positive print, made from the original negative of the final version of the film, from which a duplicate negative is made. It is then possible to make many exhibition print copies from the 'dupe' negative without damaging the original negative. Also known as the master positive.

ITV: Independent Television Commission. Collective name for the commercial producer and broadcasting companies in the UK.

Laboratory letter: an expression used indiscriminately to refer to access letters and to pledge holder agreements, without differentiating between the two. Whilst the functions of an access letter and a pledgeholder agreement may be fulfilled in a single document, the respective functions are distinct.

Lead bank, or lead manager: a bank that acts as lead manager for a potential syndicate of banks in relation to a syndicated loan. Appointed by the borrower, the lead manager, in exchange for a fee, normally settles with the borrower the outline of the basic terms of the loan, promotes the loan to potential participants, provides information relating to the borrower and its business and negotiates on behalf of the participants. Lead managers try to ensure that they are not obliged to provide the loan if insufficient participants express an interest, that they are not liable for the information provided to participants and that they are not liable for any actor omission when negotiating the loan.

Letter of credit (LC): a written undertaking to pay the sum of money, on delivery to the person giving the undertaking, of documents in the form specified in the letter of credit. When a distribution agreement is discounted, the lender may insist that the advance payable by the distributor is secured by a letter of credit from a recognized bank. The documents required to trigger payments usually include a certificate from a third party, often the completion guarantor, that delivery has been made to the distributor in accordance with the distribution agreement. Once an independent producer has convinced a financier to participate, the financier can then provide a LC upon which the producer can borrow. The costs of preparing the LC is usually borne by the producer.

LIBID: the London Interbank Bid Rate, being the rate at which a bank borrows by bidding for deposits to be placed with lending banks in the London interbank market.

LIBOR: the London Interbank Offered Rate, being the rate at which a bank is able to borrow money on the London interbank market from lending banks. LIBOR varies according to the size of the borrowing and its period.

Limited partnership: a partnership constituted by a general partner (with unlimited liability) and limited partners (with limited liability). Limited partnership is a form of association frequently used to enable investors to invest collectively. Normally, the general partner will manage the investment.

Limited recourse: a loan similar to a non-recourse loan but where there is some recourse to the assets of the borrower other than those charged, and sometimes limited recourse to other companies. The latter may take the form of a limited parent company guarantee.

Loan out agreement: an agreement where the services of an individual are made available through a production company, usually owned or controlled by that individual.
Loss payee endorsement: confirmation from a completion guarantor's reinsurer, given to a film's financiers, to the effect that they can look directly to the reinsurer to make payments under the reinsurance policy in the event that the completion guarantor has a liability to make payment under the completion guarantee.
M & E Track: a mixed music and effects track that is free from dialogue. Used for foreign language versions. See also *Triple track*.
Margin: in a banking context, the rate of interest payable to a lender over and above LIBOR or the lender's base rate – for example, 2 per cent over LIBOR.
MCPS: the Mechanical-Copyright Protection Society Limited, a collecting society that administers the licensing of mechanical reproductions of musical works and the collection and distribution of revenues derived from such licensing.
Minimum guarantee: the minimum sum a distributor guarantees will be payable to a producer as a result of the distributor's distribution of the film. The guaranteed sum may be payable at the beginning of the distribution period, as an advance against the producer's share of the proceeds of distribution. It may, however, be the aggregate sum that the distributor guarantees will be payable to the producer over the whole of the distribution period. Any shortfall of actual revenues against the guaranteed amount would then be payable at the end of the distribution period.
MLA costs: additional costs that a bank will incur in maintaining its statutory requirements in making loans.
MPAA: the Motion Picture Association of America administers the rating system for feature films in the USA in a manner not unlike that in which the BBFC does in the UK.
MPEAA: the Motion Picture Exporters Association of America, the trade association of the major studios, which represents the interests of the studios as distributors outside the USA.
Musician's Union: see *Talent Unions*.
Negative pick-up: a distribution agreement where the advance is payable only on delivery of the finished film to the distributor.
Negative pledge: a covenant contained in loan documents where the borrower agrees not to create or permit to exist any other mortgage, charge or security interest over any of its assets. The covenant is often subject to stated exceptions.

Net asset value or Net worth: the book value of the assets of a company or business less its liabilities, excluding liabilities to equity investors. The net asset value reflects the share holders'/owners' net investment in the company or business.
Net present value or NPV: today's value of money to be received or paid in the future after applying a discount to reflect the delay before it is received or paid. The accuracy of the result depends on the assumptions made in assessing the discount rate.
Non-recourse loan: a misnomer for a loan where the lender has no recourse to any party or any assets other than the assets over which the lender has specifically taken security, in effect the proceeds of exploitation of the film, and/or the single purpose vehicle which owns the assets.
Non-standard television: all forms of television other than standard television. It includes trapped audience rights, basic cable except where the programme signal is receivable over the air with a standard rooftop or set-top aerial, pay cable and over the air subscription television (STV), direct broadcast by satellite (DBS), master antenna television (MATV), multipointvideo distribution systems (MVDS) and satellite master antenna television systems (SMATV).
Non-theatrical rights: the rights to exhibit a film to a live audience by direct projection by means of sub-standard gauges (for example 16 mm or 8 mm) or by video, where the exhibition of films on a regular basis is not the primary purpose and when no specific admission charge is made for the exhibition. The exercise of non-theatrical rights is usually limited to educational establishments, nursing homes, hospitals, 'shut in locations' – such as prisons, convents and orphanages – and clubs and other organizations of a religious, educational, cultural, charitable or social nature.
Novation: the transfer of all benefits and obligations under a contract. The transfer requires the consent of the person to whom the obligations are owed. This is to be contrasted with an assignment, which is the transfer of the benefit only of a contract or other right, and may not require the consent of the person owing the obligation.
NTSC: National Television System, the code system used in the USA and Japan by which colour television pictures are distributed or transmitted using 525 lines. See also *PAL* and *SECAM*.

Off-balance sheet finance: an arrangement under which a loan is made to a company without the debt appearing on the investor's balance sheet and affecting its gearing ratio.
Optical sound negative: to make optical-sound combined prints, the final master magnetic mix is re-recorded as a photographic optical sound negative. This negative is synchronized and printed with the final cut picture negative on positive stock, to make the married print.
Option: in the context of film, an option is a right exercisable during a specific period for a specific sum to acquire certain rights, for example the right to produce a film based on a book, or a right to require an artist to contribute to a production.
Output deal: agreement between a film producer and distributor – or between a film producer and a television company – under which the distributor or television company obtains in advance the distribution or television rights to a number of films to be made or distributed over a period of time.
Overages: distribution revenues payable to the producer after the advance or minimum guarantee has been recouped.
Overspend: where the actual cost of production exceeds the budget.
P & A: printing and advertising. The cost of promotion of a film. Paying for the film to be put into cinemas and for advertising it in all media.
Packaging: the provision, usually by a talent agency, of a package of individuals to work on a film. The package may include the director, screenplay writer, stars and members of the supporting cast. The package is usually presented as a whole in that you cannot choose only some elements.
PACT: Producers Alliance for Cinema and Television, the UK trade association for film and television producers.
PAL: Phase Alternative Line, the code system used in the UK by which colour television pictures are distributed or transmitted using 625 lines. PAL is also used in an increasing number of countries in Europe. See also *NTSC* and *SECAM*.
Panning and scanning: the process by which a film shot on an aspect ratio (the ratio of the width to the height of the picture) suitable for cinema distribution (e.g., 1.85:1 or 2.3:1) is reduced and adjusted for television transmission (standard screen 1.33:1, widescreen 1.8:1). When a film is shot for both theatrical distribution and television transmission the viewfinder is often

'masked' to ensure that the main action is within the television aspect ratio.
Pay or play: a commitment to pay a director or performer made before production commences, and sometimes before all the finance has become unconditional, regardless of whether his or her services are used.
Pay television: television for which viewers pay a subscription. Normally received directly from satellites or via cable.
PFD agreement: an agreement that deals with the production, finance and distribution of a film as opposed to only one or two of these elements.
Pick-up: a film for which the distribution rights are acquired after it has been made.
Pledge holder agreement: an agreement under which a processing laboratory agrees with the financiers of a film not to part with possession of the original negative and the principal film materials without prior written consent of the financiers. See also *Access letter* and *Laboratory letter*.
Points: shares of back end or net profits in a film are measured in percentage points. To have points in a film means to have a share of the net profits.
Post-production: the late stages of film production after filming, including editing, adding music, special effects and titles.
Pre-production: the early stages of film production preceding principal photography, including casting, budgeting and finding locations.
Pre-sale: a licence or distribution agreement entered into before a film has been completed. The advance, minimum guarantee or licence fee payable under the pre-sale may form part of the finance package for the film, either as a direct contribution towards the cost of production or, if the advance, minimum guarantee or licence fee is only payable on or after delivery of the film, it may be discounted.
Prequel: the opposite of a sequel – it is set before the events depicted in the film from which it is derived.
Priority agreement: an agreement between the financiers and, sometimes, the completion guarantor, regulating the priority of their respective security interests in the film.
Private investor: an individual, often having little direct connection with the film industry, who invests his/her own money in a film. In the world of theatre he/she is referred to as an angel.

Producer's share of net profits: net profits are what is left of revenues from the exploitation of the film after distribution fees and expenses, repayment of any loans and investments raised to finance production, repayment of any sums extended by the completion guarantor and the payment of any deferments. Net profits are normally divided between the investors and the producer. The producer's share is usually between 40 per cent and 60 per cent of the net profits, out of which the producer may have to pay the profit entitlements (points) of various individuals and others who have contributed towards the film. These shares are fixed either as a share of the producer's share of net profits or as a share of 100 per cent of the net profits.
Production: the stage of film production that involves the actual filming of the piece.
Production to budget undertaking: the undertaking given by the individual producer to the completion guarantor that the sums allowed in the budget for the film approved by the financiers and completion guarantor for the cast, living expenses, music and legal fees will not be exceeded.
PRS: the Performing Right Society Limited, the British collecting society that licenses performing and broadcasting rights in musical works on behalf of composers and music publishers and collects and distributes revenues derived from such licensing.
Recoupment order: the order in which investors and financiers are repaid their loans and investments (and interest). Although all revenue may be applied in a single order, often revenue from different distribution territories or media are applied in different orders.
Remake: a new production based substantially on the script of an existing film.
Residual: a sum of money, payable under a union, guild or individual agreement, to a performer, musician, writer, composer, director or producer by reference to the means by which, or the place in which, the film is exploited.
Revolver or revolving facility: a loan facility that requires loans to be repaid at the end of given periods – usually each interest period – but enables the loans to be immediately redrawn at the end of those periods subject to a final repayment and termination date. Such facilities often arise when the borrower has the option of borrowing in more than one currency.
Roll over relief: a relief for capital gains tax purposes (or corporation tax, in the case of a company). It operates by

deferring liability for tax on a sale, where the proceeds are invested in further qualifying assets, until such time as a sale takes place and there is no such reinvestment.

SAG: the Screen Actors Guild, the American equivalent of British Actors Equity.

Sale and leaseback: a sale of an asset that is immediately leased back to the seller by the buyer.

Sales agent: an agent appointed by the producer to act as agent for the sale of the film. See also *Distributor.*

SECAM: Sequential Colour and Memory – the code system used in France by which colour television pictures are distributed or transmitted using 625 lines. See also *PAL* and *NTSC.*

Secondary rights: see *Ancillary rights.*

Security agreement: a charge or mortgage of the copyright and distribution rights in a film and of the physical materials created in the process of producing the film given by the production company as security for the repayment of a loan or investment used to finance the cost of production of the film. See also *Assignment by way of security* and *Priority agreement.*

Sequel: a film that follows another film, using the same characters but depicting later events. See also *Prequel.*

SESAC: SESAC Inc., an American collecting society acting on behalf of composers and music publishers.

Simultaneous cable relay: the relay by cable of television programme signal transmitted over the air simultaneously with (or effectively simultaneously with) the original transmission. The expression usually relates to the relay of a whole programme service or channel rather than individual programmes.

Single purpose vehicle or SPV: a company established for a particular project or to hold a particular asset. An SPV is often used by the borrower's group to contain insolvency risk and/or make it easier to give a lender the floating charge it will normally seek.

Source material: the original work on which the screenplay for a film is based.

Standard television: the American equivalent of free television.

Stop date: the last date on which a performer or director can be obliged to work. A performer or director may want the certainty of knowing when he/she will be free to accept another engagement. Stop dates are unpopular with completion guarantors, as it can be very expensive to replace an important member of the cast or the director if a film is delayed.

Strike price: see *Completion guarantee.*
Subordinated debt: debt, the repayment of which is postponed or subordinated to the claims of other creditors on liquidation or administration. The subordination may be in favour of a particular creditor or in favour of all other creditors (or a class of them).Where the subordination is in favour of all creditors, the subordinated debt is akin to share capital and is often treated as such, particularly in relation to financial covenants. The subordination will usually (but need not) encompass payment of interest, fees, etc. in respect of the debt as well as its repayment.
Syndicated loan: a loan provided by a number of banks (called a 'syndicate') as opposed to a 'bilateral loan' between one lender and the borrower.
Takeover: completion guarantors and some financiers require a right to take over the production of a film if the producer becomes insolvent, commits a material breach of its obligations to the completion guarantor or the financier encounters serious production problems. This may involve firing some of the crew and/or cast working on the film, including the director.
Talent Unions: in Britain, British Actors Equity, the Musicians' Union and the Writers Guild of Great Britain, being the respective joint negotiating bodies on behalf of actors, musicians and screen writers.
Tax transparency: a legal structure is tax transparent if it results in the same tax consequences for the ultimate investors whether they invest directly or through the legal structure. An example of an arrangement that is tax transparent is a corporate partnership (i.e., a partnership, the members of which are companies).
Tax shelter: a relief, allowance, deduction or credit for taxation purposes that has the effect of eliminating, reducing or deferring a liability to tax.
Tax haven: a jurisdiction that charges no tax or tax at very low rates. Examples are the Channel Islands, Isle of Man, British Virgin Islands, Netherlands Antilles, Bermuda and Cayman Islands.
Television rights: the collective expression includes a number of different forms of television, such as free and pay television and terrestrial and satellite television. When granting television rights, care should be taken to be specific as to the rights granted if revenues are to be maximized.

Theatrical rights: the rights to exhibit the film in cinemas and other places of public viewing to which the general public is admitted and for which an admission charge in money or money's worth is made.
Title search: a report, usually carried out by agents in the USA, on registrations of works under the proposed title of the film and on literary works, television programmes and films bearing the same or similar titles to that proposed for the film. The report may include a digest of references to projects bearing the same or a similar title that have appeared in the film industry trade press.
Triple track: separate magnetic track (sound) can come in a number of formats. Triple track is the format that contains three separate sound-tracks. Any sound can be put onto a track, for example, one track may be M & E track. A triple track is frequently used for stereo sound, one track being used for the left, one track for the right and the third unused.
Turnaround: when a project is developed, the person financing the development has an agreed period in which to put the project into production, failing which the project goes into turnaround. When this happens the producer is entitled to buy the project back from the financier, usually for all or a proportion of the sums advanced by the financier.
Underspend: the amount by which the budgeted cost of the film exceeds the actual cost of production of the film.
Window: the period for which a film is available for viewing in any particular medium.

Appendix B: Helpful Websites and Recommended Reading

Websites

Raindance: http://www.raindance.co.uk
British Film Commission: http://www.britfilmcom.co.uk
British Film Office: http://www.britfilmusa.com
CNC (Centre National de la Cinématographie): http://www.cnc.fr
Department for Culture, Media and Sport:
http://www.culture.gov.uk
Film Distributors' Association: http://www.launchingfilms.com
SAG (Screen Actors Guild): http://www.sag.org
PACT (Producers' Alliance for Cinema and Television):
http://www.pact.co.uk
Film Money & Funding faqs: http://www.filmcentre.co.uk
The British Film Institute: http://www.bfi.org.uk
UK Film Council: http://www.ukfilmcouncil.org.uk
New Producers Alliance: http://www.newproducer.co.uk
UK Film Locations and Film Resources Worldwide:
http://www.ukfilmlocation.co.uk
UK Film Funding Links: http://www.film-people.net
Film Angel Film Finance and Script Website:
http://www.filmangel.co.uk
Writer's Guild of Great Britain: http://www.writersguild.org.uk
Writers Guild of America: http://www.wga.org
http://www.filmjerk.com
http://www.webcinema.org
http://www.surfview.com
http://www.nextwavefilms.com
http://www.hollywoodinvestors.com
http://www.reelmind.com
http://www.filmdeveloper.com
http://www.thenegative.com
http://www.inetfilm.com

Books

Alberstat, Philip, 2000. *Independent Producers' Guide to Film & TV Contracts*. Focal Press.
Andersen, Arthur, 1996. *The European Film Production Guide: Finance, Tax, Legislation, France, Germany, Italy, Spain, UK* (Blueprint: Media Business School S.) Routledge.
Baumgarten, Paul A., 1992. *Producing, Financing and Distributing Film: A Comprehensive Legal and Business Guide*. Limelight Editions
Campisi, Gabriel, 2003. *The Independent Filmmaker's Guide to Writing a Business Plan for Investors*. McFarland & Company.
Clemens, John and Wolff, Melora, 2000. *Movies to Manage by: Lessons in Leadership from Great Films*. Contemporary Books Inc.
Cones, John W., 1992. *Film Finance and Distribution: A Dictionary of Terms*. Silman James Press.
Cones, John W., 1998. *43 Ways to Finance Your Feature Film: A Comprehensive Analysis of Film Finance*. Southern Illinois University Press.
Daniels, Bill, Leedy, David and Sills, Steven D., 1997. *Movie Money: Understanding Hollywood's (Creative) Accounting Practices*. Silman James Press.
Downey, Mike, 2002. *The Film Finance Handbook*. Wallflower Press.
Finney, Angus, 1996. *Developing Feature Films in Europe: A Practical Guide* (Blueprint: Media Business School S.). Routledge.
Gaines, Philip and Rhodes, David J., 1995. *Micro-budget Hollywood: Budgeting (and Making) Feature Films for 50,000 to 500,000 Dollars*. Silman James Press.
Garon, J.M., 2002. *The Independent Filmmaker's Law & Business Guide: Financing, Shooting & Distributing Independent & Digital Films*. A Cappella Publishing.
Gaspard, John and Newton, Dale, 1996. *Persistence of Vision: Impractical Guide to Producing a Feature Film for Under 30,000 Dollars*. Michael Wiese Productions.
Goodchild, John and Baillieu, B., 2002. *The British Film Business*. John Wiley and Sons Ltd.
Grove, Elliot, 2004. *Raindance Producers' Lab: lo-to-no budget filmmaking*. Focal Press.
Hancock, Caroline and Wistreich, Nic, 2003. *Get Your Film Funded: UK Film Finance Guide*. Shooting People Press.

Harmon, Renee, 1994. *The Beginning Filmmaker's Business Guide*. Walker & Co.
Koster, Robert, 1997. *The On Production Budget Book*. Focal Press.
Lee, John J., 2000. *Motion Pictures Producer's Business Handbook*. Focal Press.
Levison, Louise, 2004. *Filmmakers and Financing: Business Plans for Independents*. Focal Press.
McVicar, David, 2004. *The Cannes Film Festival Survival Guide*. Dalhousie University Free Press.
Moore, Schuyler M., 2000. *The Biz: The Basic Business, Legal and Financial Aspects of the Film Industry*. Silman James Press.
Simon, Deke and Wiese, Michael, 2001. *Film and Video Budgets*. Butterworth-Heinemann.
Singleton, Ralph S., *et al.*, 1996. *Film Budgeting: Or How Much Will It Cost You to Shoot Your Movie?* Lone Eagle Publishing Company.
Stempel, Tom, 2001. *American Audiences on Movies and Moviegoing*. The University Press of Kentucky.
Swasy, Alecia, 1997. *Changing Focus: Kodak and the Battle to Save a Great American Company*. Time Books.
Warshawski, Morrie, 2003. *Shaking the Money Tree: How to Get Grants and Donations for Film and Video Projects*. Focal Press.
Wiese, Michael, 1993. *Film and Video Financing: For Financing Films & Video Projects*. Image Book Company.

Appendix C: Example Errors and Omissions Cover Note

TO WHOM IT MAY CONCERN

This is to certify that the under-mentioned insurance has been effected with Lloyds subject to their normal policy terms and conditions for the class of business stated herein:

INSURED:	**[PRODUCTIONS LIMITED]**
NAMES OF ADDITIONAL INSURED	**[ ]**
CONDITIONS	As policy
TYPE:	Errors & Omissions
TITLE:	[NAME OF FILM]
PERIOD:	[From [ ] to [ ]]
LIMIT:	$1,000,000 any one claim, $3,000,000 in the aggregate
SITUATION:	Worldwide
EXCESS:	$10,000 each and every claim

This document is intended for use as evidence that the insurance, as described herein, has been effected and shall be subject to all terms and conditions of the policy which will be issued and that, in the event of any inconsistency herewith, the terms and provisions of such policy shall prevail.

For and on behalf of
[Insurance Company]

[ ]

Index

CPSIA information can be obtained at www.ICGtesting.com
Printed in the USA
LVOW07s0404110913

351677LV00005B/40/P

9 780240 516615